EGLIN, Anthony

The lost gardens

The Lost Gardens

Also by Anthony Eglin

The Blue Rose

THE LOST GARDENS

Anthony Eglin

Constable • London

For my friend, Roger

Constable & Robinson Ltd
3 The Lanchesters
162 Fulham Palace Road
London W6 9ER
www.constablerobinson.com

First published in the UK by Constable,
an imprint of Constable & Robinson Ltd 2005

A copy of the British Library Cataloguing in Publication
Data is available from the British Library.

ISBN 1-84119-951-6

Printed and bound in the EU

Prologue

Holland, 1944

In the dawn of a September morning, the sergeant hunched on a filthy mattress amid the rubble of what, seven days earlier, had been a handsome three-storey Dutch house. It was now a wasted husk of blackened brick and creaking wood, shelled to a near skeleton by the German tanks and mortar shells.

He reached into the pleated pocket of his tunic for the squashed pack of Woodbines. 'Bugger,' he muttered. Only three cigarettes remained – his last. He withdrew one, straightened it and, with a shaking hand, lit it.

More than a week had passed since he last looked at himself in a mirror but he didn't need a mirror to know he smelled. Living on adrenalin, fear and very little else can do that to you. After seven days and nights of fierce house-to-house combat, under a relentless counter-attack by a heavily armoured German Panzer Division, more than half his company was now wounded or dead.

The slaughter had nullified his senses. Everything in his horrifying world was muted, as though a tranquillizing cloud had enveloped it. Everything but the truth, that is – the truth never talked about among the men. But the gaunt faces and dust-circled eyes couldn't hide from each other what they all knew – that the end was not far off.

He shivered and pulled the collar of his mud-spattered greatcoat tighter around his neck, taking another long drag on the cigarette. Absently, he stared past the limp lace curtain and out through the jagged-edged hole that once was a window. The sky was turning from grey to pale gold as the anaemic sun rose over the shattered village of Kleinelangstraat.

He jumped. Someone was kicking his foot. He looked up into the grim, exhausted face of his lieutenant.

'Round everybody up, sarge. I want all the able-bodied assembled in the back of the house as soon as possible, in the big room. On the double,' he snapped. About to leave, the officer stopped and looked back. 'Corporal McBride bought it a couple of hours ago. Thought you might like to know.' There was no emotion in his voice. 'One more thing – the radio's up the spout, too. Took a direct hit.' He nodded grimly and walked away.

The sergeant watched the lieutenant duck through the doorway, brushing the door that swung crazily on its hinges, and disappear. 'Yes, sir. Yes, bloody sir,' he muttered. Stiff and cold, he started to get up. Half standing, he caught a movement through the window out of the corner of his eye. 'Jesus!' he shouted, scrambling for the front door and dashing outside.

It was one of his men. He was stumbling over the rubble-strewn road, past the smouldering skeleton of a German machine-gun carrier. He recognized who it was immediately. The lad had stripped off his jacket and was bareheaded. A dirty white rag hung limply from the business end of the rifle sloped across his shoulder.

'Kit! Don't!' the sergeant screamed, lurching forward to reach him.

Suddenly, from off to his left, another voice barked out: 'Stop, you damned fool! Drop that bloody rifle, soldier – or I'll shoot!'

Stopping in his tracks, the sergeant turned. It was the lieutenant. No more than ten paces away he stood with his feet spread apart and his pistol levelled at Kit's back. His voice was calmer now.

'Last warning, son – stop right there.'

'Christ almighty!' the sergeant cried. 'Don't shoot the poor bastard!' He leapt forward at a full run, hurling his body through the air at the officer.

In the pandemonium that followed it was impossible to tell which came first: the *crack* of the lieutenant's pistol or his shout of pain, reverberating off the walls of the shelled-out buildings, as he fell back hard on the brick and rubble, the sergeant's thirteen stones crushing him.

Arms and legs flailed under a thick cloud of dust as the two wrestled in the dirt. The sergeant soon gained the upper hand, pinning the officer down with one knee, gripping his wrist in a struggle for the pistol. He managed to force the officer's arm down, but still he couldn't wrest the pistol from him. With grunting force he kept twisting the lieutenant's arm, expecting something to snap at any moment. He could see the officer's finger curled round the trigger, only inches from his face. He summoned his last ounce of strength and gave a final jerk.

It was as if both his eardrums had suddenly burst – an explosive incessant clanging.

The blast of the shot hammered through his brain, making his eyes throb, flooding them with tears. The lieutenant's piercing scream went unheard.

He loosened his grip on the officer's wrist, looking down to see that the bullet had shattered the man's leg just below the knee. The sight of fragments of shinbone and fusion of blood and torn muscle made him want to retch.

The lieutenant's eyes were screwed tight, his grimy face contorted with pain, his body convulsing. The sergeant took the pistol, struggled to his feet and walked over to Kit's motionless body. Blood was seeping through the lad's white singlet.

He knelt, placing the tips of two fingers on Kit's neck. He waited, teeth clenched. There was no pulse. He stood for a few seconds, fighting back the tears that welled in his bloodshot eyes. He had to get the body and the lieutenant out of there quickly. It was still early but it seemed the German snipers never slept.

He knelt and hoisted Kit's body over his shoulder and carried him back to the house. Leaving the corpse inside he went back to help the lieutenant.

While one of the medics went to work on the officer's leg, the sergeant sat by Kit's side, leaning forward, head between his hands. Now he let the tears flow.

He sat like that for more than a minute, finally interrupted by the lieutenant's contemptuous voice. 'You'll go up a long time for this,' was all he said.

The sergeant said nothing. He removed the watch from Kit's wrist and went through his trouser pockets. In the front was a St Christopher medallion, some chewing gum, a bone-handled penknife and a handkerchief. In one of the back pockets he found a folded envelope addressed *To Em*. In the other, his fingers touched what felt like a small book.

He took it out. It was a black leather diary.

Chapter One

The clang of metal on metal resounded off the walls of the old stone house, echoing across the lawns to be lost in the dense forest beyond.

'Doctor!'

Lawrence Kingston brought the sledgehammer down on the iron stake one more time.

'Doctor!'

He looked up to see the carrot-haired figure of his foreman, Jack Harris, approaching. Leaning the sledgehammer against his leg he wiped his brow with the back of his hand. He was about to take a rest anyway. For the last twenty minutes he had been surveying, driving in stakes on the top lawn – one of three football-field-size levels that stepped down from the back of the big house. Once mown and rolled twice a month to look like green carpeting, they were now a waist-high tangle of weeds.

'Need you to come and take a look at something,' Jack said, nodding back over his shoulder.

'Be right there.' Kingston picked up the survey maps, put them in his canvas bag and walked over to join Jack. Was it good or bad news? From the look on Jack's face, Kingston couldn't tell. 'What you got then?' he asked.

Jack smiled. 'You'll see in a minute.'

With nothing further said, they took off.

Soon they reached a clearing some five hundred yards

from the house. It was in one of the most overgrown sections of the 'Jungle', as it was now nicknamed. Nearby, to the staccato whine of chainsaw and thwack of axe blade on wood, Jack's crew of three were chopping up the fallen trees and cutting down the dead ones, many of which were supported by their less tipsy neighbours. Wood-smoke from their bonfire was thick in the still air. When Jack and Kingston arrived, the men stopped work and gathered around.

Jack said nothing, waiting for Kingston's reaction. Facing them, built partway into a vertical limestone crag, was the façade of what appeared to be a small chapel. Off to one side was a house-high tangle of ivy brambles and vines that had been cut and ripped away from its walls by Jack's crew.

'It was completely covered,' said Jack. 'You could've walked by here a hundred times and never known it was there. Three feet thick it was.'

'Amazing,' Kingston muttered, walking up to the blackened oak door, touching the rubblestone surround. Fern-edged trails like giant snail tracks tattooed the wall where the ivy had been tugged away. On either side of the door two identical stained glass windows displayed griffins. The glass was filthy but intact.

'Did you go inside?' asked Kingston.

'No, I thought it best to wait for you.'

'Let's take a look then.'

Gripping the large iron door handle, Kingston turned the key and the door swung open, hinges creaking. Why the key had been left in the door was something that he would ponder later. He was too excited to worry about it now.

Sufficient light filtered through the open door for them to make out the interior. The space was no more than twenty-five feet wide and about forty feet long. The walls were wood and plaster, the ceiling simply raftered. For a chapel, and that's surely what it was, Kingston was surprised at the absence of ecclesiastical artifacts and trappings. The only ornamentation apparent was the handsome bronze sconces, four on each of the two long walls, none holding candles. A central flagstone aisle ending at a pulpit was flanked on either side by eight rows of simple wooden pews. The pulpit was panelled with turned balusters. But Kingston's eyes were not on the pulpit. He was looking at what was beyond.

As he walked farther down the aisle he could now see clearly what had seized his attention. Behind the pulpit alongside a small baptismal font was a large stone circular well about five feet in diameter. It looked out of keeping with the rest of the interior. He went up and rested his hand on the cold stone.

'Well, I'll be damned,' he said, turning to Jack. 'I bet this was originally a healing well.'

'A healing well?'

'Right,' he said, leaning over the waist-high ledge, peering down into the inky darkness. 'They go back to Celtic times and beyond, long before the Romans came. I'm told there are quite a few around here.' His voice echoed around the stark walls of the chapel. 'The waters are believed to have healing powers. In the Middle Ages wells were sanctified and frequented by pilgrims.'

One of Jack's crew had followed them into the chapel. 'What do the waters heal?' he asked.

'Apparently just about anything ailing you – from a hangnail to a heart condition. Skin complaints, asthma, epilepsy, stomach ailments, you name it – even paralysis! Mental as well as physical, so legend has it.'

Kingston stepped back, reached into his pocket and took out a coin. Dropping it into the well, he counted under his breath. One . . . two . . . on three, he heard the plop of the coin hitting water. 'Deep, by the sound of it.' He turned and cast his eyes around the low ceiling. 'Tomorrow, let's rig up some lights in here, Jack, and we'll show it to Jamie. She has her own place of worship now.'

11

Jamie Gibson, an American, was the new owner of Wickersham Priory, the estate on which they were all working. Her project, both ambitious and expensive, was aimed at restoring the ten-acre gardens that had fallen into decay after decades of neglect.

As he turned to go, something on the flagstones caught his eye; a slight glint, nothing more. He stooped to look closer. It was a coin. A few feet away there was another, then a third. Picking them up, he examined them in the palm of his hand. One was a shilling, dated 1963. A sixpence was dated 1959, as was another shilling.

He turned to Jack, who was about to walk off. 'Jack, how long would you say this place has been buried in that ivy?'

Jack thought for a moment. 'I dunno,' he said. 'Bloody long time, by the looks of it. You'd know better than me – why?'

'Just curious, that's all.'

By eight o'clock the next morning Jack and his men had set up a battery-powered lighting rig with two floodlights clamped to a vertical rod mounted on a tripod. Over the wellhead they had constructed a makeshift pulley with a rope tied to the handle of a galvanized bucket.

Shortly after eight fifteen Kingston and Jamie joined them. The bucket, weighted with a rock, was lowered into the well. It was some time before it reached the bottom.

Huddled around the wellhead in the chill air, the small group watched silently as two of Jack's men began pulling hand-over-hand on the pulley rope to bring the bucket up from the bottom of the well.

At last it broke the surface and they all peered over the stone ledge as it jerked and scraped its way up the last slimy ten feet – the sound echoing around the small space, misshapen shadows dancing against the white walls from the blaze of two halogen floodlights.

Sloshing water as it was lifted over the waist-high stone surround, the bucket was lowered to the floor. Jack walked over and up-ended its contents, splashing them on to the flagstones. On his haunches, he shoved the rock aside and examined the fragments of whitish material that had spilled out with the last ooze of well water and black sludge. 'Looks like we got ourselves some animal bones, doctor,' he said. 'Rat – squirrel maybe.'

Kingston walked over and knelt by the upturned bucket, poking the skeletal remains with his finger. He glanced at Jack. 'Can one of your chaps find a bag or a cloth that we can wrap these in?'

'Sure. Why?'

'Because this was no animal. It's what's left of a human hand.'

The next day, in response to Kingston's phone call, Detective Chief Inspector Chadwick and Sergeant Eldridge from Taunton police arrived at Wickersham in an unmarked car. They were accompanied by a van with personnel from Avon and Somerset Constabulary Underwater Search Unit.

Sitting in the third row of the pews, Jamie, Kingston and the chief inspector watched as the well area was cordoned off with blue and white tape and the scene photographed with a 35mm still camera, then videotaped. Soon the underwater search diver was lowered into the well.

Three minutes passed. The diver had been submerged longer than any of them had anticipated. Conversation had ceased and all eyes were now on the steel hawser that dangled from a new pulley the police had rigged over the wellhead. Suddenly it jerked and everyone exhaled. He was on his way up. It was a signal for Inspector Chadwick to get up and join the policemen waiting by the well.

Everyone watched with anticipation as the diver was lifted out. He snapped open his buoyancy vest and swung the scuba tank to the floor. Gripping his mask with both hands, he eased it up to rest it on the slick hood on his forehead, blinking his eyes to adjust to the floodlights. By the time he had removed the mouthpiece and tugged off his gloves there was a puddle of water at his feet. Those in the pews waited on his words.

'Bloody dark down there,' he said. 'Bloody cramped, too.' Though his words were meant for Inspector Chadwick who was standing next to him, his voice echoed off the bare walls of the chapel for all to hear.

'Anything interesting, Terry?' Chadwick asked.

'If you call bones interesting, sir,' he said, peeling off his hood, waggling a finger in his ear and cocking his head to one side. 'The doctor was right. There's what's left of a body down there. Mostly bones.'

'No soft tissue, ligaments, clothing?'

'Just a skeleton by the looks of it.'

An hour and a half later in the living room at Wickersham Priory Lawrence Kingston and Jamie sat discussing the grisly discovery. Between them on the coffee table was a disarray of china cups and saucers, a cosy-covered teapot, cake plates and crumpled napkins – the remains of their tea.

The DCI and sergeant had departed a couple of minutes earlier, having spent the best part of an hour asking questions about the events leading up to the discovery of the bones.

'I must say, your policemen are polite,' said Jamie, starting to stack the china.

Kingston pulled on his earlobe – a quirky habit whenever he was lost in thought – and nodded but made no comment.

Jamie paused, fingers on the handle of the china teapot. 'Can you get DNA from bones?'

'Certainly,' Kingston replied. 'Though I believe it might

be difficult coaxing DNA from the bones if they've been down there for many years, which appears to be the case.'

Jamie got up, went to the sideboard to retrieve the tea tray.

Kingston looked down at the table, speaking more to himself than to her. 'The inspector's probably right. I doubt seriously that we'll ever know who the poor soul was. Dental charts a remote possibility, I suppose.'

She looked over her shoulder. 'How on earth would you go about matching someone's teeth if they've been dead for as long as the inspector suggests?'

Kingston smiled. 'Not easy.'

Jamie faked a shiver. 'I suppose there *were* teeth? It's all a bit too gross for me.'

'I'm sure there were. And you're right, the accident or murder – whichever – could have taken place centuries ago.'

'Before this house was built?'

'A possibility.' He rubbed his chin, thinking.

Jamie screwed up her face. 'I hope you're right. I can live with a medieval family skeleton in the closet but it's another matter entirely if it took place more recently. Know what I mean?'

Kingston laughed, got up from the chair. 'I wouldn't lose any sleep over it, Jamie. Like the inspector said, we'll probably never know.'

'Will they know whether it's a man or a woman?'

'They will, quite easily.' Kingston had adopted a professorial stance, hands clasped behind his back. 'They'll determine that from the ischium-pubis index. Height too,' he added, starting to pace the room. 'That's deduced from the length of the long bones in the arms and legs. Hadden and another forensic anthropologist, whose name escapes me, developed that formula.'

Jamie's eyebrows shot up. 'God! How come you know all this?'

Kingston smiled. 'Spent a couple of years in med school when you were just a twinkle in your father's eye, my dear.'

'Really? Why did you give it up?'

Kingston grinned like a little boy who'd just landed his first fish. 'As the surgeon said, "I just wasn't cut out for it!"'

'Come on, Lawrence, be serious.'

Kingston snapped his fingers. 'Dapertuis. Professor Dapertuis. That was the other chap's name. Oh – and one other thing – they'll also be able to determine, within reason, the age of the victim at the time of death.'

'What about how long he or she's been down there?'

'That can present a problem. The longer those bones have been down there, the more difficult it will be for the pathologist to determine the time since death. Damn. I forgot to ask the inspector the rate of decomposition that bones undergo after submersion in water.' He shook his head, frowning. 'What *am* I thinking of? Chadwick wouldn't know that,' he muttered to himself.

Jamie picked up the loaded tray and started to make for the door. 'Anything I can get you, Lawrence?'

Kingston sighed. 'Thanks, no. I think we should call it a day.' He studied Detective Chief Inspector Chadwick's card one more time, then put it in his shirt pocket. 'Get back to more pleasant things like gardens and flowers.'

Straightening up after ducking under the low beam, Kingston closed the cottage door behind him. Thatched with honey-coloured stone walls, the cottage had been built over two hundred years ago to house labourers on the estate. Jamie had furnished it in a Laura Ashley style – a bit twee for Kingston's taste but appropriate and comfortable. It was now his home from home while he worked with Jamie restoring the gardens at Wickersham.

He picked up *The Times* and a pencil from the Welsh

16

dresser, went across the room and sank into the sofa. The paper was already folded to the Saturday Jumbo cross-word puzzle. He placed it on his lap and put on his glasses, ready to pick up where he'd left off the night before. Three days now and only half the answers pencilled in. Far off his usual pace. Considering that he'd been doing the mind-bending cryptic for Lord knows how many years, it was to be expected that once in a while he would be stumped. He read the 49 across clue for the third time: *One's right up the pole, as the mad may be* – 8 letters. For several moments he looked up at the misshapen timber beam that ran across the centre of the ceiling, the eraser end of the pencil resting on his lower lip. 'Bugger,' he said, finally, placing the paper back in his lap. He simply couldn't concentrate. His mind kept returning to the well, the skeleton and the coins, trying to picture what might have taken place there. He put the paper on the coffee table and stretched out, propping a pillow under his head. Once again the nagging feeling returned: that it could have been a big mistake on his part to become involved in Jamie's venture. It was too late now, though. He closed his eyes and thought back to that evening when she had first called him.

Chapter Two

When the phone had rung in his Chelsea flat that evening three months earlier, back in March, Kingston was comfortably settled in his rumpled leather chair reading *Gardens Illustrated*. It had been drizzling steadily all day. Next to him the small fire he'd lit earlier that afternoon hissed contentedly, giving a pleasing warmth and glow to the darkening room. He put the magazine aside and picked up the phone.

A woman with an American accent spoke. 'My name's Jamie Gibson,' she announced. 'Am I calling at a bad time?'

'No, no, it's fine. How can I be of help?' Kingston replied, his curiosity piqued.

'You've been recommended to me by my solicitor, David Latimer. He thinks very highly of you and suggested that I contact you.' She paused. 'He seems to know a lot about you. Tells me you're one of the top garden experts in the country.'

He made light of the compliment and asked again the reason for her call.

'I promise to be as brief as possible,' she replied.

She had recently inherited a large country house in Somerset along with its surrounding two-hundred-acre estate, formerly owned by a family named Ryder, she said. Despite its run-down condition, she had moved in and hired a local builder to start work on the house. 'I can manage the house just fine, but what really concerns me are the gardens.' She sighed. 'They're another matter entirely; that's where I'm hoping you might be of help. The reason for my call.'

'Gardens, plural, you said?'

'Yes, there're several.'

'Really? What do you mean by "another matter entirely"?'

'Well, I've been told that, in their heyday, the gardens at Wickersham Priory were among the finest in England.' She described the gardens as they had been in the years before the war and how, in the opinions of some garden writers of the time, they rivalled the best in the world.

'Where did you learn all this?' he asked.

'Mostly from the local library. A couple of seniors in the village told me about their visiting the gardens way back – but their descriptions were pretty sketchy. I also found a good book in the local bookshop, with several pages devoted to Wickersham. Gardens within gardens. They were so grand . . . so beautiful.' She spoke the words with a sensibility that he found oddly touching. Then she countered with a warm and infectious chuckle, as though she had practised it a long time to get it perfect. 'Right now, the gardens look more like something Steven Spielberg would dream up.' He smiled at the simile and was about to ask her to be more explicit but she carried on. 'It's my plan to restore them. I want to see them as they were in those days, mostly for me, but also as a way of expressing my appreciation. As a tribute, if you will, to the Ryder family. So I'm asking if you'll help me.' She paused but only for a second or so, as if not expecting a reply. 'Latimer thinks you'd be perfect for the job. Of course, I'm prepared to pay whatever it takes.' Another pause. 'Well, within reason, of course.'

Despite the temptation implicit in her last remark – and he had never been one to look a gift horse in the mouth – Kingston wasn't swayed. As the woman had been talking, he had been trying to cobble up a credible excuse and steer

19

the conversation to a polite close. He wasn't going to tell her he didn't have the time. That would sound too lame and, in any case, it would be a lie. Truth was that being retired – four years now, from his position as professor and head research botanist at Edinburgh University – he had nothing but time. No, he would simply tell her in all honesty that the magnitude of what she had described was too great for his present inclination for work and leave it at that. That could hardly offend her. In any case, Somerset was out of the question. Surrey or Bucks he might have considered, but Somerset? It was almost a half-day's trip from Chelsea. He was about to tell her all this when she cut in again.

'I'm sorry, I didn't mean to be so abrupt. I realize it's an awful lot to ask on the phone, plus you don't know me from Adam – well, Eve, I suppose,' she said, with the same infectious chuckle as before. 'It wouldn't be fair of me to expect an answer right away.' She paused. 'In fact, I would rather you didn't. What I *am* asking is that you consider it. That's all. Come down, spend a day and see the place – at my expense, of course – *then* decide whether the idea appeals to you or not. Stay as long as you want. You can have a whole cottage to yourself.'

Three days later, with the morning frost like cake icing on the hedges of Cadogan Square, he locked the front door to his flat and walked to the nearby garage where his Triumph TR4 was kept. Slipping behind the wheel, he soon joined the bumper-to-bumper traffic on Cromwell Road heading for the M4 and the two hundred-odd miles to Somerset, to see Jamie Gibson's estate.

Chapter Three

Once the cheerless sprawl of London's suburbs was behind him, Kingston's frame of mind improved with every mile. Midway on the long stretch between Reading and Swindon he pulled off at a service station and took the top down. It would be well worth braving the chill in the air. Back on the motorway his spirits climbed another couple of notches. Not surprising. His prized TR4 was getting a much-needed chance to blow out some cobwebs; he was on his way to a part of Somerset that he'd never seen, to meet a young woman he'd never met, and what's more, after weeks of wretched weather, the skies in every direction were cloudless.

A crab sandwich lunch, a glass of Sancerre and a refuelling stop in Bridgwater and he was on the last leg of the journey. Now the roads were narrow, cars few and far between. The exhaust crackled as he shifted down to third, then second, to negotiate a sharp hairpin. Every curve in the road revealed yet another vista of postcard perfection. He was now in the very heart of the Quantock Hills, an ancient wooded corner of the West Country.

The last few miles of the journey had been full of pleasant surprises. On one occasion, on a lane barely inches wider than the car itself, he had had to pull up sharply to give right-of-way to a string of wild horses. Every so often the banks on either side of the road were thick with wildflowers that spangled through the ferns and into the woods like confetti. A sweet fragrance perfumed the air that was loud with the gurgle and bubble of water and the twittering and warbling of a thousand birds. Twice he had driven through shallow fords on the road. Crossing heather-cloaked moors, through gentle pastures and ferny forest, he hadn't seen a house or any signs of people for miles.

Running a hand through his tangle of windblown hair, he peered over the top of his sunglasses. Yes, there they were, set back from the road, about fifty feet ahead on the left: the two blackened stone pillars each with a stone griffin perched on top – exactly as she had described. He slipped into second, passed between them and up the straight driveway leading to Wickersham Priory.

He drove slowly, taking in the scenery. A clutch of cottages tucked in the fold of a distant hollow appeared ahead: signs of habitation at last. Lulled by the meagre warmth of the grudging sun he tried to conjure a mental picture of the woman he was about to meet.

Caught up in the flight of fancy he very nearly overran the right-angled bend in the driveway. Quickly gaining control, he jammed his foot on the brake and skidded to a stop. He squinted in disbelief through the dirt-speckled windscreen. Fifty yards ahead was a wall of overgrown vegetation. In a heartbeat he had emerged from English countryside to rainforest. Cheek by jowl with native shrubs and trees stood all kinds of sub-tropical species. Coconut palms swayed on their spindly trunks amidst native pine, cedar, beech and laurel. In the shadow of an enormous oak the fronds of giant tree ferns and the elephant-ear leaves of *Gunnera* looked incongruous. Here and there tips of golden bamboo undulated above brambles and thicket. Thick vines snaked up tree trunks, trailing fountains of vivid colour. He estimated the maidenhair tree towering high above the scene to be at least a hundred feet tall. One scarlet-budding rhododendron was the size of a two-storey house. He stared at the sight for a minute or more then continued up the drive.

As he passed through a gap in the green wall the sunlight was abruptly extinguished, as if at the flick of a light switch. Out of the shadows, columns of tree trunks – some with a girth approaching that of ancient sequoias – loomed from the ferny black undergrowth, their lower bark sheathed in a velour-like mantle of bright green moss, algae and lichen. A cathedral-like silence added to the primeval gloom. Kingston shivered and drove on.

All at once it was light again. Now, tall clipped hedges of yew flanked the driveway. After the cheerless atmosphere of the last several minutes, Kingston found the orderliness heartening. Ahead, the gravel drive split to form a sweeping circle. On the grassy island within stood a massive ornamental stone fountain topped by a trio of sculptured dolphins, open mouths pointing skyward. Imprisoned by weeds at the base, it was blackened with age and neglect. He pictured the fountain in its former glory, jetting columns of water high into the air. What a splendid first impression it must have made.

On the other side of the circle a manor house loomed large. The sprawling structure was built of stone the colour of parchment yellowed with age. Mullioned and leaded windows of varying size gave relief to its stern façade. In colonnades, tall chimneys jutted from the slate roof like guardsmen. A blanket of ivy with scaffolding erected alongside shrouded the set-back part of the house on his left. At the buttressed entrance a Gothic archway led to a recessed front door.

'Mid-eighteenth century,' Kingston muttered to himself, rounding the circle.

Ahead, standing by the arch, was a smiling young woman wearing a loose white T-shirt and blue jeans. She was holding a broom.

'Could be earlier,' he mused, glancing up at the windows. He pulled the TR4 to a stop alongside her. Glad to be able to stretch his legs after being cooped up for the last couple of hours, he got out and took in a long breath, stretching his six foot three inch frame. 'Good afternoon,' he said, slamming the car door with a thump, running a hand through his hair in a vain attempt to make it appear less tangled. 'I'm here to see Jamie Gibson.'

The young woman grinned. 'You're talking to her.'

He summoned a weak smile and shook his head. 'I'm sorry. I apologize.'

'No need. I'm hardly one's idea of the lady of the manor.' She offered her hand. 'So, what do you think of the jungle?'

'Quite a jolt, I must say.' He smiled, creasing the laugh lines at his eyes. 'I've never seen anything like it.' He shook her hand, noting the unusual firmness of her grip and absence of nail polish. 'Lawrence Kingston,' he said.

'I'm delighted that you're here,' she countered, sizing him up. He towered over her by several inches, his features angular and pleasingly lined. Most noticeable was the hair, a thick snarl of white, though his eyebrows were oddly dark. No longer smiling, his face wore an air of authority. There was a vague but nevertheless intimidating lucidity in his blue eyes.

'Do I call you doctor?' she asked.

'No, no, Lawrence is fine.'

'Good. Well, come on in. You must be tired after such a long drive.' She paused, glanced at the sports car, then ran her eyes over Kingston's frame, but all she said was, 'Nice car.'

Kingston followed her into the house, their footsteps echoing across the tiled floor of a sparsely furnished entrance hall, through an open door into a living room. The room was grand, an ornate frieze girdling its high ceiling. A clutter of Persian carpets – most of them a bit the worse for wear – covered much of the parquet floor. The furniture, all of it antique, was a jumble of styles and periods. Gilt-framed paintings hung from walls that were the colour of old piano keys. An enormous crystal chandelier dominated the air space in the centre of the room. All the natural light came from one end where tall french doors, flanked by leaded windows, opened to a flagstone terrace looking out on to what used to be gardens, now an ugly wall of weeds, bramble and vines.

Jamie gestured to the large damask sofa. 'Please sit down, Lawrence. May I get you something to drink?'

'A cup of tea would be nice.'

'Breakfast tea or Earl Grey?'

'Earl Grey's fine, thanks. Oh, lemon, please, if you have it.'

Jamie nodded toward the coffee table. 'The top book contains several references to the house. I've marked the pages. I think you'll find it interesting. I'll be right back,' she said, leaving the room.

Jamie Gibson was not at all as he'd imagined. In the first place, she was considerably younger and prettier than her somewhat husky American voice on the phone had suggested. Mid-thirties, he would guess. She had soft features with trusting brown eyes that, he would soon learn, could turn in a flutter of long lashes to businesslike and penetrating. Of average height and slim of hip, she had an athlete's suppleness. Her blonde hair was fashionably short and her skin evenly tanned, leading him to wonder just how long she'd been living in Somerset. Beyond a trace of lipstick, she wore no make-up. It would be a fairly safe bet that she was from either California or Florida. He would inquire when she came back.

He leafed through the thick book to the first yellow Post-it note and started reading.

Five minutes had passed when he heard the rattle of china and looked up to see Jamie coming through the door carrying a tray with cups, saucers and a plate of scones.

'I see the house was built in the mid-1700s,' Kingston said, looking up. 'From these old drawings, it doesn't appear to have changed much?'

Jamie lowered the tray to the coffee table. 'No, hardly at all.'

Kingston crossed his long legs, leaned back into the sofa and put on his best smile. 'Forgive me for being curious,' he said.

She tilted her head to one side as if to say, 'Well?'

'California's my first guess, Florida second. Am I close?'

She sat down opposite him, folded her hands in her lap, returned the smile and then nodded. 'Right first time,' she said. 'Sonoma County, north of San Francisco.'

'Wine country. Know it well.'

'Really?'

'Yes. I had the good fortune to spend the best part of a summer there, about seven or eight years ago. A friend of mine, Gene De Martini – Gino, God rest his generous soul – owned a small winery close to Buena Vista on the east side of town. His kids run it now. I just love the place.'

'I don't know them personally, but I know the winery. They're getting quite a reputation. They won a couple of medals recently and they just opened a tasting room.'

'Good for them. I must drop them a line sometime.'

'I'll certainly look them up when I go back.'

'Don't you miss it? That beautiful weather – your friends?'

Jamie's expression suddenly clouded and she looked away. For what seemed like a long time, he waited for her answer. At last she turned back to face him. She had regained her poise but Kingston knew that he had stirred up memories she preferred not recall.

Trying to avoid his gaze, she lightly brushed a finger under one eyelid then looked up with a forced smile. 'I think about it from time to time,' she said, 'but I haven't been away long enough to be homesick. Besides, everything here is so new and this place is so demanding that I haven't had much time to think about home.' She offered a little smile. 'Sooner or later, I'm sure I will, though.'

Kingston knew when a change of subject was called for. He uncrossed his legs, leaned forward and smiled. 'So,

Jamie, tell me how a nice young American woman came to acquire such a big chunk of Somerset?'

She picked up the teapot, pouring Kingston's tea and then her own, as if buying time before answering his question. She slid the cup and saucer towards him, then a small glass dish with lemon slices. 'I hope it's strong enough for you,' she said.

Kingston watched and waited as she stirred two teaspoons of sugar into her cup.

She settled into the armchair, resting the cup and saucer in her lap. 'When we talked on the phone, I believe I told you that I'd inherited this place.'

'Yes, you did.' Kingston was consumed with curiosity to know more about her good fortune but with their acquaintanceship barely started he didn't want to risk the slightest chance of appearing forward or nosy, traits not entirely foreign to him. He had been hoping that, given her own good time, she would tell him her story. That moment might be now.

'It all started about six months ago,' she said. For a second or so she looked away, staring out through the casement windows where the skies had darkened and the leaves were starting to swish against the panes. 'I received a letter from a lawyer in Taunton – David Latimer. It was quite short, actually. Said that I'd been left the estate and all its assets and would I get in touch with him, which I did the next day. I thought it must be a horrible mistake or some kind of joke but right off, he confirmed that it wasn't. When he told me the size of the estate – what it was all worth and how much money was involved – I nearly died. I couldn't believe it.' She paused then laughed. 'I remember telling him jokingly that it came just in time because I was facing a fifteen hundred dollar repair job on my car.'

'What did he say?'

'Pretty soon, you'll be able to go out and buy a Bentley, if you like.'

'What an amazing story,' said Kingston.

'It certainly is. I still have to pinch myself sometimes to make sure I'm here – that it's all happening.'

'This was an aunt . . . an uncle?'

'Neither. No one related to me, as far as I know. That's what made it even more far-fetched.' She took a sip of tea, holding the cup in both hands.

'How extraordinary.'

'I know. Isn't it crazy? I still don't know who the man is.' She paused, a slight tilt to her head.

'What do you mean?'

'Sorry. What I should have said is that I know *who* he is but I haven't the foggiest idea why he named me as heir to this lot,' and she swept an arm round to take in the room.

For a moment Kingston held his cup poised in mid-air. 'How curious. Who is this chap? – I should say, *was*, I suppose.'

'Captain Ryder – James Grenville Ryder. His ancestors built this place over two hundred years ago. Up till now, Ryders have always lived here. He was the last, though. The end of the line,' she said, a tinge of sadness in her voice.

'You don't know anything at all about him?' asked Kingston, breaking off a piece of warm scone.

'Very little. He came back here some time after the war. I'm not sure exactly when, but David Latimer seemed to think it was in the early sixties.'

'More than forty years ago.' Kingston looked up to the chandelier, calculating. 'Must've been in his eighties when he died.'

Jamie nodded. 'He had two brothers, both killed in World War II. Their names are on the memorial in the village. One was in the RAF.'

'So Ryder lived here by himself?'

'No. He had a live-in butler called Mainwaring who apparently looked after everything on the estate. The nice man who runs the wine shop in the village told me that Mainwaring was very close-mouthed about Ryder and Wickersham. Came in, bought what he wanted, paid cash and walked out. Hardly ever said a word. The lady in the newsagent's said much the same thing. "Creepy old bugger", she called him. Always wore a heavy black overcoat, even in the height of summer.' She paused to finish her tea.

'What happened to him?'

'I think Latimer said that he just took off. Left the area. To tell the truth, I don't recall.'

'Did Ryder leave him anything?'

'David did say that Mainwaring received a modest bequest, yes.'

Kingston rubbed his chin thoughtfully. 'Did Ryder ever venture into the village?'

'Not that I know of, which leads to speculation that he might have been an invalid.'

'Hmm – that would certainly explain it.'

'There was also an elderly cook and housekeeper, called Dorothy Parmenter, affectionately known as Dot. I kept her on, as a matter of fact. She'll be cooking dinner tonight.' She smiled. 'I should warn you though, she's not the easiest person to get along with.'

'In what way?'

'She's very strait-laced. A widow. Doesn't talk much. Sometimes I think our roles are reversed.'

'I know the type.'

'On the plus side, she's a fabulous cook. And after she's done with cleaning, you could literally eat off the floor.'

Jamie brushed a strand of hair from her eye and placed her cup back on the saucer. 'That's about the size of it,' she said with a shrug.

'Must have been quite a shock to the locals when they learned you were the new lady of the manor.'

Her eyes widened and she laughed out loud. 'Are you kidding? They'll be talking about it for years.'

Kingston was beginning to wonder whether he was coming off as being a little too inquisitive but since the young woman didn't appear to be fazed by his questions he saw no reason not to satisfy his curiosity. He frowned. 'If this Dot of yours worked for Ryder, surely *she* must know something about him?'

'That's what I thought. First thing I did after hiring her was to quiz her about Ryder. She told me that during the two years she worked for him, all her instructions had come from Mainwaring. She swore that in all that time she saw Ryder on no more than three or four occasions. Hard to believe, isn't it?'

'Not really. Quite a few people choose to be reclusive. Particularly if they've got something to hide.'

She raised her eyebrows as if taking exception to his remark then broke into a smile. 'You make it sound like he was up to no good.'

'No, that's not what I meant at all. I'm just saying that there could have been a physical reason for his wanting to avoid people. A disfiguring war injury, something like that.'

'I suppose that could be a possibility.' She hesitated, then frowned. 'But surely Dot would have mentioned that?'

'Perhaps his mind was gone. That happens a lot in war.' He shrugged. 'Maybe Alzheimer's.'

'Could be, but he was sane enough to leave me all this. More than enough for the upkeep and expenses and a lot left over, too. '

'It's a mystery, all right.'

'So now you have the whole picture.' She slapped her hands on her knees. 'You know all about me.'

It was clear that, as far as Jamie was concerned, that was the end of the subject. But he dared ask one more question.

'What about your solicitor?'

'David?' she said, shaking her head. 'He assures me that he's as much in the dark as I am. According to him, his office received the sealed will, signed by Ryder and a notary, about a year ago, to be opened only upon his death. Apparently the family solicitor passed away just prior to that and David's office was assigned to handle the estate, so naturally he doesn't know that much about Ryder. Everything was perfectly in order, though, the title papers, bank and securities information, all the documents – they all checked out.'

'Obviously no Ryders in the dark recesses of your family, then?'

'Not that I know of.' She looked at him for a moment and grinned. 'If there were, they would more likely be Riders of the Purple Sage!'

Kingston laughed. 'Well, Jamie, I suppose if Latimer is satisfied that no Tom, Dick or Harry is going to come along in a year or so trying to prove he's the rightful heir – then not to worry.'

'That was one of my first questions. Latimer's already ruled out the chance of that happening.' She paused for a moment. 'Anyway,' she said, 'enough about all that, let's talk about why you're here.'

During the next half-hour, Jamie told Kingston what she had learned so far about Wickersham's history and her plans for its rehabilitation. Built in 1758 on the site of an old Benedictine priory, the house boasted twenty rooms on the ground floor alone, including a library and a billiards room. There was also a large well-stocked wine cellar (Kingston's ears pricked up at this), and three cottages in the grounds plus ancillary outbuildings. Work on the house was already under way, the first job replacing sections of the original slate roof.

The gardens, she said, were another matter (there was that phrase again). From everything she knew, the original gardens flanking the house on the south and west covered approximately ten acres. Nowhere had she been able to find mention of the original – or any, for that matter – garden designers or landscape architects. Pulling out some sheets of paper from one of the books on the coffee table, Jamie read aloud from the notes she'd made at the library. 'Here's what I know about the gardens as they existed in the years before the war,' she said, glancing up at Kingston. 'As best as I can make out, there were at least eight separate and distinct gardens.' She looked down at the paper again, running a finger down the list. 'A walled vegetable garden, an Italian garden, a rose garden, a sunken water garden, an herb garden . . . to mention a few. Plus I found references to an orchard, a yew alley, lots of topiaries, a circular thatched summer house, a gatehouse, a grotto, a pleached lime walk, various and sundry trellises, arbours and pergolas, some built on big stone piers . . .' She paused, studying the list. 'Oh, and there was a brick potting house, several large greenhouses, a long grass walk and huge lawns that stepped down in three levels from the rear of the house.' She looked up at Kingston.

'Goodness gracious, they weren't kidding when they said it could have rivalled the best,' he said. 'I'm surprised it's been such a well-preserved secret all these years.'

'Probably because it was never open to the public.'

'That could explain it.'

She looked puzzled. 'Hidcote's a garden, I take it?'

Kingston nodded. 'It's in Gloucestershire, in the Cotswolds. It's considered one of, if not, *the* finest example of all English gardens and yet, curiously, it wasn't created by an Englishman.'

'Really?'

'Would you be surprised if I told you it was an American?'

'I would, yes.'

'Well, indeed, it was – a Major Lawrence Johnston. His well-heeled mother bought him the estate just before World War I. There are more than twenty-five gardens within gardens covering the ten-acre site.'

'I must look it up in the library.'

'No book can do it justice. You *must* see it in person.' He paused and took a sip of tepid tea, quickly putting down his cup. 'You will, Jamie, because I'm going to take you there. The head gardener's an acquaintance. We'll also make a day trip to Sissinghurst. It's another brilliant example of twentieth-century English gardening.'

'I'd like that very much.'

Kingston raised a hand, briefly. 'I'm sorry, I seem to have interrupted.'

Jamie went on to tell him about the other two people on her staff. One was Eric, a young chap from the village, a part-timer who did odd jobs, ran errands and helped Dot. The second was an elderly caretaker, China, who lived with his ailing wife in one of the cottages on the estate. He also did some light garden work.

'I noticed, driving in, how nicely the yew hedges were clipped,' Kingston commented.

'Yes, he just did those. I was very pleased with them. China's not getting any younger but I must say he's a stickler for doing things right.'

'Odd name?'

She shook her head, glancing up to the ceiling as she did so. 'You Brits and your nicknames. His real name is Stanley – Stanley Wedgwood. Anyway, getting back to the gardens,' she said with a little sigh and a creasing of her brow, 'you saw for yourself, driving in, just how far gone they are. And you saw only a little corner. Before dinner, we'll go for a walk. Not too far, but enough to give you a better understanding of what you're getting into.' She paused, fixing him with her brown eyes and then smiling enigmatically. 'That is, of course, if you accept my generous offer.'

Chapter Four

Their short walk around the perimeter of the house confirmed Jamie's description. Much of it resembled what Kingston had seen earlier: thick stands of trees, so close together as to form a black wall, trunks, limbs and branches arching and writhing in a futile attempt to escape the strangling embrace of ivy, vines and creepers that lashed them together. It was as if the house were under siege, about to be swallowed up any day by this diabolical mass of plant life. As the light began to fade, the sight became even more menacing. For a while Jamie said nothing. Not that anything she might have said could further explain what they were looking at. After five minutes Kingston announced that he'd seen enough.

As they walked back to the house, his mind was occupied with two opposing thoughts: first and foremost, that this was without question a horticultural opportunity of a lifetime. In years to come, the gardens at Wickersham could become – as once they had been – on a par with the best. It could well be his chance to secure a place in the annals of world gardening. A chance that could also lead one day to his name being added to the list of pre-eminent English garden designers of the last four hundred years. Among the many was the seventeenth-century plantsman designer, John Tradescant; a hundred years later, the landscape genius of Lancelot 'Capability' Brown. Then, in the nineteenth century, the feisty William Robinson, whose ideas of a naturalistic, 'cottage garden' style became the dominant influence of the time, and one that survives to this day in many English gardens. The last century emerged with a new brilliance and the enduring designs of Gertrude Jekyll, Sir Edwin Lutyens, Harold Peto, Lawrence Johnston and Vita Sackville-West. In more recent years, Graham Stuart Thomas, Rosemary Verey, Christopher Lloyd and Penelope Hobhouse further inspired and influenced gardeners around the world.

But then there was the other side of the coin. Was he fully prepared to spend the next God knows how many months – even years – of his precious remaining time on earth dedicated to taming a jungle? He had no illusions about what it entailed and what he was going to have to sacrifice to see it through. Though their relationship was barely hours old, he had a good feeling about Jamie. She was forthright and sincere in her desire to restore the gardens and charming into the bargain. But would she be the same six months down the road? What effect would the colossal upheaval and financial drain have on her? Right now, she might think she was wealthy but did she really comprehend the kind of expenses she was going to be faced with? The upkeep of the estate and the enormous tax burden alone must be a daunting figure, but add to that the costs of refurbishing the house and a major garden restoration and the numbers would be staggering.

From his impression so far, Jamie didn't seem the type to press him for a quick decision. Nevertheless it would be expected of him as a potential employee, and rightfully so, to give some indication of his thoughts and intent. She would realize, of course, that he couldn't make a final decision until he knew what fee or salary she had in mind. He was already thinking that, if it was at all reasonable, he was prepared to conditionally accept her offer. He sighed. It was a huge decision.

Jamie picked up on the sigh. 'Quite a mess, isn't it?'

'Certainly is,' replied Kingston.

At the front door of the house Jamie stopped and turned

to him. 'Tell me honestly. What were you thinking back there?'

'I was thinking of Heligan,' he fibbed.

'Heligan?'

'A garden and a house in Cornwall, not unlike yours, actually. Maybe a shade larger.'

'Tell me.'

'It's a remarkable story. Just before World War I the gardens were abandoned and in the ensuing decades became completely buried. They would probably have been lost forever if not for two men, Tim Smit and John Nelson. By a stroke of luck, in the early nineties they were shown the land where the gardens once existed. There was a problem, though. It was all but inaccessible. The land had been literally consumed, buried by rampant growth and rotting with the decay of almost eighty years. From that moment they began a quest, not only to restore the gardens – as you're doing – but also, as it turned out, to resurrect a lost way of life. It's one of the most fascinating garden stories of all time.'

'Why didn't you tell me this earlier, Lawrence?'

'I suppose, until now, the resemblance just hadn't struck me. But there's no question that there are many similarities. Tim Smit wrote a book about Heligan. It's brilliant.'

'I'd very much like to read it. Don't you think we should go there, too?'

'We should, without question.'

'Let's go inside and you can tell me more about it over dinner.'

Throughout the main course Jamie did most of the talking, unusual for her. She seemed happy with small talk, mostly about her first impressions of Somerset and Wickersham. Kingston avoided asking further questions about her past, realizing that he had come close to overstepping the bounds of propriety earlier, though he was dying to know what she did in California – what kind of work? Her family?

The conversation drifted back to gardening.

'You seem to know quite a lot about gardening,' he said.

'Not really. I'm one of those self-indulgent people who like gardens solely for the pleasure they give. It's not that I don't like plants and flowers, the nitty-gritty, the hands in the dirt thing, it's just that I prefer the sensory aspect of gardens, as a means of escape, for the serenity, as a quiet and beautiful place for contemplation.'

'You'll have a wonderful time over here then. There's no end of extraordinary gardens to see. Quite a few in this neck of the woods, too.' He looked up at the ceiling moulding. 'Let's see, Hestercombe is close by and there's a lovely small garden at Tintinhull that was under the care of Penelope Hobhouse for a number of years. Then there's Hadspen House – as I recall, the gardeners there are Canadian. Barrington Court, East Lambrook Manor. You could spend all summer doing nothing but visit gardens, Jamie.'

At that point, Dot made a well-timed entrance to take away their empty plates and inquire about tea or coffee, telling them that 'afters' was on the way.

'That's such a quaint phrase,' Jamie commented the moment Dot had left.

Kingston took a sip of wine. 'You've got to admit, it's right to the point. Personally, I've always thought "dessert" was a trifle pretentious, if you'll pardon the pun. Plus, it comes from the French,' he said with a sniff. '*Desservir*, loosely translated as clearing the table.' For a split second his mind flashed back to a vaguely similar set of circumstances two years ago, sitting across a dining-room table from Kate Sheppard, an equally attractive young woman. She and her husband, Alex, owned the garden where a blue rose was discovered. He glanced briefly at Jamie who was lost in thought, studying her wineglass. They sat in silence for a few moments, each with their own thoughts.

'Tell me about the blue rose,' she said, suddenly looking up.

The question caught him off balance. The damned woman was reading his mind. Latimer must have mentioned it to her. 'You mean my fifteen minutes of fame,' he replied with a smile.

Over the rim of her wineglass, Jamie's brown eyes looked larger than normal and inquisitive. 'That's not what I heard,' she said with the slightest smile. 'You made a big splash according to all reports. Tell me about it.'

Kingston smoothed the tablecloth in front of him, long fingers spread, deciding which version to give her, the abridged or the unexpurgated. Having recounted the story so many times now, he had both by rote. He was about to launch into his narrative when Dot reappeared with the afters.

For the next five minutes Kingston recounted his short version of the drama that had taken place in Wiltshire. Save for the occasional question, Jamie listened attentively and with occasional amusement as he relived – not without liberal fustian flourishes – the bizarre turn of events, the despicable treatment suffered by Kate Sheppard and the loss of lives that had taken place that summer. By the time Dot entered the room again, ten minutes later, balancing a tray with a silver coffeepot, cups and saucers, Kingston had finished summing up and was answering what would be Jamie's last question on the subject. 'As far as I know, it wasn't reported by the press, Jamie, but a few weeks after we handed it over, the blue rose was destroyed by the people at the Department of Health.'

Jamie eyed Kingston as she poured coffee into their china cups. 'And the two missing cuttings? Did they ever show up?'

'No,' he sighed. 'I hope to God they never do.'

As the evening drew on Kingston was starting to wonder if she was ever going to ask him about his impressions of Wickersham and how he felt about her proposal. He

38

decided that if she didn't bring it up before the evening was over, he would take the initiative. Not a minute or so later she got round to the question of his involvement.

Step by careful step, she unfolded her plan, 'visualizing', as she put it, what his role would be, stressing more than once that he could go at whatever pace he felt most comfortable. He noticed, too, that she used mostly 'whens' as opposed to 'ifs' in talking about his participation. Still, there was no mention of reimbursement.

Before long, the tall-case clock in the hall was announcing eleven o'clock, the somnolent chimes reminding Kingston, as did his eyelids, that it had been a long and remarkable day and that he was ready to pack it in. He glanced at his watch and then at Jamie, who looked wide awake. He leaned back in his chair and smiled. 'As the classic line goes, Jamie, you've made me an offer I can't refuse. There are some important things we need to get resolved before signing on the dotted line but, by and large, I'm very interested in your project and would like to be part of it.' He paused to take a sip of coffee, wondering whether she had got the hint. 'I'm not quite sure if you realize just how huge an undertaking this is but, regardless, I get the impression that you'll be able to handle it. I think we'll make a good team.'

'I know we will,' she replied with a smile.

'Would it be all right with you if we picked up our discussion in the morning?' he asked, stifling a yawn.

For a second, Jamie's expression was blank. Then, as quickly, she smiled again. 'Yes, of course. But there's one thing we haven't talked about yet, perhaps the most important of all. I apologize for not bringing it up sooner.'

Finally, thought Kingston.

'The question of compensation,' she said. 'Your fee.'

For reasons unknown – but no doubt to do with his lifetime in the halls of academia, where discussing one's income was considered boorish and salaries were rarely negotiated – he had always found discussing such matters uncomfortable. With his curiosity piqued, now could be an exception, though.

'I must confess, Jamie, I hadn't given it much thought.' The minute the words left his mouth he knew they sounded hollow. 'Well, that is to say – it wouldn't necessarily be the deciding factor.'

She said nothing, as if enjoying his momentary and rare lapse of equanimity.

Kingston broke the awkward silence. 'Perhaps you should tell me what you had in mind.'

To his surprise, Jamie got up from the table and went over to a nearby bureau. She opened the top drawer and withdrew an envelope. Returning to the table, she slid the envelope towards him. 'I suppose I should have given you this much earlier.'

Kingston opened the envelope, took out the letter, unfolded it and started to read. After a few seconds he looked up at Jamie, astonishment registered on his face. 'This is – well, what can I say – this is more than generous. Are you sure –?'

'We don't have to discuss it now. It will keep overnight, Lawrence.' Suddenly, her eyes hardened, locking on to Kingston's. 'I would like to say one thing, though,' she said. 'I don't want the money to influence you unnecessarily. I want you to be well compensated but above all I would want you to accept the assignment *only* because you believed in it and would put your heart and soul into it. I would like to think of you as a partner, not an employee. The two of us can create something of extraordinary beauty here. I'm certain of it.' Just as quickly, the brown eyes were soft again, still fixed on Kingston but not demanding a reply. She fell silent.

Kingston took a deep breath and placed the letter on the table. The sum she was offering was more than double his former annual salary. He was still struggling to contain his shock. 'Jamie, it's far more than is necessary,' he said softly. 'And you're right. If I accept, you have my word for it that it will only be for the reasons you have stated.' He smiled. 'Can we sleep on it, then?'

By noon the next day, he and Jamie had reached a handshake agreement. He would return one week hence to further familiarize himself with the estate and start to address the myriad tasks confronting them. During his absence she would start checking with the county and the local borough to find out what permits or special procedures might be required. Equipment and materials would be purchased as needed, starting with two pickup trucks, a small backhoe loader, and a laundry list of items like axes, chainsaws, power and gardening tools.

They said goodbye at the front door portico under gloomy skies. Kingston slipped effortlessly behind the wheel of the TR4 – a remarkable feat, considering his size – slammed the door, turned the key in the ignition and with a wave of a kid-gloved hand, drove off round the circular drive and out of sight.

Passing through the two stone pillars, leaving Wickersham, he looked in the rear view mirror at the black wall of the jungle. It had started to drizzle. He flicked the wipers on and headed for the A39 to Bridgwater, wondering whether to put the top up. 'What *am* I getting myself into?' he muttered under his breath.

Chapter Five

On his return to London, Kingston made all the necessary arrangements for the care of his apartment, forwarding of mail and other exigencies required during his extended absence. A friend and neighbour promised to keep an eye on things. Within six days he was back at Wickersham, comfortably lodged in one of the estate cottages that Jamie had decorated in a cheerful country look.

First order of the day had been to hire a foreman for the project who, in turn, would assemble a work crew. Of the dozen or so applicants, Kingston had chosen Jack Harris, as best of a mediocre bunch. Jamie's impression was not quite as charitable – a little too cocky, she had commented after meeting him. Despite her misgivings she went along with Kingston's decision.

Jack was single and had lived in the Taunton area for the last several years working in construction and general landscaping but the London accent was still there. Kingston was soon to learn that though Jack might be sparing on words and somewhat lacking in good manners and diplomacy, his energy and drive were Herculean. He claimed the immediate respect of his crew by demonstrating that there was nothing he would ask them to do that he couldn't do himself. On one occasion, to prove a point, he scrambled up a fifty-foot Chinese cedar tree without the help of ropes or a harness.

Within five days of Jack's hiring, work commenced on the uphill task of clearing the land. Bulldozing was kept to an absolute minimum. It would have been the quickest and simplest method but by and large it was out of the question since there was no way of knowing what was buried underneath the rampant mass of bramble, ivy, laurel, impossibly tangled vines and fallen trees.

Teams called 'bramble bashers' did a lot of the preliminary clearing work. The nickname had survived from the Heligan days. Working in pairs, under the watchful eye of a gardener lest they should start hacking away in the wrong places or at plants that were to be saved, one 'basher' would slash away at the dense growth with a machete while his mate cleared the hacked-out debris with a long rake. Chainsaw crews were at the ready should they hit fallen trees. Once an area was cleared, a dumper truck would appear to cart away the debris.

Extreme care had to be taken not to destroy anything above or under the ground that might be a remnant of the former gardens. It was Kingston's hope, indeed, expectation, that they would be able to salvage all kinds of plants, shrubs, and garden treasures that were entombed under the sixty-plus years of rampant vegetative growth. While various pieces of mechanical equipment were employed for some of the heavy-duty work, most of the clearing was done by sheer hard labour.

Once it was completed, a comprehensive survey of the site would be undertaken. First, all the landscape features: the pathways, steps, walls and rock areas like the grotto would be established on the map. Next the structures and garden features that had been unearthed would be catalogued. Then, finally, the most labour-intensive of all, identifying and marking the precise location of every tree and shrub. These would all be tagged and numbered and entered into a computer database.

The hope was – although at this early stage in the restoration, rather slim – that later, if and when plans of the original gardens were found, the new plan could be figuratively superimposed over the original, thereby establishing the evolution and development of the garden through to the present day.

The early stages of the restoration process would have taken months longer were it not for the help of Gillian Thomas. An amateur historian, she worked at the library in Bridgwater. Gillian had volunteered to conduct historical research and to compile an official record, written and photographic, of every stage of development on the estate. As a start, she had undertaken a thorough search of the vaults of the Somerset Record Office in Taunton and other public record offices. Three weeks into the task, she unearthed two detailed plans of the estate drawn in the early part of the nineteenth century. Later she procured an 1840 Ordnance Survey map and an 1852 tithe map of Wickersham. These documents were invaluable in forming the foundation for the new design.

One of the first priorities had been to raze the grounds immediately surrounding the house. This done, the house took on a much more pleasant aspect. Opened up to the skies on all sides, it seemed to flourish in its new environment, assuming an even grander mien, looming larger than before. For Jamie – and she made no secret of it – progress was unbearably slow but as every day passed, nature grudgingly surrendered piece after piece of the puzzle. Victorian and Edwardian garden features, structures, ornaments and artifacts, abandoned long ago, were salvaged, photographed, catalogued and subjected to critical scrutiny by Kingston and his crew.

Some discoveries were not of great significance – like that of a derelict potting shed entombed in a sarcophagus of nettles and blackberry. It surrendered hundreds of terracotta pots, a stockpile of glazed Victorian edging and a trove of vintage garden tools. Another find provided much-needed clues to the botanical history of the gardens. In a derelict, fern-shrouded structure, built up against a high brick wall – Kingston thought it might have been a peach house – several wooden crates, too rotted to even lift, contained a hundred or so old zinc plant markers. Back in the days before the war, a gardener had had the foresight to wrap them in oiled paper and tie them in neat bundles. Not only were they beautifully preserved, each bore the name of a plant variety that had been planted or was about to be planted in the gardens. As he read off the Latin names like *Lychnis chalcedonica*, *Campanula lactiflora*, *Nigella damascena*, *Astrantia major*, Kingston's eyes lit up. 'Better than digging up a box of gold coins,' he declared to Jamie. Over the last weeks, the lack of plant information had become a recurring topic. Surprisingly, up until now, not a single work ledger, planting layout or sales receipt had surfaced. Now, at the very least, they possessed the beginnings of a list that would enable them to start planting.

On two occasions over more recent days, work had come to a complete halt. A jubilant shouting had signalled these events, bringing everybody within earshot running to the scene. These were important finds. The first was unearthed after a full day's hacking away at a fifty-foot stretch of house-high bramble. All these years the impenetrable mass had mothballed the rotting remains of a large Victorian greenhouse. Most of the algae-stained windows were still intact and its shiny cobbled floor was none the worse for its incarceration. Gillian had snapped off at least three dozen digital photos that afternoon.

The second recovery was even more impressive. In an area of the garden close to the house, a twelve by thirty-foot mosaic-tiled reflecting pool looked skyward again after sixty years in hibernation. The central motif of the design, the head of a griffin, was identical to those Kingston had encountered earlier on the stone pillars – the Ryder family crest. The decorative Italian tiles were in remarkably fine condition.

And now, of course, there was the chapel and the well. Since that discovery Kingston had returned to the site twice. Although he had said nothing yet, it had struck him straight away that there was something not right about the dates of the coins. Since it was already known that the gardens had been abandoned in the years prior to the war – the late thirties – it seemed a reasonable assumption that the chapel would have been buried since that time, too. But the coins were dated 1959 and 1963. The only explanation was that there had to be another way of entering the chapel. The coins had appeared sometime *after* it was sealed by nature.

For this reason, Kingston's visits to the chapel served only one purpose: to see if there had once been another means of entry; a way in that was used by the man who had either fallen down the well or whose body had been dumped there. So far he had not been able to come up with any evidence of another means of access. As a result, he had concluded that Jack and he were wrong and that somehow nature had given the chapel a reprieve and had not consumed it until much later than the rest of the garden.

Kingston was looking forward to the coming evening. It was Friday and David Latimer and his wife were invited to dinner at Wickersham. It would be the first time that Latimer had seen the property since the week Jamie arrived in England.

David Latimer was one of those men whose age could be anywhere from forty years to sixty. Grey hair on the one hand; yet evenly tanned skin that was as smooth as alabaster on the other. A fastidious dresser, he wore a double-breasted navy blazer that showed the proper measure of shirt cuff below the four regimental brass buttons on the sleeves. His wife, Arabella, was dark-haired, bubbly and as thin as a wafer. An ascetic diet and too many hours at the gym, thought Kingston, when first introduced. He was soon to find out that she ate like a horse.

A few forkfuls into the main course, the conversation –

having exhausted speculation about the skeleton – inevitably found its way around to Ryder.

Latimer glanced across the table at Jamie. 'Have you come up with any more information about Major Ryder?'

'No, nothing whatsoever.' She shrugged, then said, 'Not that I've been really trying.'

'Nothing turned up in all those hundreds of boxes?'

'No,' said Jamie, taking a sip of wine.

'Not even a *photo*?' Arabella piped up. 'No family pictures?'

Jamie shook her head. 'No. To tell the truth he's been about the furthest thing from my mind, of late.' She glanced at Kingston. 'There's been so much to do – Lawrence will tell you.'

Arabella dabbed her chili pepper-painted lips with her napkin leaving a visible print. 'It would be odd, don't you think, with several generations of Ryders having lived in this house, if there wasn't a single photo, some clippings, a scrapbook? Not one?'

'Bella makes a good point,' said Latimer. 'Particularly with the three sons – men, I suppose – being in uniform. It would be unheard of *not* to have photos scattered around the house.'

Kingston swirled the wine around in his glass then held it up to the light. An excellent '93 Beaune. The rich tawny red reflected a glint off the steady flame of the Georgian candelabra close to him. 'Unless, at one point, they were all – re-moved,' he said, pronouncing each syllable.

Latimer frowned. 'Removed?'

'Who would have done that?' Jamie asked, concealing her amusement at Kingston's posing. 'And, why, for that matter?'

'I don't know,' Kingston huffed. 'Not yet, anyway.'

For several moments conversation ceased as knives scraped on plates, wineglasses were topped up and second helpings were offered around the table. Kingston helped himself to more Yorkshire pudding and gravy.

'Lawrence, when you said "Not yet, anyway," does that mean that you know something that we don't?' asked Latimer.

'No, David,' Kingston replied. 'All I meant was that there could be more to this whole Ryder business than any of us realize. Don't you think that –'

'Good heavens!' It was Arabella who interrupted Kingston mid-sentence. A quizzical look had crossed her face. 'A thought just occurred to me.' She put a hand up to her mouth.

'Well?' asked her husband.

'No, that would be absurd,' she said, with a shake of the head.

'Come on, Bella, what would, for crying out loud?' asked Latimer.

'What if the bones belonged to Ryder?'

Jamie started to laugh. 'That's an odd way to put it, Bella. You're suggesting it could have been Ryder's body in the well?'

Latimer looked confused and glanced at Kingston.

'I'm sure the police won't overlook that as a possibility. Frankly, it's a theory I hadn't ruled out myself,' said Kingston coolly.

'If it was, then . . .' Latimer groped for words.

'Then it raises all kinds of questions,' Jamie interrupted.

'The first being, who's been living in the house all these years, posing as Ryder?' Latimer shook his head and looked at his wife disdainfully. 'No, the idea's patently absurd,' he said. 'For starters, Mainwaring identified Ryder's body.'

'But suppose the servant was lying. Wouldn't it be easy to find out?' Bella asked.

'How?' Jamie inquired.

'Well, just have his body exhumed.'

'Oh come on, this is *silly*,' Jamie said, shaking her head.

'I don't see why,' Bella snipped.

Jamie frowned at Latimer. 'Is that possible, David? Now I come to think of it, we never did discuss his death – the funeral.'

Her question hung in the air for several moments, while Latimer was clearly trying to frame an answer.

He leaned back in his chair and ran a hand across his forehead. 'No, we didn't, Jamie,' he said. Then, after a pause 'And no, we can't, I'm afraid.'

'Can't what,' asked Jamie.

'Have him exhumed.'

'Why not?'

'Because Major Ryder was cremated.'

Chapter Six

After dinner Jamie offered to show Bella around the upstairs rooms. This gave Kingston the chance he had been hoping for – the opportunity for a private talk with David. There were questions – one in particular – that he wanted to ask that would have been out of the question in the company of Jamie. The last thing he wanted was for her to get the impression that he was nosing into her affairs.

With fresh coffee for Latimer and a cognac for Kingston, the two of them sat across from each other, chairs angled toward the fireplace. For a while he and Latimer talked about the restoration, Kingston briefing him on the encouraging progress they'd made so far and describing some of the structures and features that they had uncovered and were going to rehabilitate.

Soon, the conversation shifted to Jamie.

'How did you track her down?' asked Kingston.

'It took longer than we anticipated because we initially assumed that she was English or British. When we drew a blank with our inquiries, we turned it over to a private investigator.'

Kingston nodded. 'I'm not one to be nosy, David, but I'm curious. How is it that Jamie was able to make what appears to be such an easy and rapid transition from her life back in California? I've tried to picture myself suddenly thrust in her position and how I would react, what a huge impact it would have on one's life in general. There's her job – presuming she had one – her family and friends, her house or apartment, all those things. As I understand it, she made a fairly quick decision to chuck it all up and come over here, thousands of miles away, where she doesn't know a soul. I must say, for a single woman, it's damned adventuresome.'

Latimer put down his cup and saucer. 'As you've probably found out already, Jamie is not your typical American. She tends to keep herself to herself. In a way, I suppose, she's more like us. You know, the stereotypical reserved Englishman or woman in this case. In due course I'm sure she'll come around.' He chuckled. 'With someone as charismatic as you, Lawrence, rather quickly, I would imagine.'

'Seriously, is she going to be able to afford all this? You and I both know what kind of money it's going to take.'

Latimer paused for a moment, as if debating just how much of Jamie's personal information he could pass on. 'Let me put it this way,' he said. 'The two of us have spent a lot of time going over the estate's assets. Early on she gave me a rough idea of what she wanted to do and later she presented me with what I would call a very pragmatic and sophisticated business plan. It not only detailed all the various projects and changes that she was recommending but included their projected costs. The breakdown of the expense estimates was quite extensive and specific. Working with her builder, she produced a timetable and work order list several pages long. I wouldn't mind betting she's done this kind of thing before. She's exceptionally bright, you know.'

'I've already come to that conclusion, David.' Kingston took time crossing his legs. 'By the way, what did she do in the States?'

'You know, she's been rather vague about that. She just said that she worked in the wine business. She did tell me her father worked for a wine import company, though. Perhaps she did, too. Her parents are both dead, by the way.'

'I'm sorry to hear that.'

'Anyway,' said Latimer, with a slight shrug, 'just what motivated her to drop everything back there to come over here and take on this challenge, I really can't say. I'm more than satisfied that she can afford it though, don't you worry on that score. I don't know where this Ryder chap got his money from – family money for the best part, I suppose, but somehow he managed to invest it very wisely over the years.' He chuckled. 'All I know is that it didn't come from his army pension.'

Kingston nodded in agreement. 'Well, the important thing is that the money's there, right?'

Latimer smiled. 'Oh, you'll get paid all right, if that's what you're worried about, old chap.'

Kingston returned the smile. 'Never gave it a moment's thought, David.'

'Kidding aside, you've a right to ask. You know as well as I do that more often than not the gentry who own these big estates are virtual paupers. Every day there's another one selling off bits and pieces at auction, flogging cream teas and opening the ancestral pile to the public. Damned shame if you ask me.'

At a pause in the conversation, Kingston got up and prodded the smouldering logs, bringing them to flame, spitting sparks up the chimney. 'This chap Mainwaring,' he said, sitting down, leaning back in the overstuffed chair. 'How long was he with Ryder?'

Latimer took a sip of coffee. It must have been his fourth or fifth cup of the evening but he seemed remarkably relaxed. 'Can't be certain – about fifteen years, I believe.'

'Jamie said that he wasn't very well liked. "Creepy bugger" I think were the words she said one of the villagers used.'

'A reasonably accurate description, I would say. Not exactly Prince Charming, that's for sure.'

Kingston crossed his legs, turning sideways to the fire, which was now throwing off enough heat at trouser cuff distance to toast bread. 'David, I should mention that Jamie has been quite open with me about her new-found wealth. I'm continually amazed how she seems able to take it all in her stride. Most young women today would have a difficult time adjusting to it all, I would think.'

'Couldn't agree more. When I first learned that she was to inherit the estate, I've got to admit, I expected the worst. I pictured having to deal with one of those frightful tabloid bimbos with a hundred-word vocabulary.'

Kingston nodded. 'About the exact opposite, eh?'

'Yes, thankfully. I think the world of Jamie and I really admire what she's doing here.' He smiled. 'Roping you in, included – and I know that's no easy task.'

'She's quite a saleslady, too. But getting back to this Mainwaring chap, she mentioned that he also received a sum of money from the estate.'

'He did, yes, a decent amount. Anyway, sufficient to make most people happy.'

Kingston cleared his throat. 'I know I probably shouldn't be asking you this but if he was in Ryder's employ for fifteen years, wouldn't it be expected that he would anticipate getting a sizeable chunk of the estate when Ryder passed away? Particularly since he would most certainly be aware of Ryder's having no heirs within the family.'

Latimer was smiling again. 'Well, since confidentiality as far as Ryder is concerned is no longer a consideration I can tell you that Mainwaring *was* surprised. Not only surprised but very upset.' He stared into the fire for a moment as if he were choosing his words then looked back at Kingston. His smile was gone. 'There's no reason for you to mention this to Jamie, or anyone else for that matter, but when I read Mainwaring the part of the will that concerned him, it clearly came as a terrible shock to him to learn that Jamie was going to inherit Wickersham. He wasn't mad or furious – anything like that – it was as if he simply couldn't believe what he was hearing. As if there'd been some awful mistake. I remember the long silence that followed when I'd finished. To tell the truth, I was a bit worried at the time because he looked as if he might explode any moment and things could turn nasty. But he didn't.' Latimer thought for a moment then sighed. 'In retrospect, I think it *was* a huge letdown for him.'

'Did he finally calm down?'

'Somewhat, but not after accusing me of influencing Ryder. I told him that I'd never met Ryder and that a former partner, who was now deceased, handled Ryder's affairs. Despite my explaining that there was no doubt or ambiguity to Ryder's will, he didn't want to listen to reason. He insisted that he'd been swindled.'

'He never got violent, though?'

'No, thankfully. He finally took all the documents and the unopened envelope addressed to him and left.'

'Envelope? What was that all about?'

'It's not uncommon for the testator to request sealed letters of a personal nature be given to one or more beneficiaries in a bequest. It could well have been a letter from Ryder explaining the reasons for his decision. Maybe he felt Mainwaring was owed that courtesy.'

'Mainwaring didn't open it in front of you, then?'

'No, not that I necessarily expected him to. It was irrelevant, none of my business.'

'He just left after that?'

'For God's sake, Lawrence, why on earth does all this matter, now?'

Kingston shrugged. 'You're right. It's water under the bridge. Too many questions can become annoying.'

Latimer smiled. 'So can clichés.'

The grandfather clock in the hall struck ten. Latimer continued, 'Anyway, to answer your question, Mainwaring did leave but not before informing me that he was going to contest the will and that he would be back.'

'And did he?'

'No. I never expected him to, really. Never heard from him again.'

'Did he leave the area, do you know?'

'Come on, Lawrence, how the hell would I know that?'

Jamie and Bella came back into the room. Bella gushing about how 'darling' the house was. There was no more talk about Mainwaring.

The party broke up shortly after eleven. After accompanying Jamie to see David Latimer and a rather loud and legless Arabella off at the front door, Kingston walked the short distance to his cottage. Listening to Bella babbling on for the last hour, plus the wine and a stiff after-dinner cognac, had given him a mild headache. Sleep would be a welcome and merciful end to the day.

He locked the front door, turned off the lights and went upstairs to bed. He was asleep in a matter of minutes.

Kingston had just put three pound coins in the pay and display machine at the Coal Orchard car park in Taunton when his mobile rang. He took the ticket and fumbled for the phone buried in the pocket of his Barbour jacket along with loose change, miscellaneous receipts and half a roll of Polo mints. Odds were it would be Jamie because hardly anybody else knew the number. Were it not for her insistence, he wouldn't have had the phone in the first place. He hated the damned things, particularly in the hands of drivers. He would have been just as happy with a walkie-talkie for the estate.

It *was* Jamie. She was calling to ask Kingston to pick up a book that had just come in at the library. She had also heard from Inspector Chadwick.

'He said the bones are those of a male; approximately sixty years of age; height, five eleven.' Jamie paused. 'We don't seem to have a very good connection, Lawrence.'

'I can hear you fine,' said Kingston, walking back towards his car. 'Did Chadwick have any idea how long the bones had been down there?'

'A long time, was all he said.'

'I guessed as much. Anything else?'

'Not really. He described the condition of individual bones but it was way over my head. You know – medical jargon. Words like sutures and ossification. He said you could call him if you like.'

'That's it, then?'

'I guess so. We'll probably never know who the poor man was.'

'Or did 'e fall or was 'e pushed.'

'Chadwick said that if anything else turned up – and that was unlikely – he'd let us know.'

'Case closed then.'

'Looks like it.'

'Okay, I should be back about fiveish.' He said goodbye and switched off the phone. Putting it back in his pocket, he opened the driver's side door and placed the ticket on the inside of the windscreen. He checked his watch. Five hours should be more than enough time for what he had to do, including his lunch in Taunton with Malcolm Bailey, a reporter for the *Somerset Herald*.

He hadn't told Jamie, but in addition to the lunch and a couple of small errands he was making one other stop that afternoon: the Somerset Light Infantry Office on Mount Street. He was hoping to find out more about the reclusive Major Ryder.

In due course he knew he would have to tell Jamie what he was up to, particularly if anything of interest turned up; anything that might shed light on a connection between Ryder and Jamie. But for now, surely a little innocent inquiry couldn't hurt.

Kingston's pub lunch with Malcolm Bailey went on longer than anticipated. He was a jovial man with a lusty appetite and, as it turned out, a hollow leg when it came to Golden Eagle bitter.

The newspaper was planning a special series on the restoration at Wickersham, to be published starting the week of the opening. Bailey, along with the paper's gardening columnist and staff photographer, had been gathering material and taking photos since the start. A number of the gardening magazines, *Gardens Illustrated* and *The English Garden* among them, had also lined up interviews and photo sessions. Jamie had already been the subject of at least a dozen interviews.

By odd coincidence, Malcolm had been working at the *Wiltshire Gazette and Herald* when the story about the blue rose broke. He was the lead reporter on the case and had interviewed Alex and Kate Sheppard. The two men had much to talk about and it was not surprising that their lunch lasted over three hours.

After parting company outside the Masons Arms, Kingston walked to Mount Street to see what more, if anything, he could find out about Major Ryder.

His meeting with an affable Lieutenant Colonel Jarvis was brief and disappointing. Kingston learned very little. Their records confirmed that Ryder, at the time a lieutenant, was with the 4th Battalion Somerset Light Infantry. His regiment had landed in Normandy two weeks after D-Day. Three months later, in Holland, his company had been separated from the battalion and had eventually been captured by the Germans but not without putting up a courageous fight. Ryder was subsequently awarded a Military Cross. That was it.

From there, Kingston walked to a bookshop in East Street where, after browsing for fifteen minutes, he bought a new thriller and an Amy Tan book, as a surprise for Jamie. A quick trip to the library and he was on his way back to Wickersham.

At three fifteen that afternoon a silver BMW had pulled up to the front door at Wickersham. The man who got out of the car was average height with a compact build. Balding on top, the remainder of his grey-speckled hair was shaven, military style. He wore dark aviator glasses, a leather bomber jacket and tan trousers with a mobile phone hooked on to his belt. In several athletic strides, he reached the door and rang the bell. A wait of less than a minute and Jamie opened the door.

'Good afternoon,' the man said, smiling. 'Are you Jamie Gibson?' There was a gravelly sound to his voice, as if he were getting over a cold. Despite the fashionable five o'clock shadow, the man looked pleasant enough.

'Yes,' Jamie replied, a little uncertain of what to expect.

'Forgive me for arriving unannounced. I should have called you to let you know I was coming. I'm Julian Fox. We talked on the phone about two weeks ago.'

'Oh, yes, of course,' said Jamie. 'I apologize. Now I remember.'

'Here,' he said, handing her a card that he had extracted from the wallet in his hip pocket.

She did remember the phone call but not too well. The man had said something about wanting to ask her about some paintings that Major Ryder had owned jointly with an art dealer in France. She recalled agreeing to see him. She had meant to tell Latimer about the call when he was over for dinner but what with work on the gardens and all the excitement about the skeleton, it had completely slipped her mind.

'Come on in,' she said, letting him pass, then closing the door behind her. She showed him across the entrance hall into the living room, gesturing to the sofa. 'Please, sit down. May I offer you some coffee?' she asked.

'That would be nice,' he nodded.

Jamie left the room to find Dot and within less than a minute, returned. She sat down opposite him, hands in her lap. 'What's this all about, then?'

Fox leaned forward slightly, 'I'm here on behalf of a client of mine, a Monsieur Girard.'

'Are you a lawyer?'

He smiled and shook his head. 'No – no, I'm not.' Without further explanation as to the relationship with his client, he went on. 'Through a mutual acquaintance we recently learned that Major Ryder had passed away. Soon after, we discovered that you had inherited his estate.' He paused briefly, rubbing his hands together. 'You see, many years back, Girard was in business with Major Ryder.'

As he spoke, she was conscious of looking at his eyes more than one would in an ordinary conversation. They were unnaturally blue, with rather a disconcerting frankness to them.

'They were partners in an art gallery,' he said.

'An art gallery?'

'Yes, in Paris.' He paused. 'You were not aware, then?'

'No, I wasn't.' She had to take her eyes off his for a moment. Picking up his card, she studied it as she spoke. 'In fact, I know very little about Major Ryder. Tell me more.'

The card was very plain. Just his name, a London address and phone number. No title or company name.

Fox leaned back in the sofa and crossed his legs. 'After World War II, Ryder and Girard went into business together. I'm sure you're aware that Ryder was an army officer.'

She nodded. 'Yes.'

'Well, Girard had a small gallery at the time and scratched out a living but couldn't afford to buy paintings of any importance, nothing of quality. Then Ryder came on the scene. It was evident from the start that he knew a lot about art – he said he was a collector himself. Within a short time, Ryder invested a substantial amount of money in the business, allowing them to move to a larger and better location and start purchasing and selling paintings of much better provenance, higher value.'

'That must have taken a lot of money, surely?'

'Yes and no. You have to realize that this was nearly sixty years ago and there were lots of paintings and other works of art coming back on the market after the German occupation. But, yes, you're right. I understand that Ryder's investment was sizeable. But then again, according to Girard, he always seemed to have money when it was needed.'

Jamie was wondering what had happened to the coffee when Dot entered carrying a tray. Lowering it slowly to the coffee table, she was about to pour the coffee when Jamie told her not to worry, that she would take care of it. Dot left the room.

Jamie filled the cups and waited while Fox stirred three teaspoonfuls of sugar into his coffee. 'Why are you telling me all this?' she asked.

He uncrossed his legs and leaned forward.

'There are three paintings that belong to Monsieur Girard that Major Ryder was storing for the gallery. According to Girard, they were being held here on the estate for safekeeping. Now, with Major Ryder's passing, we would like to have those paintings returned.'

'What kind of paintings are you talking about?'

'They're oil paintings and the artists are French.'

'Are these old paintings you're talking about? Like those up there?' She pointed to the two eighteenth-century pictures on the facing wall.

He turned to look at the paintings. 'No, not as old as those.'

'If this man has retained your services to locate his paintings, it suggests that they must be valuable. What are they worth?'

'No specific price has been mentioned. But yes, in answer to your question, they are of considerable value.'

'Well, I'm afraid you may have come on a wild goose chase. The only paintings here,' she gestured with a hand, 'are the ones that you're looking at.'

He smiled thinly. 'I'm afraid they are not the paintings in question, Miss Gibson.' He got up and walked over to examine one of the gilt-framed oil portraits.

'Well, I don't know what more to tell you,' said Jamie, raising her voice slightly. 'I can assure you that there are no other paintings in the house. Everything was carefully inventoried after Ryder's death and I would certainly have been made aware of any paintings like those you've described. I can't believe for one moment that anyone, least of all the lawyers, would have made a mistake or concealed the fact.'

He returned and stood by the edge of the sofa. By his expression, she could tell that he was not at all satisfied with her answer. He said nothing, just stood staring at her with those confounded eyes.

Jamie was standing now. As far as she was concerned, the interview was over, coffee finished or not. She took two steps towards the door. 'Anyway, Mr Fox, I'm sorry I can't be of more help.' She paused for moment. 'I only wish they *were* here.'

Jamie was fully expecting the man to thank her and politely leave but he didn't. For an awkward moment they faced each other across the room.

Then he spoke. 'Look, Miss Gibson,' he said, 'I should have told you this earlier. Monsieur Girard does not have much longer to live, a few months at the most. He is a sick old man and I have promised him that I will do everything I can to find the paintings. They mean a lot to him and he wants to pass them on to his son. He told me he was a fool for not having settled the matter with Ryder long ago but, for whatever reason, he didn't. Now he simply wants what is rightfully his. You must agree that is not too much to ask.'

Jamie shrugged. 'I'm sorry, I've told you everything I know.'

'Much as I want to believe you, we know the paintings are here and not anywhere else. If you have any knowledge of them, please tell me now, it'll save a lot of trouble for both of us.'

Jamie pursed her lips. How many times did she have to

tell him? 'Look, I don't know what more I can say. I've told you they're not *here*. In any case, had it occurred to you that Ryder might have sold the paintings without Girard's knowledge?'

He smiled and shook his head. 'There were safeguards against that ever happening.'

'Like what?'

'Never mind, it's not relevant. But take my word for it, Ryder could not sell the paintings without our knowing.'

'Well, what more can I say, Mr Fox? If you'd like to talk to my lawyer, I'd be happy to give you his number.'

He shook his head. 'That won't be necessary,' he said, offering his hand. 'Thank you for seeing me.'

'If they do turn up, naturally I'll call you right away,' she replied, shaking his hand. Together they walked to the front door where she watched him get into his car. With a quick wave of the hand from the open window, he drove off.

Chapter Seven

Driving back to Wickersham, Kingston was mulling over his visit to the Somerset Light Infantry Office. Jarvis had suggested that Kingston contact the Historical Disclosures Section of the Army Personnel Centre in Scotland, who, he said, might be able to give a more detailed account of Ryder's military career.

Kingston would do that in due course but from now he would be best advised to proceed with Jamie's blessing. Though they had developed what he felt to be an easy-going relationship he was, after all, an employee and he knew it was none of his business poking into her personal affairs. Besides, for all he knew she might prefer *not* knowing more about Ryder.

When he arrived at the house, Jamie was waiting for him. She was fidgety and said little. They went into the kitchen where Kingston sat down, placing the bag containing the Amy Tan book and Jamie's library book on the floor beside him. Before giving them to her, he decided to wait until he knew what was bothering her.

She'd already made a pot of tea and poured him a cup without asking. It wasn't like her. Had she somehow found out about his visit to the Light Infantry Office? Maybe Jarvis had called back? Then she proceeded to tell him about Fox's visit.

Kingston's initial suggestion, that she should consider hiring a contractor to undertake a top to bottom search of the house and the cottages to look for the paintings, was met with a blank stare. She reasoned – and he had to admit that her argument was sound – that, even if Girard's assertion that Ryder had stored the paintings in the house was true, by no means did it imply that they were still there. She reminded Kingston that half a century had passed since Ryder's Paris days and what was a much more likely scenario was that Ryder had either sold the paintings, or if that was not possible – as Fox contended – then they were simply moved elsewhere. 'You've got to remember, Lawrence, all this took place long before I was born,' she added.

Up until now Kingston hadn't thought about the age difference but Jamie's comment made him pause. For most of her generation, the war in Europe had little or no meaning. Even the Vietnam war was probably not something that had played a significant part in her education, her upbringing. She saw these things from an entirely different perspective.

'The whole idea of a search is silly, Lawrence,'

'How about letting me take a look around?'

His question was greeted with an amused look followed by a measured shaking of her head. 'You're incorrigible.'

'Well, it couldn't do any harm, could it?'

She let out a sigh. 'If that's what you want to do, you have my blessing – on two conditions. One, you do it in your own time and two, stay out of my bedroom.'

Kingston stood, about to leave, then remembered the books. He bent and picked up the bag. 'I picked up another book for you,' he said, handing her the bag. 'Hope you haven't read it.'

She took the bag and removed the books, examining the Amy Tan cover. 'No, I haven't – thank you, Lawrence. What a kind thought,' she said with a smile.

For four days and nights, starting at the attic, Kingston conducted his search. Every break he had from the demands of the garden restoration he would return to the house. Every evening, he would do the same thing. Frequently on his hands and knees and often up on ladders, he went over every inch of the place like a man possessed. Occasionally, Jamie would watch with concealed amusement as Kingston systematically measured and remeasured, knocked on wall panels, cleared out bookcases, shone a flashlight in cupboards and pantries, even took up all the rugs, one by one, to examine the oak flooring planks. In the early evening of the fourth day, he was ready to admit defeat. If the paintings *were* in the house, it was doubtful that they would ever be found. Jamie opened a bottle of Veuve Clicquot that night as consolation.

Next morning, good to his promise, Kingston took Jamie to see the gardens at Hidcote Manor. They left early enough in the morning to allow time for a stop in Chipping Campden first. Twenty minutes after their lunch at the Seymour House Hotel, Kingston and Jamie arrived at the fabled gardens near the northern border of Gloucestershire. They had struck lucky with the weather. Earlier that morning, the sky was overcast and now and again the windscreen wipers were called for. Now, with a blue sky cushioned with fluffy white clouds, it couldn't be a better day for a garden visit.

Standing in the rectangular gravel Garden Courtyard, they lingered a moment to admire the small chapel and the old butterscotch-coloured stone house, behind which lay what has long been considered the most influential garden in England.

Kingston introduced Jamie to the head gardener, Peter Jenkins, and they chatted for a while about the project at Wickersham before entering the gardens. As they did so, the bell in the chapel chimed two thirty.

Over lunch, Kingston had filled Jamie in on the history

of the garden, starting with a short biography of its reclusive and unlikely creator.

'He was American born but he became a naturalized British citizen soon after arriving at Hidcote. His name was Lawrence Johnston. Of all things, he was a career military man. Got to the rank of major, eventually. He and his well-heeled mother, Mrs Winthrop – she was twice widowed actually, one husband was a wealthy banker, I believe – arrived at Hidcote in 1907. Johnson was thirty-six at the time. It was an inhospitable piece of land. The three hundred acres of mostly windswept fields were awkwardly sloping and not at all suited to the cultivation of a garden. Plus, neither had any experience in gardening.'

Jamie smiled. 'Sounds a bit like me.'

Kingston returned the smile. 'You didn't tell me about those two husbands!'

'I will, one day,' she replied.

'So where was I? Oh, yes. Someone once commented that "with their peripatetic lifestyle, it seems unlikely that the two of them had ever stayed anywhere long enough to see a tree grow". I thought that was a clever line.' He paused. 'But Lawrence Johnston was set on making a garden. In the seven years leading up to World War I, he worked tirelessly, planning and planting the beginnings of his garden. At the start of hostilities, he went off to the wars again – I forgot to mention, he had fought earlier in the Boer War. He was an officer in the Northumberland Fusiliers. Quite a hero, too – he was wounded twice, and once nearly buried alive.'

'Good Lord! It's a wonder he found any time for gardening.'

'I know, but it was in the years to follow that Hidcote really took shape, when he left the army. After the war, he came back to Hidcote and spent the next thirty-four years expanding and nurturing the gardens to their present glory: twenty-eight separate gardens within gardens spread over ten acres. In his later years, he turned the gardens and the house over to the National Trust.'

'Sounds like he was what we call an "A" personality type.'

Kingston shook his head. 'On the contrary. He was not at all what one might expect. He was shy and modest and shunned publicity. But he had impeccable taste and over the years participated in several plant-hunting expeditions in various parts of the world. Several plants are named after him and the garden, the most famous, of course, being Hidcote lavender. It seemed he had very little interest in anything other than his garden.'

'When did the National Trust take over?'

'In the late forties. They've maintained it superbly ever since. He died in 1958 in Menton, France, where he had created another garden, Serre de la Madonne. He's buried in a village churchyard a few miles from here, beside his mother.'

'What an amazing story. They should make a film about it.'

'You know, Jamie, Hidcote is a little like Wickersham in one respect.'

'Why's that?'

'In the forty-plus years that Johnston gardened at Hidcote, he left no diaries, few letters and wrote no articles about his extraordinary creation. No plans of work in progress or finished designs, and no plant lists have ever surfaced.'

Leaving the courtyard, they walked through a narrow blue-painted door into the Old Garden. Circled by old rosy brick walls the garden was a profusion of blue, white, pink and mauve from the exuberant plantings in five jam-packed long beds. Kingston pointed out campanulas, Cambridge Blue iris, hardy geraniums, anchusa, astrantia major and white philadelphus, as they ambled the grass and gravel paths that circled the garden.

Next they entered the White Garden, a small symmetrical enclosure bounded by box hedging with stylized topiary birds. Here, all the plants were either grey or white. On to the Maple Garden with its feathery mounds of *Acer palmatum*, Japanese maple, and stepping-stones set in gravel that led past a sunken stream with wands of Solomon's seal and lush clumps of skunk cabbage.

During the course of the next three hours, Kingston led Jamie through Hidcote's breathtaking wonderland: the long and deep red borders crammed with spiky cordyline, crimson canna, cherry trees and dazzling oriental poppies; the magnificent and spacious Theatre Lawn with its formal clipped yew hedging and towering old beech tree; the Long Walk, a wide swath of mown grass flanked on either side by tall boxy hornbeam hedges leading to a wrought-iron gate through which they could see only sky and the farmlands beyond.

They lingered in the serene Pool Garden with its large circular pool and central fountain surrounded by more cleverly clipped yew hedges and the large yew Palladian portico atop a flight of semicircular steps leading to a grassy roundel at the back. On to the formal Pillar Garden and the Stilt Garden where the intertwining branches of facing rows of hornbeam trees were clipped into overhead box shapes. Closing in on the three-hour mark they also managed to cover the magnificent Rose Borders, the Pine Garden with its rectangular lily pond, floods of agapanthus and spiny agaves, the Fuchsia Garden, the Poppy Garden, the Stream Garden, the Kitchen Garden and the Terrace Garden.

With many parts of the garden left unseen, they finally decided to call it a day and retreat to the tea rooms for a rest before they took the long drive back to Wickersham.

Jamie had long ago run out of superlatives and now fully understood what unerring taste, design skills, plantsmanship, passion, drive and dogged persistence it required to create a garden like Hidcote. Back at the parking area, she got into the car, buoyed with a new enthusiasm and determination to shape her own gardens, hoping that one day, long into the future, they would attain the magnificence and breathtaking loveliness of those she'd seen today.

Another week passed with the restoration proceeding at a brisk pace. Jamie was visibly pleased when Kingston told her that most of the clearing was now complete. The original network of gravel paths that crisscrossed the gardens – several thousand feet – was now identified. Locating them had been a slow and laborious process but without the aid of Gillian Thomas's Ordnance Survey and tithe maps the task would have been nigh on impossible.

The challenging problem of locating old drainage and water supply pipes, culverts and irrigation systems was made easier with the use of a metal detector. While it worked like a charm with the Victorian cast iron and later date galvanized pipes, finding the earlier ceramic and clay pipes was very much a hit and miss affair.

Over the past weeks Kingston had been interviewing a steady parade of gardeners. Now that all the clearing, grading and groundwork was done, more knowledgeable hands were soon going to be needed for planting, training, fertilizing, watering – all the myriad tasks required in the making and maintaining of a garden the size and scope of Wickersham.

From information that Gillian had dug up, Kingston had learned that just after the turn of the century the garden staff had reached its peak of twenty-two persons. All lived locally, in nearby villages, a few in the then four cottages on the estate. As in many of the large estate gardens at the time, a strict Victorian caste system of employment was enforced where every man knew his place and his job. A gardener's life at the time was quoted as being the equivalent to serfdom. Working hours were long and holidays few. When the weather was too bad for the gardeners to go outside, they were put to work making labels, mending tools and implements, scrubbing plant pots and cleaning the insides of the greenhouses.

All the garden staff had to wear a clean collar and tie, waistcoat, cap to doff with, and a serge apron with large pockets known as 'brats'. All these were required to be worn daily, even when working in hot weather or in the boiler house. No smoking was permitted and more often than not, each gardener had to purchase his own knives for such tasks as budding and light pruning. A member of a glasshouse team could rise to become a head gardener, whereas those who worked in the kitchen garden and pleasure gardens could only aspire to the position of foreman. The Victorian head gardener was as strict a disciplinarian as any regimental sergeant major and he was given a house or cottage and all his coal and vegetables for free. Invariably, he would have risen through the ranks from under-gardener, journeyman gardener, to foreman, gaining many years of experience along the way before attaining the important and influential role as head gardener.

Word about the restoration had got around quickly and on most fair weather days a small gallery of locals would show up, curious to check up on the progress. It reminded Kingston of city construction sites where the contractors drilled peepholes in the barricades so that passers-by could observe the show.

In the course of his interviews with prospective gardeners and labourers, Kingston was pleasantly surprised and encouraged that many of the job-seekers were not only young but well qualified – some with degrees in garden design and horticulture – and all eager to take on the hard work and long hours that would be demanded of them. In his day, it had been hard to get youngsters interested in gardening. To start with he hired a total of seven – two men with considerable journeyman experience, a young

man and two young women with some horticultural training, and two local lads as labourers.

A giant cat's cradle of pegs and strings outlining beds
and borders was strung out in various parts of the garden.
Many of the beds were already double-dug with manure
and other additions worked in to enrich the soil.

The one-acre walled vegetable and cutting flower garden that not too many weeks ago had resembled an overgrown bombsite was starting to take shape. The nine-foot
high brick wall on two sides, preserved in remarkable
condition, had been cleared of all weeds, brambles and ivy
and had been high-pressure washed. On sections of the
inside wall, espalier and cordon wires were in place for the
apple and pear trees waiting in the wings. The three glass-
houses were in various stages of completion and all the
cold frames and rehabilitated Victorian cloches were
painted and ready to go. Outside the walls several bonfires
burned, the smouldering ashes rekindled every morning
with an inexhaustible supply of fuel hacked and sawn
from the jungle-like gardens.

Working from sun-up often to sundown, Kingston had
little or no time to dwell on the perplexing developments
of the past weeks. Much as he wanted to delve into the
mystery of the skeleton, the coins and Girard's claim it
simply wasn't possible. Every time he took pause to give
them further thought, something came up in the gardens
to sidetrack him. Then, of course, there was the overriding
mystery of Wickersham: why did the reclusive Major
Ryder elect to leave his estate to an American woman,
ostensibly unknown to him?

In the coming days, however, certain items and a scrap
of information would come into his possession that would
further pique his curiosity, which he would be the first to
admit took very little piquing.

The first happened early on a Saturday morning when
Kingston was face up under the kitchen sink at the big
house, trying to fix an obstinate leak. He'd insisted – now

71

unwisely, he was beginning to think – on taking care of it when Jamie told him she was about to call a plumber. Earlier that morning she had gone into Taunton to do some shopping and have lunch at David and Bella Latimer's. Just as he was about to apply leverage on the wrench, the doorbell rang. Cursing and extricating himself from the sink cupboard, he went to the front door and opened it. On the doorstep stood an ordinary-looking grey-haired man in his mid-sixties hugging six bound volumes close to his chest as one might carry a baby. The spectacles on the end of his nose were in danger of falling off at any moment. The books looked quite old. The man introduced himself as Roger Ferguson, an archivist at the Somerset Record Office in Taunton. Kingston ushered him into the living room where Ferguson lowered the books on to the coffee table. 'Phew! Bloody heavy, those,' he muttered in a West Country accent. He picked up the top book. 'Thought these might be of help,' he said, handing it to Kingston. Kingston took the book and opened it to the first page. His jaw dropped. It was as if the man had handed him a mint copy of the Gutenberg Bible. He was looking at a head gardener's work book for the years 1905 to 1908. 'They're all from Wickersham,' Ferguson said. 'The other three go up to 1917. The two with the black bindings contain quite a lot of historical information on the house and the estate. I think you'll find them most interesting.'

Ferguson, sitting on the edge of the sofa, went on to explain that he had heard about what was going on at Wickersham from Nick Sheffield, one of Jack Harris's crew. They had met by chance at his local one night. Being a keen gardener and intrigued, Ferguson had taken it upon himself to do a little overtime research and had struck gold.

In amazingly good condition, the volumes detailed plant purchases, work and holiday schedules, invoices, and perhaps most important of all, job allocations. Important, because the job allocations specified all Wickersham's

72

numerous garden sites. It was a virtual map of the entire estate – a comprehensive list of all the individual gardens, the various buildings, greenhouses, structural features, the engineering of the water system: the hydraulic ram pumps, drive and supply pipes. A quick riffle through one of the black leather-bound books was all that was needed to tell Kingston that it contained a wealth of historical data, including drawings and photos – the kind of information that until now had been a distant dream. He couldn't wait to see Jamie's expression when he handed them to her.

It was all Kingston could do to stop himself from throwing his arms around the man and hugging him.

Over coffee and digestive biscuits, they talked for the best part of an hour. Ferguson, who was born and raised in Somerset, had always been fascinated by Wickersham. Over the years he'd read a number of articles about the house, its gardens and the more recent generations of Ryders. He had always wanted to see it, he said. It was no surprise that Kingston's offer of a conducted tour of part of the estate close to the house was met with boyish enthusiasm.

Back at the house half an hour later, having seen Ferguson off, Kingston decided the sink would have to wait – the books were too important. He went into the living room to study them.

For the rest of the morning Kingston buried himself in the gardener's work books. They were exactly what they had been hoping for all along. As he read on, the depth of information about the gardens back in those days astonished him. The meticulous records not only reflected a precise accountability for the upkeep and enrichment of the gardens but also demonstrated just how big a part they played in the lives of the Ryder family of that time, both aesthetically and nutritionally. The books represented an extraordinary diary, a way of country life that has been lost forever. Jamie was going to be flabbergasted.

Finally, laying the work books aside, he picked up the

first of the two black volumes, the historical records, and began to read. Most of the introductory text dealt as much with county historical events and influences of the time as it did with Wickersham itself. Interspersed, were a number of stylized architectural drawings and photographic plates of passing interest. Collectively, they showed how very little the house had changed over the centuries. Sections on the chronology of the Ryder family were particularly absorbing. Jamie, who seemed to be developing a curious fondness for the family, would enjoy reading those pages.

Kingston read on, skipping parts that appeared of little interest. Finished for the time being with the first book, he picked up the second. Opening it at the contents page, he noted that, in chronological order, this was actually book one, since it commenced the history of Wickersham at the beginning of the sixteenth century. Not more than four pages into the first chapter, chronicling the Reformation period, his eyes scanned a long paragraph. He stopped, then read it again.

Between 1536 and 1539 the monasteries were dissolved and their lands and buildings either confiscated or destroyed. Throughout the violent upheaval, Thomas Cromwell combined governing genius with Machiavellian ruthlessness. The years to 1540 saw his enforcers travel the country assessing and plundering the church's vast wealth. It was possibly the greatest act of vandalism in English history. Wickersham Priory was destroyed in 1540. Like other monasteries at the time Wickersham scrambled to protect and hide its tithe monies and priceless ecclesiastical treasures. To this day, no evidence has ever surfaced to prove that the monks of Wickersham were successful in their attempt.

Over recent years there has been much speculation on the actual site of the monastery. Archaeologists and historians are generally agreed that it was located in the vicinity of the present house which was constructed in 1758.

Kingston's mind was in overdrive. He needed to talk to Roger Ferguson again. But he didn't have his home phone number and, even if he did, wouldn't disturb him at the weekend. He would call him first thing Monday morning. He went back to reading.

Two hours later, eyes strained, he took a break. Glancing at his watch, he saw it was past two. No wonder he felt so damned hungry.

Rummaging around the kitchen – it was bigger than the entire ground floor of his flat – he found some weepy Stilton and what he took for Edam in the cheese safe and a reasonably fresh cottage loaf in the bread bin. He was in luck: in the refrigerator there was a solitary bottle of Pinot Gris and on the lower shelf, of all things, a jar of Branston pickle. Dot must have bought that. Assembling an impromptu ploughman's lunch on a china plate, he poured himself a glass of wine and took it all back to the living room.

Settling into the wingback, he opened *The Times*, folding it to the Jumbo crossword puzzle, and began his lunch. He got 1 across right away: *Horse given unsuitable diet on board ship* (10). Answer, Lipizzaner. By the time his wineglass was empty, he'd solved at least a dozen clues. Not too bad, he told himself.

He woke with a start, a hand on his shoulder, gently shaking it. He looked up and saw Jamie standing next to him.

'Thought you might like something to eat,' she said. 'It's almost six. You've been out since I got back at five. I didn't want to disturb you.'

Kingston got up and rubbed his eyes. The room was dimly lit. 'How are David and Bella?' he asked.

'Fine. Bella lasted longer than I thought. David took me aside when I arrived and told me that she was on her third gin and tonic of the morning.' Jamie shrugged and smiled. 'She conked out right after lunch. I'm amazed how tolerant David is with her. I can't believe she's like that all the

75

time.' She picked up one of the books from the coffee table. 'What are these?'

Before she could read the title, Kingston reached over and calmly took it from her. She looked surprised.

Holding the book up as if it were prima facie evidence in a court trial, he waved it once for effect. 'This, Jamie, is a gardener's work book. Dated 1905 to 1908. It's from Wickersham and there are four of them.'

'Where – where did you get them?'

He held up a hand. 'In a moment. There's more.' He put the book on the table and pick up the two black-bound volumes. 'These chronicle the history of the house and the original priory, including the Ryder family.'

'Really? Let me see.' She reached out and took one of the books and started to leaf through the pages. After a few seconds she looked up. 'These are extraordinary, Lawrence. What luck.'

'Luck is right. A chap called Ferguson showed up on the doorstep with them this morning. He works at the Somerset Record Office in Taunton. He'd heard about what we were doing here and thought they might be of interest.'

'*Interest?* That's putting it mildly.'

'Believe me, Jamie, they're going to keep you occupied for quite some time,' said Kingston, excusing himself. 'I'll be back in half hour,' he said, getting up and picking up the plate and glass. At the door, he paused and looked back at her, rubbing his chin. He was debating whether he should tell her about his new theory; the reason he wanted to talk to Ferguson again. He decided it could wait till later.

Monday morning, at ten thirty, after a short walk from the car park, Kingston arrived at the Somerset Record Office. Ushered into a modern and tidy office, Kingston sat across from Ferguson. 'I somehow expected more books, more files, papers,' said Kingston with a smile, gazing around the room. 'Something more – Dickensian.'

Ferguson returned the smile, looking over the wire rims of his perfectly round glasses. 'Most people do. The word "archivist" conjures up a stereotypical image, I'm afraid. All our files and records – Lord knows how many millions there are now – are stored throughout this and other buildings. All we really need at our fingertips, nowadays, is the computer.'

'How far back do the records go?'

'Eighth century AD up to yesterday,' Ferguson replied.

'Quite remarkable.'

'So, what is it that brings you here, doctor? On the phone you sounded quite wound up.'

'I don't want to waste your time, Roger, so I'll get to the point.'

Ferguson sat back and gave a brief gesture with an open palm. 'Fine.'

'Recently we discovered an old well at Wickersham. It's located in a small chapel that was buried under a fifty-year tangle of ivy and brambles. My guess is that the well predates the chapel by at least a couple of centuries. So, it would seem that the chapel was built to accommodate the well.'

'My God, that could be a *very* significant find, you know.' Ferguson gave Kingston a questioning look over the top of his glasses. 'I'd really like to have seen that on Saturday. Is there a reason you didn't mention it then?'

Kingston had anticipated the question. He had since realized that it was foolish of him not to have shown it to Roger at the time. After all, he knew full well how important it was. He had to tell him about the skeleton, too. Roger would learn about it sooner or later. Skeletons didn't show up in wells with great frequency in Somerset.

'I didn't mention it then because it's the subject of a police investigation. It was locked up.'

'*What?*'

'You see, when the well was discovered, it was found to contain the skeleton of a man. The police pathologist has determined that the bones were down there a long time. It's doubtful that we'll ever know who it was.'

'Very Agatha Christie. Do they suspect foul play?'

'Apparently there's no evidence to suggest there was but they're keeping the case open. I must say, though, when I last talked to the inspector in charge, he didn't seem too optimistic about their getting much more information. Any clues that might tell them who it was or how it came about.'

'My goodness, a lot of excitement up there?'

Kingston nodded in agreement. 'For a while, yes. Things are more or less back to normal now, though. We've all got over the initial shock.'

'So, when would it be convenient for me to see it?'

'Unfortunately, tomorrow's out. Don't worry, though, we'll do it in the next couple of days.'

'If it's okay with you, I may bring a couple of other people with me.'

'That's fine. There's something else,' Kingston added. 'Nothing to do with archaeology, nothing like that. It's – well, we have something of a riddle on our hands, too.'

'Riddle? What kind of riddle?'

'How shall I put this?' Kingston drew in a long breath. 'I mentioned that when the crew first found the chapel, it was concealed behind a three-foot thick wall of vegetation, built into the side of a small cliff. There was only one way in, through a heavy oak door. By the girth of the ivy at its base – *Hedera colochica* "Dentata" . . . the bloody stuff is a house eater – our crew foreman estimated, and I tend to agree with him, that the chapel was probably buried over fifty years ago. Knowing that the gardens were abandoned shortly prior to World War II would seem to corroborate the fact. In fact, that would make it over sixty years.'

Ferguson unclasped his hands and leaned forward slightly, frowning. 'Where is this all leading?'

Kingston sniffed. 'Sorry, I didn't mean to be so pedantic. Anyway, when we opened up the chapel, we found three coins in there, on the floor. One is dated 1963, the other two 1959.'

'Meaning . . .' Ferguson looked up to the ceiling, calculating. 'They couldn't have been there for more than forty years?'

'Exactly.'

'Well, if your guess is right, that is a puzzle. You said there's no other way into the chapel?'

'No. We've gone over every inch of the damned place several times. It's quite small and austere, so another entry would be easy to find.'

Ferguson said nothing for a moment. 'But you didn't come all the way here to tell me just that, I take it?'

'No, you're right, Roger.' Kingston got up, stuffed his hands in his trouser pockets and commenced pacing the small room, chin up, as if addressing an invisible jury. 'There are two things, both related to something that I read in one of the books you lent me. There's a section dealing with the Reformation stating that with the dissolution of the monasteries, Wickersham, like all the monastic buildings in England, was destroyed. It didn't state if the land was sold or became the property of the Crown.'

'That's correct,' said Ferguson. 'The priory church here in Taunton was destroyed around the same time.'

'What got me thinking was a paragraph concerning the upheaval, that the churches had to scramble to protect and hide their monies and priceless treasures.'

'That's true.'

'And none have ever been found.'

Ferguson laughed. 'No,' he said. 'And I doubt ever will.'

Kingston had stopped pacing and stood facing Ferguson, his back to the window. 'Bear with me, please, Roger. There's a reference in the same book stating that the house at Wickersham was built in 1758. Further, it states that the house was built in the vicinity of the old monastery. Jamie's book says much the same thing, that Wickersham was built on the grounds of an old priory.'

'What are you getting at?'

'Isn't it possible, even remotely, that part of the old priory was built underground and still exists? I know priests' holes are not uncommon. Weren't they devised for the same reason? To conceal things?'

'Priests, mostly.' He rubbed his chin with his forefinger. 'I see what you're getting at, though. The chapel could stand on the site of the old priory.'

Kingston returned to the chair, placing his hands squarely on the back, looking at Ferguson. 'And about the only way of proving that, short of knocking the damned place down and excavating, would be if there were some records – drawings, maps, sketches – of the old priory which we could compare with a present-day plan of Wickersham.' He sat down again. 'Think you can offer any help?'

Ferguson swivelled his chair so that he was side-on to Kingston and looked up at the ceiling as he spoke. 'The monastery at Wickersham has always been a bit of a mystery. For as long as I've been here – which is too long, I might add – the exact location has been subject to considerable debate. Indeed, there's very little left of the monastery here in Taunton but there's no question of its location and its size. It was an Augustinian priory founded in the reign of Henry I by the Bishop of Winchester.' He frowned. 'William Giffard, I believe his name was. That's why we have the street names, Priory Avenue and Priory Bridge.'

Kingston was impressed but not really surprised that Ferguson had instant recall of all this information. 'So, do you think your chaps could do some digging and see if they can turn up any more information about the location of the priory at Wickersham?'

'I doubt seriously that we're going to be able to find out

more than we know already. It's a subject that's been heavily researched over the years – by historians, archaeologists, theologians, architectural types, you name it – but I don't see the harm in conducting further searches. One never knows. That's what we're here for, doctor.'

At the door they shook hands. 'Don't you forget now,' said Ferguson. 'I have to see that chapel and the well – very soon.'

Chapter Eight

Kingston had been less than forthcoming when he told Ferguson about the chapel being locked up. It was, indeed, locked but it was Kingston who had the key, a very large iron key, which hung on a carved wooden rack in the hall of his cottage.

It was the day after his meeting with Ferguson and were it not for the fact that the chapel and the monastery were very much on his mind, he might not have noticed, early that morning, that the key was missing. Throughout breakfast he kept wondering about it. He decided that before going up to the house to have his usual meeting with Jamie, he would stop at the chapel first.

Arriving at the oak door, he was surprised to see it was open. He went inside, careful not to make any sound. Directly across from him, on the other side of the wellhead, his back to Kingston, was a man in a plaid shirt, shining a flashlight on the wall, running his hand over the plaster.

'What do you think you're doing?' Kingston barked.

The man spun round. It was Jack Harris.

'Christ! You scared the shit out of me, Lawrence.'

'What are doing here, Jack?'

Jack passed a tongue nervously over his lips. 'Just trying to help,' he mumbled.

'How?'

'Well – you know – trying to find out how those coins got in here. Seeing if there's another way in. You got me curious, that's all.'

'How did you get in here? It's supposed to be locked.'

Jack's eyes flickered slightly. 'It was open, I swear.'

Kingston was about to mention the missing key but decided that it would be tantamount to an accusation. 'Who else knows about this place?' he asked.

'You mean other than the crew who were here when we discovered it?'

'Yes, who else?'

'Well – nobody, as far as I know.'

The two of them walked out of the chapel, Kingston up to the house, Jack to the vegetable garden, where most of the crew were presently working.

The door to Jamie's office was open. Kingston peeked in and saw her at the computer. He gave a gentle tap on the door. 'Ready when you are, boss,' he said.

Jamie swivelled on her chair. 'Come in, Lawrence, I'm just about done here.'

He waited while she typed in a couple more entries of whatever it was she was working on. It looked like a table of some kind.

'Okay, done,' she said, turning the computer off. 'Let's go see how the vegetable garden's coming along.'

Outside, the sun had just come out and it had the makings of a beautiful day.

'Just ran into Jack, up at the chapel,' Kingston said, as they walked across the top lawn.

'Really? What was he doing there? I thought the place was locked up.'

'It was but the key's missing from the rack in the cottage. Jack swore he knew nothing about it. Said that the door was open.'

'Hmm.'

Kingston went on to tell her about their conversation, that he thought Jack was lying through his teeth.

'I didn't think it worth mentioning, Lawrence, but over the last couple of weeks or so, it seems like Jack has gone out of his way to be nice to me. When he was first hired,

I got the distinct impression that he was trying to avoid me. I recall I told you at the time that he was a bit too macho for my liking. I put it down to resentment, the fact that a woman could have inherited such a large estate – even more so, an American woman.'

'Yes, I remember.'

'Well, of late, he's done a complete flip-flop. He couldn't be nicer. Often, he'll stop by the office to chat at the end of the day.'

'Well, I'm pleased to hear that. He's doing a good job, I must say.'

'At one of those friendly little chats, he asked me if I could loan him some money. I should have told you, I suppose, but I didn't think much of it at the time.'

'Really? When was this?'

'Three or four days ago. Said he'd got behind on his credit cards and some other debts. For a guy who's usually so sure of himself, he was very nervous.'

'What did you tell him?'

'I was actually considering it until I asked how much he had in mind. When he told me two thousand pounds, I was shocked. I thought he was talking about fifty or a hundred pounds – that sort of thing.'

'That's serious money. I don't like the sound of it at all. In any case, he should have come to me first.'

'I think you'd better sit down and talk with him, Lawrence. Find out what's going on.'

'I will, Jamie. First thing tomorrow.'

The high brick wall of the vegetable garden came into view 'There's something I don't like about that man,' she said.

'He may be hard to replace but if that's what we have to do, we will.'

When Kingston got back to the cottage at seven o'clock that night, the letter was on the hall table. Post forwarded to him was usually held at the house. But now and then China or Eric would drop off letters – almost always bills. The front door was only locked at night.

He opened the envelope, noting the Army Personnel Centre address, and read the contents. As he did so, a smile spread across his face. Not only did it contain more information about Major Ryder, but it listed the names of eight men who had served with Ryder during the war – all of whom were believed still living. This was what he had been hoping for.

Kingston read the letter again. Ryder's war ended on 14 July 1944 when, as a lieutenant, he was wounded in action in the Dutch town of Kleinelangstraat. After his unit was captured, he was taken to a German field hospital where he was patched up and then shipped off to an *Oflag*, a POW camp for officers. His condition worsened to a point that, to save his life, he was transferred to a hospital in Paris. After two operations and a lengthy period of rehabilitation, he was released. Awarded a Military Cross for bravery he was promoted to the rank of captain. By this time Paris had fallen to the Allied armies. Records from then on were non-existent but the letter went on to state that, after the war, Ryder spent some time in Paris before returning to England where he eventually retired from service. Immediately, Kingston thought back to the French dealer, Girard. This tallied with what the man Fox had told Jamie: that Girard and Ryder were in business together after the war in Paris. It would explain why Ryder didn't return to England right away after his rehabilitation.

Kingston scanned down the list of the veterans' names on the second sheet. He would start calling in the morning. He put the letter back in its envelope, turned off the lights and went upstairs to bed. This was information that Jamie was entitled to know about. Besides, it supported his theory about the missing paintings. Before long he would have to tell her what he was up to. She was leaving early the next morning but he would tell her when he felt the time was right. In a matter of minutes, he was asleep.

A crack of thunder woke him with a start from his dream. For a few seconds, the room was harshly lit by a strobe of lightning. In the dream he had been alone in the dimly lit living room at Wickersham. The room was as he remembered it, save for the pictures. Every surface of every table, the mantelpiece, the grand piano, even the window seats were stacked with framed photographs of varying shapes and sizes. All the head and shoulder sepia tone photos were identical – each of the same man, stern-faced, and with humourless dark eyes that followed Kingston around the room. The man in the photo was wearing an army uniform with major's pips on each epaulette. Then Kingston heard Jamie's desperate voice calling his name.

He sat up in bed sweating, a hand on the bed rail. He could hear his heart beating. He glanced at the chartreuse-lit numerals on the alarm clock: 3:20. Then another crash of thunder, this time farther off. Now the rain was slapping against the open window, the curtain whipping like a flag. He slipped out of bed and went to the window. Reaching to close it, the rain soaking his forearm, he peered outside. It was too dark to see much at all. All he heard was the sheeting rain and the wind. He was about to return to bed when a far-off flash of lightning illuminated the sky. In seconds it was dark again. But in that brief moment Kingston was certain he saw a shadowy figure retreating into the jungle, opposite. 'That's strange,' he whispered. The person's head was covered with a hood, like a monk's cowl.

Chapter Nine

Early the following morning Kingston examined the area outside his bedroom window at the edge of the jungle, the place where he thought he'd seen the prowler. At first, he found nothing to indicate that anyone had been there. He looked up at his window, trying to recall his angle of view last night. He started walking slowly along the edge of the jungle, eyes to the ground. A few more steps and he stopped. In front of him the grass was flattened in places. A few feet farther on he saw a muddy scuffmark that could possibly have been made by the back of a heel. This was most certainly the spot where the man had made his exit.

Arriving at the vegetable garden a few minutes later, he inquired after Jack. It soon became clear after questioning the half-dozen gardeners and labourers at the site that Jack hadn't shown up yet. Kingston thought nothing more of it, concluding that he was probably sick. He could have his chat with Jack later.

Jamie was gone for the day. She'd left early for a dental appointment, after which she was having lunch with David Latimer and in the afternoon doing errands in Taunton, so telling her about the mysterious prowler would have to wait until tonight. It was her birthday and he was taking her out to dinner at the White Swan. At first, he had debated whether he should tell her at all. Why give her cause to worry unduly about an incident that may well be unfounded or ultimately explained? But he had decided that telling her was the right thing to do. She would want know about it.

Kingston closed the door of the workshop behind him, went across the large airy room with its three vertical skylights and sat down at the drawing board. The workshop was one of the first new buildings to be constructed on the garden site. He had designed it to function as the nerve centre, as it were, for the entire garden operation. It served as an office for him; a place to store records, which were becoming more voluminous every day; a design centre with computers appended with all the obligatory peripherals and a large drawing board; a library for garden books and catalogues; and a place where they could hold meetings and the occasional celebration – as they had when the reflection pool was uncovered.

In front of him on the architect's drawing table was a large sketchpad with rough designs for what would soon be the rose garden. It was one of his pet projects and so far he had given Jamie no hint of what he was planning. As far as he was concerned, roses would get top billing and he was spending a disproportionate amount of time making sure that both his design and his selection of shrub varieties, climbers and ramblers were impeccable. He wanted it to come as a complete surprise.

Just when he first became infatuated with roses, he couldn't remember. Much as with one's taste in art, music and other pleasures mature, what had started as an amusing dalliance had developed over many years to become a passionate love affair. In this respect, he was certainly in good company – that much he knew. He had lectured on the subject so many times that he could still rattle much of it off by rote. The names of writers, poets and artists who have commemorated and eulogized the rose would fill volumes. Starting with Sappho, Horace and Virgil, the rose weaves its literary way through the centuries in the prose of Shakespeare, Herrick, Wordsworth, Yeats and the Brownings. To this day books about roses appear and will continue to appear on bookshop shelves with predictable certainty. In the history of art the rose reigns supreme. Botticelli, Manet, de La Tour, Georgia O'Keefe were all enthralled by the queen of flowers.

Botanists, plant biologists and historians generally agree that roses were cultivated five thousand years ago. (Fossil evidence in North America suggests that roses flourished at least thirty-two million years ago.) Over the centuries they bloomed in the land of the Pharaohs and were cultivated in Bronze Age Crete; Grecian coins of the fifth century BC depict a rose on one side. Roses just kept growing and growing in the plots and hearts of gardeners all over the globe. By the end of the eighteenth century there were more than a thousand varieties.

Today's would-be rose aficionado is faced with a dazzling choice of old and new hybrids. Take your pick: from chaste whites and negligee pinks all the way to peppery and damson reds. Blooms the size of a fingernail or as large as a pie plate. Many voluptuously perfumed, most bristling with thorns. Miniature, ground cover, shrub, landscape, patio, standard, climber, rambler – there's a shape and size for every space.

Next the neophyte rose buyer has to decide what species or variety to choose. Navigating the thicket of options is a bewildering exercise, one that requires considerable study and deliberation, professional help or a sharp pin. Four basic groups define the genus: species roses, antique roses, early nineteenth-century hybrids, and modern roses. Within each of the first three groups there are up to as many as two dozen different families of rose, and within those families, more roses. In the last group, modern roses, the division is enormous, resulting in many thousands of varieties.

Kingston had spent several weeks ruminating over his choice of roses for Wickersham. There was no shortage of space for planting so the starting list was lengthy. Winnowing down the candidates had been both a trial and a

89

pleasure. Adding names and crossing them off conjured memories of garden visits past. He could picture the lovely single Gallica, 'Complicata', threading its joyful way up through the branches of the old apple tree at Graham Stuart Thomas's rose garden at Mottisfont Abbey and the exuberant *Rosa felipes* 'Kiftsgate' zooming fifty feet into the copper beech at the charming Gloucestershire garden after which it was named.

The few pictures they had of the original rose garden at Wickersham all showed a typical layout. Orderly beds, some surrounded with low clipped box hedges, filled with nothing but regimented rows of roses. Kingston abhorred this kind of municipal garden look, judging the practice barely one step above the use of multicoloured bedding plants designed to replicate the Union Jack or the city name.

The new rose garden at Wickersham would be one of the few areas that didn't mirror its predecessor. Roses would be mixed in with shrubs, perennials and other plants, allowing them to show off their individuality and form, a technique now in common practice as exemplified at the garden at Sissinghurst. He was, however, going to make one small concession, in recognition of Britain's celebrated rose hybridizer, David Austin, who created an entirely new category of roses known worldwide as English Roses. In any gardener's dreams, the perfect rose would combine beauty of form, subtlety of colour, irresistible fragrance, resistance to disease and, above all, the ability to flower repeatedly. Such are the roses of David Austin. And Kingston was going to showcase them.

At noon, he took a break to check on progress in various parts of the gardens. Still, there was no sign of Jack. A couple of phone calls went unanswered. He decided that if Jack didn't show up in the morning, he would drive over to his house and find out what was going on.

*   *   *

Seven o'clock on a Wednesday night at the White Swan in Coombe St Mary was just as busy as Saturday – or any other night, for that matter: three-deep at the bar, a surround-sound din of conversation and a minimum twenty-minute wait for the dining room. The quintessential horse brasses type pub, it had, hands down, the best food within fifty miles in any direction.

It was Jamie's birthday and the dinner was on Kingston. He'd brought along a small gift: Mirabel Osler's *A Gentle Plea for Chaos*, one of his favourite books, musings about the joys and trials of her garden. They'd had a glass of house white in the bar while waiting for the table and, now seated, were on a second, from the bottle of Sancerre that Kingston had just selected for their first course.

Their conversation was mostly about food and wine, which suited Kingston fine. He didn't often get the chance these days to flex his epicurean muscles. He was quickly finding out, however, that there was more than just Dot's talent at work in the kitchen at Wickersham; that Jamie probably had a great deal more influence than he'd given her credit for. 'By no means a foodie,' as she had put it, she credited her father – more so than her mother – as having the most influence on her when she was growing up. 'He just *loved* to cook,' she said with a wistful smile. 'He was real easy to buy Christmas gifts for. Of course, growing up surrounded by grapevines and wineries in one of the world's great wine-growing regions didn't hurt either.' Whether it was the wine or not, she seemed comfortable talking about her past.

Kingston placed his fork and spoon on the white china bowl in front of him and leaned back in his chair. 'What did you do in California, Jamie? Your job, I mean?'

For a moment she said nothing, then broke into a smile. 'I was a winemaker.'

It was if she already knew what his reaction would be. She waited, the teasing smile still on her lips. 'You look surprised, Lawrence.'

91

'Well – I am. A winemaker?'

'That's right.' She was clearly enjoying watching Kingston fumbling for the right words. She saved him the trouble. 'Did you know that in French there's no word for winemaker? Nor is there in Spanish, Italian or German. The French use the word *vigneron*, which means wine grower.'

'I'd never thought about that,' said Kingston, rubbing his chin. 'Interesting.'

'Most men think of it as being a male-dominated profession, which it still is in Europe. It used to be that way in California but nowadays more and more young women are graduating from U.C. Davis and Fresno each year, with degrees in enology and viticulture. Same thing happened in the restaurant business. Some of best chefs in the bay-area now are women. Alice Waters of Chez Panisse is probably the most famous. As a matter of fact, she was invited to open a restaurant at the Louvre, in Paris. You can just imagine what the Frenchmen would have said about that.'

'I must say I'm very impressed. I should've had you pick the wine.'

'No, you made an excellent choice.'

'So, where did you work? Would I recognize the name of the winery?'

'I doubt it. It's quite small. About twelve thousand cases a year. It's called Hargrove. Near a small town called Glen Ellen.'

'What varietals?'

'Old Vines Zinfandel, Syrah and Merlot, mostly – but we've planted several acres of Carignane and Mourvedre and they'll be ready in a couple of years.'

'All reds.'

'Yes. I want to start blending varietals, soon. If and when I go back, that is.'

'The Rhone style varietals lend themselves to that, as I understand.'

92

'They do. Sounds as if you know quite a lot about wine.'

He shrugged. 'All learned by drinking it for many years, I'm afraid.'

'The best way.'

'I would imagine it's a frightfully competitive business these days, with so many countries producing good wines.'

'It is. And it can get expensive. We have a saying, that if you want to make ten million in the wine business, start with twenty.'

Kingston laughed. 'Clever,' he said. 'You've been holding out on me, then? You do know something about horticulture. That's certainly part of winemaking.'

'A very big part. Most people don't think of winemaking as farming but that's essentially what it is. The enology part comes later and, as you know, that's got to be right, too. But it all starts out there in the vineyard. Agriculture pure and simple – well, not quite so simple as it looks.'

'Did you quit to come over here?'

'No. I took a leave of absence. The couple that owns the winery, the Hargroves, treat me as if I were the daughter they never had. Neither of their two sons wanted to be in the wine business.'

'So, do you plan to stay here indefinitely?'

'It's hard to say. When I first saw the estate and how big it was –' She picked up her glass and sipped some water. 'By the way, I don't think I told you, David hired a helicopter that very first day. He said that was the only way I could grasp an understanding of what I owned. It was quite a trip, I can tell you. All those acres of beautiful land.'

'I can imagine what a thrill it was. Good for David.'

'Naturally, the first few weeks here I was really homesick. Then David told me about a winery not too far from here called Moorlynch. He took me there and I met the owners. It's quite lovely and their wines are excellent – all whites. That's when I got the idea.'

'What idea?'

'To try making wines here one day. At Wickersham.'

'That's a *wonderful* idea.'

'I hadn't brought it up so far because I want the gardens to be the only priority. But down the road, that's what I might do.' She smiled. 'Providing you haven't spent all my money by that time, Lawrence.'

'Did you have a garden back home?'

'I did. A tiny one, at the house I rented on a big piece of property not too far from the winery. I grew mostly herbs and perennials, a few roses, too – some climbers. Mediterranean, I suppose you'd call it.' She grinned. 'Stuff that's hard to kill.'

'It sounds delightful. I envy you that weather.'

'Like they say, the grass is always greener –'

'Which usually means the water bill is higher.'

She chuckled. 'How true. You wouldn't believe the number of times I've prayed for rain during our endless summers.'

They fell silent as the waiter arrived to take away the plates, topping up their glasses before making a polite exit.

'What do your parents think of all your good fortune? Your friends?'

He couldn't miss the flicker of apprehension in her eyes. She looked away and then, as quickly, back to him. 'My parents died quite a while ago,' she replied softly. 'Nearly seven years.'

'I'm sorry,' he said, glancing down at the tablecloth for a moment to give her pause to reflect. There was no point in telling her that he knew already, that Latimer had told him. He looked up at her.

'No, it's okay. It took a long time but I'm fine talking about them now.'

'I know how it is, Jamie.' Aware that it would come

across as an empty platitude he found himself saying it anyway, if for no other reason than to fill the void: 'I lost my wife ten years ago.'

'I'm sorry, Lawrence,' she said. She toyed with her wine-glass, looking into it as she spoke, her voice now more upbeat. 'They were killed in a plane crash. My dad's Cessna. They went down in a snowstorm in the Sierras. It was a crushing irony, because they were on their way back from Lake Tahoe. They'd spent the weekend there celebrating their anniversary. It was one of their favourite places.' She looked at him with a fragile smile and eyes that tried desperately but couldn't hide her love and her sorrow. 'My dad fancied himself as a poker player,' she added.

'How terribly sad.' Kingston shifted in his seat, thinking a change of subject might be prudent. But she went on talking about them for another minute or so. He learned that her mother met Jamie's dad-to-be – Warren Arthur Gibson, nickname, Wag – in San Francisco. At the time he was vice president of a wine-importing company, her mother, a private secretary for Bechtel, the international engineering company. Within a year they married and Jamie was born the following year.

The waiter reappeared with their main courses.

'As for friends,' said Jamie, 'I keep in touch with Todd and Suzanne Hargrove on a fairly regular basis. I'm in touch with other friends, mostly by e-mail, and once in a while, when I get really homesick, I'll pick up the phone. Matter of fact, Matthew, one of the guys I worked with – neat guy, you'll like him – may come over in a couple of months. He's got three weeks' vacation due.' She smiled. 'I told him we were a little short on rooms but we'd fix him up somehow.'

'Is *he* in for a surprise.'

For several moments they ate in companionable silence.

'I forgot to ask you,' said Jamie, giving him a questioning look. 'Did you get to talk with Jack yet?'

Kingston shook his head. 'No, I didn't. He didn't show up for work this morning.'

'No phone call?'

'No. I tried calling him a couple of times but either he's not answering the phone or he's not home. If he doesn't show up tomorrow, I'll go over and find out what's going on.'

Jamie talked a little more about growing up in San Francisco and her time at U.C. Davis where she was in the tennis and soccer teams. But her next question was transparently shaped to steer the conversation in a new direction. She looked up from her plate and said, 'Do you have any children, Lawrence?'

Kingston welcomed the question, always eager to talk about his daughter. 'Yes, a daughter, Julie. She lives in Seattle, works for Bill Gates – Microsoft. I've no idea exactly what it is she does but he pays her a small fortune, so I know it's important,' he said, with a quick smile.

'Do you get to see her at all?'

'Nowhere near enough but I've been over three times and she's been back here once. I'm eternally grateful for e-mail. We talk on the phone every once in a while, of course.'

Over dessert and coffee, Kingston did most of the talking. He spoke at length about his life in London, how he passed his time, and talked openly about his past. Jamie listened with keen interest as he described his work at the University of Edinburgh, where he had held the lofty position of Professor of the Institute of Cell Molecular Biology, and his eventual and reluctant retirement. He also told Jamie about his wife Megan, who had been killed in a boating accident on a lake in Switzerland, and the bleak and lonely years that followed, adjusting to and accepting life as a bachelor. He had lived in his Chelsea flat since he retired, quietly for the most part and on the whole happily.

After a long wait – the waiter had already apologized

twice – the bill arrived. Kingston put on his glasses and gave it a cursory glance, reaching in his wallet for his credit card. Jamie averted her eyes, drinking what little was left of her coffee.

'I meant to ask you,' she said. 'Did you have any problems in that storm last night? No leaks, or anything? We hardly ever get storms like that back home. I don't mind admitting, that first crash of thunder scared the hell out of me.'

He was grateful for the opening. Now telling her about the prowler might not make him come across as alarmist. At least, he could ease into it.

'No, everything was fine,' he answered, looking up. 'The curtains got soaked because, foolishly, I left a window open. But otherwise, fine.' He was about to bring up the incident but before he could get out a word she interrupted.

'Sorry, I didn't mean to butt in,' she said. 'I've always wondered about thatched roofs. They seem awfully primitive.'

'Primitive, maybe, but damned good. A good thatch will last at least fifty to sixty years, maybe longer.'

'Really?'

Kingston decided to give it a second go. 'There was something else that happened last night. I didn't mention it earlier because I didn't want to worry you unnecessarily.'

Jamie frowned. 'Worry me?'

'Well, not so much worry you, but have you think I might be making too much of what was probably a trifling matter.'

'What *are* you talking about, Lawrence? A trifling matter?'

'Well, when I got up to close the window, I saw somebody outside. I just caught a glimpse of him.'

'Him?'

'Well, I couldn't be certain. It was really dark. And the far-off flash of lightning lasted only a matter of seconds.'

'Who do you think it was?'

'I've no idea. I asked China but he said he slept through it, if you can imagine.' He hesitated. 'Whoever it was, was dressed like a monk.'

'Are you serious? A monk?'

'I'm sure I wasn't mistaken.'

'It was probably one of those hooded sweaters. A lot of young men wear them these days.'

'It could have been. But the important question is who would be snooping around in pouring rain in the early hours of the morning and why?'

Looking perplexed, Jamie pondered the question. 'I don't like the sound of it. I've always felt perfectly safe alone in the house, particularly since you've been here, but the idea of a prowler is a bit scary. Don't you think we should report it?'

'It might not be a bad idea. I'll give the police a call in the morning.'

They left the White Swan at nine fifteen.

Back at Wickersham, under a crescent moon and hurrying clouds, Kingston said goodnight to Jamie at the front door of the house and walked to his cottage. Inserting his key in the lock, he was surprised to find the door already open. An uneasy feeling came over him as he pushed the door ajar and paused before entering the darkened room. Something was not right. He reached for the light switch and turned it on. 'Good God!' he gasped. 'What in hell's name . . .'

The room was a shambles. Desk and bureau drawers had been pulled out, emptied, and thrown across the room. The wingback chair was on its side. His records, papers and books littered the floor.

He went across the room, picked up the phone and called Jamie, then called the police. In less than two minutes she was there. After surveying the mess and speculating on who could have done it, Jamie accepted Kingston's offer of a nightcap and they sat amidst the shambles in the small living room; he with a Macallan and she with a glass of dry sherry – the only other drink he had to offer without opening a bottle of wine.

'I don't think the police are going to learn much tomorrow,' said Kingston.

'You've no idea what they could have been looking for?'

Kingston shook his head. 'I don't, Jamie. Question is – why didn't they take my camera or the sound system – or that little carriage clock up there,' he said nodding to the mantel, 'the things that are easily sold? They were all in full view. This obviously wasn't your common or garden break-in.'

'You think this has something to do with the paintings, don't you?'

Kingston didn't answer right away. 'I don't think we can rule it out altogether, Jamie. You have to admit the possibility.'

They talked for another half-hour. At eleven fifteen Kingston walked Jamie back to the house, making sure that she was safely inside before returning to the cottage. He stayed up another ten minutes, pondering the break-in, before turning in.

By ten the next morning Kingston had made a rough inventory. Most important among the missing items were the two Wickersham history books and one of the garden record books loaned by Ferguson. Also stolen were several folders containing plans, maps and other documents relating to the house and the estate. More perplexing, one item was replaced. The key to the chapel was back in its rightful place on the hall rack.

Chapter Ten

Responding to Kingston's phone call reporting the theft, Sergeant Eldridge and a policewoman showed up the following morning and questioned him about the incident. With scant information, other than a description of the prowler, which Kingston reported to Eldridge, and no suspects that Kingston could think of, the interview was brief.

By the time Kingston arrived in the village of Little Charrington, the earlier showers had given way to cool and blustery weather. At the post office, a cubicle not much roomier than a phone box wedged in a far corner of the newsagent's, he got directions to Briary Avenue, where Jack Harris lived.

There were only a dozen or so houses in the short street, so finding number 12, the house that Jack rented, was easy. In any case, ahead on his right, he could already see Jack's red Toyota pickup parked alongside the kerb. A good sign, it signalled that his journey hadn't been a waste of time. Pulling up behind the pickup, he turned off the engine and was unbuckling his seatbelt when the front door to number 12 opened. A stocky man wearing a leather jacket emerged, closing the door behind him. Kingston watched as the man walked the short path to the open garden gate and then to his car, a silver BMW. By the time Kingston had stepped from his car, the BMW had disappeared round the corner.

Kingston rang the doorbell and waited. Right after a

second ring, the door cracked open not more than six inches. Kingston could see part of Jack's face and a dark bruise on his cheekbone. 'Are you all right, Jack?' Kingston asked. 'We're all worried about you.'

'I'm fine,' Jack replied. 'Just been laid up for a couple of days, that's all.'

'Are you sick? What happened?'

'Fell off the bloody bike.' The answer came too fast to be a lie but it could also have been a prepared answer. Kingston knew that something wasn't quite right or Jack would have asked him in.

'Is there anything I can do? Have you seen a doctor?'

'No, I'm fine, really. I'll be back to work in a couple of days if that's what you're worried about.'

'I'm worried about *you*, Jack, not the work. That bruise looks pretty nasty.'

'Look, Lawrence, I'm sorry I didn't call you. I was pretty shaken up.' He licked his lips. 'I've got to go.' He started to ease the door closed. 'Like I said, I'll be back on Monday.'

Kingston was left no choice, he could hardly barge his way in. Even if he did, what could he expect to find? 'All right, Jack. You take care – and do me a favour. Save me the trouble of driving all the way up here and answer your damned phone from now on, will you?' For a split second he glanced past Jack into the shadows of the hallway and noticed a coat rack. The top garment was a grey sweatshirt. It had a hood.

'Yeah, okay. I will.' With that, Jack slowly closed the door and the latch clicked shut.

True to his word, Jack showed up for work on Monday morning at eight thirty. There was no hiding the bruises, which were worse than Kingston expected. Right off, the men started ragging him. 'Run into Mike Tyson, did yer?' 'What does the other guy look like?' But Jack stuck to his story about falling off his bike. It seemed a credible explanation.

At the end of the afternoon, just before Jack was leaving, Kingston asked him if he could have a word. They sat down together in the workshop, each with a beer from the small refrigerator Jamie had insisted on installing.

Kingston took a draught of beer, wiping the foam from his lip. 'So, what's going on, Jack?' he asked.

Jack, who was drinking from the bottle, took his time answering. 'It was just like I told you. Dumb as it may sound, I took a header off the bike.'

'I don't mean that. What I'm talking about is your being up at the chapel and asking Jamie Gibson if she could loan you money.'

Jack's eyes darted around the room for a couple of seconds. 'Yep, I did ask her. Soon as I'd done it, I knew it might have been a mistake.' He paused, his eyes finally meeting Kingston's. 'I assumed she had more money than she knew what to do with. Why not?'

'Why did you need the money?'

'It was like I told her. I've been getting behind in my card payments – you know, the penalties and the interest an' all – things were starting to add up. They were going to pull my card.'

'I see.' Kingston took another sip of the Bass ale. 'Tell me, what did you expect to find at the chapel?'

'To find?'

'Yes. What were you looking for?'

'I told you, didn't I?'

'You told me you were just trying to help, to see if there was another way into the chapel. Wouldn't the logical thing have been to ask me first?'

Jack looked uneasy. When he picked up his beer bottle, Kingston noticed the slightest tremble in his hand. 'I suppose so,' he replied.

'Perhaps you were looking for yourself?'

Jack shook his head.

'Or someone else, perhaps?'

He continued to shake his head. 'No, it was mostly curiosity on my part. That's all.'

Four days had passed since the ransacking of the cottage. Kingston had called Ferguson and informed him of the theft of the three books. Ferguson was not too happy with the news but soon became resigned to the fact that nothing further could be done about it and that was the last he might see of them.

At eight o'clock on Tuesday morning Kingston sat at the long pine table in the kitchen of the big house reading the paper. Today, he was going up to London on the train. First stop on his list was an overdue visit to check up on his flat. After that he was to meet his accountant. Time permitting, he would try to squeeze in a haircut. Not so much a cut as a trim. He preferred to keep it a little on the shaggy side. Then, at three forty-five, he was going to meet one of the veterans on the list, a former lance corporal, Arthur Loftus, who was under Ryder's command during the war.

Soon into their phone conversation three days earlier, it became apparent that Loftus not only had lots to talk about, but also found solace in doing so. When Kingston asked if he could pay him a visit Loftus was quick to agree. 'Could do with a bit of company,' he said.

Kingston was waiting for Jamie, who had offered to drive him to the station in Taunton. When she came down, he would tell her everything. About his first contact with Lieutenant Colonel Jarvis in Taunton, the letter from the Personnel Centre, the phone calls and the appointment he had made to meet Loftus, who lived in Kingsbury.

Jamie entered the kitchen, humming and looking well rested. 'Want some coffee and toast before we leave? Plenty of time,' she said, glancing up at the wall clock.

'Lovely,' Kingston replied, lowering the paper.

103

She went to the counter, opened the cupboard door and reached up for the coffee tin.

'You're chipper this morning,' he said.

She looked over her shoulder, still humming. 'Glad to see the back of you for a few hours.'

'Now, come on.' He smiled. 'You haven't seen me since yesterday morning.'

In a few minutes, coffee was poured and the toast was on the table. Kingston took a slice, spread marmalade on it and cut it in two. He looked across at her. He hoped his gaze wasn't too searching. 'There's something I need to tell you, Jamie,' he said.

'By the look on your face, it must be serious.'

'I wouldn't call it serious, but I thought it best that we talk about it.'

'I hope you're not up to something illegal,' she said with a nervous smile.

'No, nothing like that. It's just that I've been doing a little – well, detective work.'

'Oh, about Jack? The books?'

'No. About Major Ryder, actually,' he said, taking a bite of toast.

She must have heard what he'd said but she didn't react unduly surprised. 'So what's this detective work you're up to? Ryder, you said?'

'Yes.'

'Why is everybody so obsessed with Ryder? Like Bella at dinner that night, suggesting it could be Ryder's bones in the well. That was plain ridiculous.'

'Far fetched, I agree. And I'm not obsessed, Jamie, just curious. The reason I'm bringing it up now is that if you feel that – that it's none of my business and you don't want it to go any further, then I'll drop it.'

Jamie frowned. 'Exactly what is it you're doing, Lawrence?'

'I've simply been trying to find out more about Ryder's army career. He intrigues me. I know it's a bit presumptuous on my part to be poking into your affairs but I saw no harm in it.' He made an attempt at a smile, a means of lightening the conversation. 'Particularly if it were to uncover a long-lost English relative of yours.' His comment didn't appear to have the effect intended. Her sober expression hadn't changed so he decided not to pursue the point, simply staring into his coffee, waiting for her to say something.

'You're right, Lawrence. You are being nosy. Perhaps you could be more specific?'

He told her about the Army Personnel letter and that, in the afternoon, he was going to meet a former lance corporal, who he believed could shed more light on Ryder. 'I promise you, if this chap Loftus has nothing to add to what we already know about Ryder, then it's a dead issue as far as I'm concerned.'

'Not exactly what I would call a good choice of words.' She looked at him for what seemed a long time. Then a faint smile appeared. 'Have you always had this ambition to be a private eye?'

He smiled. 'Let me talk to Loftus today and that will probably be the end of it.'

'All right, since you've already gone to all this trouble, you go meet him. I'm not sure that I like it but then I don't see what harm it can do.'

'Thanks, Jamie,' said Kingston, relieved.

'One other thing,' she said. 'This is all between you and me. I don't want Latimer or anybody else made aware of what you're doing.'

For the next ten minutes Kingston gave her a progress report on the restoration project. Spreading the plans on the kitchen table he showed her the designs he'd drawn up for a pleached lime walk and a thatched-roof summerhouse. 'When we have more time I have to tell you about the rose garden, too,' he said. 'You're going to like what I've got planned for you.'

Jamie picked up her plate and coffee mug and went to

105

the counter. 'What time do you think you'll be back from London?'

'There's a five fifty out of Waterloo that arrives in Taunton at eight twenty or thereabouts,' said Kingston. 'Shouldn't be any problem catching that.' He paused. 'By the way, I'll get a cab from the station. No point in dragging you out.' He got up. 'I suppose we'd better get going. James, my tax chap, is a stickler for punctuality – the politeness of kings, as he puts it.'

In Jamie's car, a Volvo estate, Kingston strapped on his seatbelt and glanced across at her, a grin on his face. 'You *will* try to stay on the right side of the road, my dear?'

'Surely you mean the left,' she deadpanned, looking over her shoulder, backing up.

A ten-minute walk from Wembley Park tube station had brought Kingston to Loftus's semi-detached house. He hoped the knee-high weeds surrounding a pathetic patch of brick that was the front garden was not an indication of what he might find inside. He winced and rang the doorbell.

When Arthur Loftus opened the door Kingston was taken aback for a moment. The man in front of him somehow didn't match the voice on the phone. With his stoop, he couldn't be much more than five feet tall. His face was deeply wrinkled and his eyes were soulful and abnormally large. Wisps of grey hair clung to the side of his shiny pate like fluff from a bird's nest. His clothes, a baggy cardigan and worn corduroys, looked as if they doubled as sleepwear.

Loftus's eyes sized up Kingston, then with a nod of his head – on a level with Kingston's chest – he said, 'Come on in, doctor.'

'Thank you, Arthur. A pleasure to meet you,' said Kingston.

'Likewise,' said Loftus, stepping aside and pointing with

a malacca cane gripped in his liver-spotted hand. 'Down the hall, second on the right.'

When Kingston had rung Loftus, the first question he had asked was whether Loftus remembered an officer by the name of Ryder. 'Ryder, blimey, how could I forget him, that bastard,' was Loftus's answer. From then on Kingston hadn't been able to get a word in edgewise. After listening for a minute or so, he was convinced that a meeting with Loftus was essential. There was no question that Loftus was in full possession of his faculties. His memory, in particular, was remarkable – sharper than his own, Kingston reckoned. Just before hanging up Loftus had mentioned that he lived alone but that taking care of the house had become just too much for him of late. 'Gettin' the upper hand it is,' he said. He also allowed that Kingston's timing was fortunate because he was about to move up to Nottingham to live with his younger sister. 'She's only eighty-one,' he chuckled, giving his address and directions, and wishing Kingston a polite good day.

This man was Kingston's final chance. He was the last of the eight men referred to him by the Personnel Centre. In the course of his phone calls, he had found out that two of the men had recently met their maker, one was in an intensive care ward and not expected to last many more days, while another was in the advanced stages of Alzheimer's disease. Three more, a lance corporal and two privates, he had talked to on the phone and in each case had decided that further questioning would serve no purpose.

Near the end of the dimly lit hall Kingston entered a small sitting room. 'Ain't much but make yourself at home,' Loftus said cheerfully.

Kingston stood for a moment taking stock of the room and debating where he should sit. Jaundiced lace curtains drawn across the bay window made the floral-papered room even gloomier than the hallway. The sofa facing him had lower back pain written all over it. On a spindly-

107

legged table near the window an aspidistra appeared to be in a valiant struggle for survival against a redoubtable trinity: a radiator, light deprivation and Loftus's indifference. Kingston chose the wingback chair noticing, too late, the dark patch of grease on its upholstered back where countless heads had rested over countless years. Stacked on the low coffee table in front of the sofa, where Loftus was about to sit, were several bulging and dog-eared scrapbooks.

'How about something to wet your whistle, doc?'

'No, I'm fine, Arthur. Thanks anyway.'

'Art. Call me Art.' He laughed a little laugh but it couldn't conceal the flicker of sadness in his round eyes. 'Used to call me Dodger, me mates did.'

Kingston smiled and nodded.

'You know? Artful Dodger.'

'Yes, I got it,' Kingston said, with a tactful smile. 'Art, it is then.' He crossed his long legs and shifted to get comfortable, leaning to one side to avoid the grease patch. Before he could broach the subject of Ryder, Art had launched into a loosely chronological account of his army career. It took him the best part of ten minutes to get from square bashing at Aldershot to landing in Normandy. Kingston became so absorbed in Art's anecdotal mastery that, at one point, he had to remind himself why he was there in the first place.

Finally, it looked as though Art was running out of words. 'Sure you don't want a cuppa, doc?' he inquired.

In his mind's eye, Kingston pictured a thick-rimmed mug with chips on the lip, filled with a lukewarm mahogany liquid. 'No. No thanks, I'm fine, Art,' he said, perhaps a little too hastily. 'Can I ask you about this officer named Ryder?' he added quickly, before Art could start rattling off again.

Whether Art had heard him or not, Kingston couldn't tell. Until now there had been nothing to suggest that Art might have a hearing problem. Nevertheless he had completely ignored Kingston's question.

'So, where was I, now?' Loftus said, picking up a photo from the open scrapbook and handing it to Kingston. The faded black and white picture was of three grinning uniformed young men, outstretched arms on each other's shoulders. 'Here, this was taken a couple of days after we landed.' He leaned across the table and placed it in front of Kingston, prodding at it with a bony forefinger.

'That's me on the right – and Charlie, with the bottle-bottoms, he's on the left. And there's young Eddie in the middle – Eddie Butler.' He let out a long sigh and massaged his brow. 'Blown to smithereens – 'bout a week later. Poor sod. Only sixteen, he was. Silly bugger lied to get in.' His eyes searched the photo as if seeing it for the first time, and he slowly shook his head.

Kingston remained respectfully silent, studying the young devil-may-care faces, one by one, as he waited for Art to say something. When, at last, he looked up he was surprised to see a smile on Art's face.

'Great on the mouth organ, he was,' Loftus said, nodding to himself.

Kingston cleared his throat. 'Was Eddie . . . did that happen when you were trapped in that Dutch town? I forget the name – Klein something – it was mentioned in the letter I told you about. Bloody awful business, by the sound of it.' Immediately the words left his mouth, he regretted having uttered them. He watched as Art stared off into space. Kingston could only ruefully guess at what ghosts his words had aroused.

Art broke the silence. 'Klein Longstreet, that's where it were all right. Never forget that place.'

Kingston noticed that Art was looking at him in an odd way. 'Would you prefer we not talk about it?'

'No, it's okay. It don't bother me any more. Funny, ain't it, how the mind works. You'd think that after all these years I'd want to forget the bloody war. But, if you wanna

109

know the truth, doc, thinking back on them times – not that I do it that often, mind you – gives me a certain amount of pleasure. I suppose I've learned to blot out the bad parts.'

Kingston handed the photo back to Art. 'Tell me about Ryder,' he asked offhandedly.

'I'll tell you one thing – none of us could stand that snotty bastard. *Lieutenant Ryder.*'

'Ended up as Major. Did you know he was awarded a Military Cross?'

'Yeah, one of me mates told me, after the war. What a joke!'

'Why is that?'

'Kershaw's the one who should've got a medal.'

'Kershaw?'

'Right – Sergeant Jeremy Kershaw. I wouldn't be sitting here now if it weren't for him. He's the one who shot Ryder.'

Kingston raised his eyebrows. 'Shot Ryder?'

'That's right. Should have finished him off while he was at it, if you ask me.'

'He *shot* his superior officer? It was . . . some kind of accident, I take it?'

'It was, according to Jeremy. Happened in a struggle but Ryder swore Jeremy did it on purpose. They put him under close arrest.'

'My God! What exactly happened?'

Loftus looked up toward the ceiling. Kingston waited silently, respectful that the man was fanning embers of an old fire that would never be fully extinguished.

'It all took place in that village you mentioned,' he said looking at Kingston. 'We were just about done in. What I'm saying is that all of us – all, except that arrogant sod, Ryder – knew that we didn't have a chance in hell of surviving. After we'd been fighting for our bloody lives all week, the Jerries had finished off more than half of us. We only had enough food to last another day or so, the radio had gone for a burton and we were almost out of ammunition. But Ryder wouldn't surrender. He wouldn't hear of it. Kershaw had given up trying to convince him. Ryder even gave us this bullshit speech about never giving in, fighting to the bitter end an' all that. He was a right nutter, that one. It was bloody awful, I tell you.' Loftus paused and looked down at the coffee table as if the memories had become too real, too painful. Then he looked back up at Kingston, his face showing no signs of distress.

'One of the lads, not much more than a kid he was . . .' He glanced at the ceiling again. 'Nah, his name escapes me. Anyway, he'd cracked. Gone round the bend. Couldn't take it any more, poor sod. We all felt sorry for him, Kershaw more than most. You'd have thought he was his brother. Which didn't figure 'cause Kershaw was a kinda loner. Tough as nails – afraid of no one.' Loftus paused to scratch his head. 'Anyway, early one morning when it was real quiet this young feller takes it into his head to pack it in – surrender. He takes off his helmet and jacket and starts walking over all this rubble toward the Jerries, waving a white flag. Well, according Kershaw . . .' He paused and wagged a finger in Kingston's direction. 'Now this is second hand, mind you – Ryder, who's got a pistol, spots the poor bugger as he's halfway up the street and yells out that either he stops or he's gonna be shot for desertion. Unfortunately for Ryder, Kershaw shows up and tries to stop Ryder from shooting the lad. He jumps the lieutenant, the gun goes off and the lad gets killed. Then, Ryder and Kershaw are rolling round on the ground wrestling for the gun. That's when Ryder gets shot and how come Kershaw gets sent up.' He sighed and stood up. 'Couple of days later we were captured anyway.'

'What happened to Kershaw?'

'He was court-martialled. Heard he got twenty years.'

'I take it you haven't heard from him?'

Loftus shook his head. 'No. I didn't expect to. We didn't

111

know each other that well. Like I said, he kept pretty much to himself.'

They talked for another ten minutes or so then Kingston glanced at his watch. He was startled to see it was past five. He was cutting it fine to make the five fifty from Waterloo. He thanked Loftus profusely, apologizing for leaving so hurriedly, handed him his card and left.

Chapter Eleven

By the time the cab pulled into the driveway at Wickersham it was ten thirty. With only the porch light lit, Kingston concluded that Jamie had probably turned in early. Just as well – he was far too tired to have to relate the events of the day right now. He paid off the driver and went to the cottage.

In the small living room he poured an inch of Macallan from the bottle on the mahogany butler's table that served as the bar. He added a splash of Malvern water, took a sip, exhaled a loud sigh of satisfaction, then crossed the room and sank into the chintz sofa. For a while, he thought about Loftus, and the legions of servicemen who would live out their private lives forever haunted by memories and nightmares of wartime horror and death. Considering their short span of time together, he had developed a genuine liking for the little man.

All in all, the day had gone well: haircut satisfactory, as always; nothing untoward at the flat, save a few rolled-up newspapers on the doorstep (despite his having suspended delivery) and a couple of bills that hadn't been forwarded and a folded note from his neighbour, Andrew. He was in line for a couple of tickets for the opera and did Kingston want to go?

Tomorrow, after he'd told Jamie about his conversation with Loftus, he was going to take her up to the water tank to show her how the water supply and irrigation worked, how it was captured and how it was distributed. He wouldn't normally have bothered her with it but she had expressed interest and insisted on seeing it, which impressed him.

He also planned to inspect the chapel again, and that made him think of Roger Ferguson. How was he coming along with his search, he wondered? Something else struck Kingston as odd, too. Why hadn't he been calling? Surely there couldn't be many other things that would have higher priority for him than the chapel. He made a mental note to ring Roger tomorrow. He spent five minutes reading the first few pages of *The Times*, finished his whisky, turned off the light and went upstairs to bed.

At nine o'clock the next morning, the sky was darkening like a spreading ink-stain. No question a bad storm was in the offing. After spending an hour with the construction crew going over new plans for the lime walk and the summerhouse, Kingston walked up to the house. It was raining heavily now and ponderous clouds were hanging low in the sky. As he approached the house, he saw that many of the windows were lit. He found Jamie in the living room, by a table lamp, reading. She looked up when he entered.

'Morning, Lawrence.' She rested the book in her lap. 'Miserable morning. I didn't hear you last night. What time did you get back?'

'About half ten. I was exhausted. Saw all the lights off, so I went straight to bed.'

'Everything all right at home?'

'Yes, fine, thanks, No problems.'

'Good.'

Wasn't she going to ask him about Loftus?

'Did you get a haircut? Doesn't look like it.'

'Wish my barber, Jackie, could've heard what you just said.'

'Why, for heaven's sake?'

'Well she maintains that with a proper haircut, it shouldn't look as if one's just had one, nor should it look like one needs one.'

'Very profound.'

He was beginning to feel awkward just standing there discussing his damned haircut. Perhaps he should cobble up an excuse to leave and tell her about the meeting later. She saved him the trouble.

'The coffee's hot in the kitchen. Why don't you go get some and then tell me what happened with the soldier. You did meet with him?'

'Yes, I did. He's a very nice man. I learned quite a lot.'

Kingston returned with a mug of coffee and sat down in the wingback opposite Jamie. There were others, but somehow he always ended up in the same chair.

'I've forgotten. What was the man's name?' asked Jamie.

'Loftus – Arthur Loftus – a lance corporal back in the war days. It was most –' A low rumble of distant thunder smothered the end of his sentence.

Jamie glanced to the window where the wind was picking up, slapping fat blobs of rain on the panes. She looked back at Kingston. 'That was nearly sixty years ago. How old is he, for God's sake?'

'I didn't ask. But he has to be over eighty. Sharp as a two-edged sword, though.' He took a sip of coffee and started to recount what Loftus had told him. She leaned forward perceptibly and for the next five minutes listened without interrupting.

'Well, that's about it – as near as dammit,' said Kingston. He searched her face trying to gauge her thoughts but her expression was ambiguous. 'Well, what do you think?'

She gave his question a few seconds' thought before answering. 'I'm not sure. You see, all along I've thought of Ryder as being a good guy. And from what you're suggesting – I should say Loftus – that may not have been the case.'

'True, but remember, at this point, it's only his word we've got to go on.'

'I understand, but can't you see, this changes things. Sure, much of what I'm doing here is of my own choosing but in the back of my mind, there's always been the other underlying reason, the question of doing what's right, morally, that gives the entire project much more meaning and gratification. A sense of purpose.'

'I know what you're saying, Jamie. You'd mentioned it earlier. About "doing it as a tribute to the Ryder family", I think you put it.'

'That's right. But now, if it turns out that Ryder wasn't the war hero that we all thought and instead, was – well, someone just short of being a murderer – how do you think that makes me feel?'

'Jamie, I think you're getting upset needlessly,' he said, suddenly thrown on the defensive. 'Ryder may have had every right and good reason to shoot the chap. I don't know what regulations would apply in a case like this but I do know that at one time, desertion in the face of the enemy meant execution on the spot.' He paused briefly and shrugged. 'This is one man's account, Jamie – only Loftus's side of the story.'

Kingston was quickly realizing that it would be unwise to pursue this line of reasoning. If he did, she would become increasingly and unnecessarily agitated. He lowered his voice. 'Look, unless by some stroke of luck more information about Ryder comes to light, we may never know what *really* happened back in that Dutch village.' He gestured to her with open palms. 'So we might as well leave it buried in the past and get on with things. In any case, we're talking about the Ryder *family*. And in that context I don't see any reason for you to feel any differently. After all, there were two other brothers who fought and died for their country and I'm willing to bet that, if we

116

were to research the family's genealogy, you would find that there were other Ryders who fought gallantly in other wars. So your motivation remains just as principled as before, Jamie.'

'All right. Maybe I *am* making too much of it. But there's nothing else you've mentioned that further explains why Ryder did what he did – that is, name me as his heir. Isn't that why you went to all this trouble in the first place? You may be looking for something that's simply not there.'

'You're probably right,' he said, just to make her feel better but not agreeing. He glanced out of the window ready to change the subject. 'If this rain keeps up,' he said, 'you may want to think twice about going up to the water tank. It's a bit of a hike and it can get quite slippery.'

'Let's just wait and see, maybe it'll clear up this after-noon. Your weather has a strange habit of doing that.'

'Why don't I check in with you after lunch, then?'

'Fine – oh, I forgot to tell you. A man called for you yesterday, from the Record Office. Sounded like death warmed up – Roger, I think he said his name was.'

'Yes, Ferguson. Did he leave a message?'

'Just for you to call, that's all. He left his number, I've got it in the office.'

Kingston was standing. 'Don't worry, I have his card.' For a moment he considered telling Jamie his theory about the old priory but considering her mood he thought better of it. Plus, there was the distinct risk of her thinking that he was developing a complex of some kind.

With the absence of mains water in rural areas, nearly all of Britain's large country houses had to rely on nearby local sources for their water supply: rivers, streams, lakes and wells. Kingston had researched several such houses, including Heligan, to learn more about how the water supply was delivered to the house and how the irrigation systems worked.

117

From everything he'd learned, the estate at Wickersham – if it were to have employed the same water supply systems as many of its contemporaries – would have a large reservoir located in one of the highest points in the gardens. He was soon proved right. Though not an early priority, it had been located quickly approximately half a mile behind the house on the north side: a massive stone and brick holding tank that Kingston estimated would hold close to fifty thousand gallons of clean water.

The rain had stopped shortly after noon and the sun had broken through the clouds when Kingston and Jamie set off for the water tank. On the hike up they had paused on a knoll that offered a splendid 180 degree panorama of the estate.

'There's some of your vineyard slopes,' said Kingston, pointing to a series of gently rolling, grass-covered hills that encompassed at least forty acres of land.

She didn't answer right away, giving the scene what Kingston took to be a long critical appraisal. 'Could be a great place to start,' she said. 'The exposure's good.'

'Shouldn't be too difficult to get access,' said Kingston. 'And with what we know already, irrigation shouldn't be a problem.'

The talk for the remainder of the climb up to the reservoir was about growing grapes.

Five minutes was more than enough for them to inspect the reservoir. Jamie was polite but Kingston got the impression that she would much rather be doing a closer exploration of the land for her vineyards than looking at a stone and brick edifice full of murky water.

'Come on,' said Kingston. 'I'll show you something a trifle more interesting.' He started up a narrow dirt path that wound its way higher up the hill. After ten minutes or so, during which they descended into a small valley, passed through dense overgrowth, and then climbed up the other side into open land, they finally arrived at a small clearing. In the centre was a three-sided structure built of stone. The two narrow long walls, only two feet high, enclosed steps that went down about five feet and then stopped; the opening was filled with mud and debris.

'This is the ram chamber,' said Kingston, ready to show off the knowledge that he'd gleaned from his Heligan research. 'When we dig out all the crud, we'll find two or three ram pumps down there, two to five inches in capacity. They're capable of pumping close to ten gallons of water a minute, to a height of three hundred feet, over a one-mile distance.'

'That's an awful long way. How are they powered?'

'That's the beauty, Jamie. They're powered by nature, by gravity, from the stream that feeds them.' Kingston was already on the move again. 'One last short climb.'

Heading north away from the ram house Jamie followed as they wound their way farther up the hill. After another five minutes they arrived at a small stone building with a sloped roof. Along one side of it was a deep trough.

'This is the catch basin,' said Kingston.

Jamie was sitting on the edge of the stone wall of the trough, seemingly happy just to rest after the steep climb, which hadn't seemed to affect Kingston at all

'Here's how it works. When you consider that this was probably engineered well over one hundred years ago, it's sheer genius.' He was pointing farther up the hill. 'Up in the valleys above us somewhere – Jack and I haven't explored there yet – one or more streams will have been dammed and the overflow is channelled down here through large pipes, at least four inches in diameter. From here the water is directed down individual pipes called drive pipes. Each one of these is connected to the back of a hydraulic ram pump down below. Bear in mind that the system relies entirely on gravity, so the drive pipes must be set at an angle of no less than 45 degrees. This was no mean feat of engineering when you consider that back in those days the pipes had to be cut into the rock face of the hill and that meant either pickaxes or dynamite.'

119

'It's amazing,' said Jamie.

'The bad news is, we're going to have our work cut out for us to bring it all back to working order. All the mud is going to have to be taken out by hand. It's going to be a long and back-breaking bucket brigade, I'm afraid. Then we have to lug out the ram pumps and those things weigh a ton, they're made of iron and brass.'

'What about them? The pumps? I would imagine that they'd be in pretty bad shape after being buried in mud for sixty-plus years.'

'That was the case at Heligan and I'm sure that's going to be the case here. Amazingly enough, the company that built their original system in 1880 is still in operation. More unbelievable is that spare parts are still available.'

'Let's keep our fingers crossed that it's the same company that built ours.'

On the way down, at Kingston's urging, Jamie talked more about winemaking: this time about the complex steps and the decision-making that confront the winemaker once the grapes have made their journey from the vineyards to the winery.

'Practically all red grapes and white grapes have clear colourless juice. The red pigment is the grape skins. But you probably knew that,' she said, glancing at Kingston, who nodded. She continued. 'I'll try to keep it simple. Unlike white grapes that we usually press within hours of their arrival at the winery – the juice separated from the skins – red grapes require extended contact with the skin. So red wine is made by fermenting the juice, pulp and skins together. After several days of fermentation the red wine is then pressed.' She went on to talk about the strains of yeast used in the critical multi-step biochemical process that convert the sugars into alcohol; the importance of temperature control during fermentation; the traditional use and repeat use of French or American oak barrels, the insides of which are toasted at the cooperage, and how they contribute to the flavours, aromas and complexity of the wine as it ages.

They stopped to take a pause on the knoll where they'd rested on the way up. Sitting on the grass, they looked out over the tree-studded hills and green pastures where curls of clouds were starting to creep through the divides in the valleys. Whereas it was warm on the way up, it was now cooling quickly.

'Pinot Noir country,' Jamie muttered.

'You want those cool nights, eh?'

'That's right. It's one of the trickiest of all wines to make well.'

'Aren't Burgundy wines mostly Pinot Noir?'

'They are. It's one of the oldest grape varieties yet one of the most demanding and elusive. Even in Burgundy a good vintage comes only once every three years.' She smiled coyly. 'Back home we call it Pinot Envy.'

Kingston made no comment, a little taken back.

Jamie went on. It was clear that she enjoyed these little chats about wine and Kingston was only too happy to sit and listen, his normal role reversed.

'With Pinot, there're so many difficulties, it's a wonder growers struggle with it. It's genetically unpredictable from vineyard to vineyard – you never know what off-spring you're going to get from a parent plant – big or small grapes and clusters, different aromas, flavours and levels of crop.'

'So, once planted, you've got what you've got,' said Kingston.

'Exactly right. Plus it's susceptible to just about every affliction known, including Pierce's disease which can wipe out a vineyard in a couple of years.' She paused to flip a pebble off the knoll. 'Worldwide, there are only twelve identifiable clones of Cabernet Sauvignon. With Pinot Noir there's close to a thousand.'

'And *you* want to try it?'

'I have a feeling it might do well here because one of the

critical things with Pinot is the climate. It needs relatively cool weather and chalky soil that drains well. That's why they can make such good Pinots in Oregon and the cooler parts of Northern California, like the Russian River area by the coast and Carneros in Napa and Sonoma right next to the bay.'

'Maybe you should start with something a little more friendly?'

'Don't worry, Lawrence, Pinot will only be an experiment, a challenge. It can become a very expensive business. When I left, the going rate for Pinot grapes was close to three thousand dollars a ton.'

'The more I hear you talk, the more I like your idea of developing a vineyard here, Jamie. I'd love to be around when you start in on it.'

'You can be if you want to. I'd love to have company. I've toyed with the idea of bringing a couple of people over but that can wait.'

'You may even find who you're looking for here, locally. There're plenty of wineries in Britain today. I read somewhere that they number over four hundred. Hard to believe, isn't it?'

'Really, I had no idea there were *that* many.'

'Well, if nothing else, some of those people would be aware of some of the more unusual problems of growing grapes in England. As one of our chaps once said to a French grower: "Where is it written that the sun stops shining at the Channel?"'

She chuckled. 'How true. Without question, I'll be picking their brains.'

Kingston said nothing further, having conjured a mental picture of endless rows of vines stretching off into the distant hills surrounding the estate – he and Jamie tasting their very first bottling. Wickersham Vineyards: it had a classy euphony to it. Jamie's words woke him from his fanciful digression.

She talked about wine all the way back to the house.

Kingston could tell that if there was anything at all she was missing from her old life back in California it was making wine.

It was two days before Ferguson returned Kingston's phone call. Kingston took the call on his mobile at Sherratt's, the wholesale nursery that was supplying most of the roses for the garden. The conversation lasted little more than a minute.

Jamie had been right about his voice; he said he'd been off work with flu.

'It's your lucky day,' Ferguson said with a nasal twang. He went on to describe a single, undated document that one of his researchers had found. It was in the form of a crude fold-out plan showing the layout of the priory: the great hall, kitchen, various rooms, stables, livestock and storage areas and a garden. 'But that's not all,' Ferguson said, pausing for effect by the sound of it. 'The drawing indicates a second level plan that shows a network of rooms, vaults and passages. And most interesting of all is that the second level is underground.'

'Underground?'

'That's right. Just like you guessed. So I wouldn't rule out the possibility that part of Wickersham is standing on the former basement of the priory, as it were. Now I *have* to see it.'

Chapter Twelve

Walking through the house, Kingston saw no signs of Jamie or Dot. In the living room the windows were opened wide; the lowering sun varnishing the walls and furniture tops with an amber sheen. Approaching the open french doors, he saw the back-lit silhouette of Jamie on the terrace. She was sitting on one of the Chippendale teak benches they'd bought a couple of weeks earlier. As he stepped on to the flagstones he felt a surge of pride at the sight of the three levels of lawn descending from the terrace. Though the sod had been laid barely five weeks ago, they looked surprisingly well established, almost as good as those in the old photos. He looked away with a smile. After mowing and rolling for a few decades, they would look just like those at Sissinghurst Castle garden, as smooth as bowling greens.

Seeing him, Jamie looked up from the pad on her lap and put the ballpoint pen on the table by her side. 'Hello, Lawrence. Looks like you had a good day?'

He sat down facing her. 'I did, very good, in fact. At long last, I think I have a final list of the roses. Went over it today with Sherratt's. There's a couple that they might have to hunt around for but they don't see any problems in getting the rest.' He leaned back and rubbed his eyes, which were tired after the long drive with the sun in his face most of the way. 'How about you?'

'Not much to report.' She took a sip of water from the plastic bottle, which Kingston found a little unrefined despite the fact that he knew most young people nowa-days drank their water and beer that way.

'Oh, I almost forgot, your fellow Loftus called. That's quite an accent. He left a number.' She leafed through the pad on her lap and tore off a sheet. 'Here,' she said, handing it to him. He couldn't help noticing the indif-ference in her voice. 'Said he was up at his sister's in Nottingham.'

Kingston glanced absently at the number. 'Hmm. Did he say what it was about?'

'No, just to call him.'

They were interrupted by Dot, who wanted to ask Jamie a question about laundry. The conversation was brief and soon Dot went on her way.

'Her usual vivacious self,' Kingston muttered.

'Be nice, Lawrence. We can't all be Miss Congeniality.'

Jamie got up from the chair and for a moment it looked as if she was about to say something; instead, she looked away, out to the lawns. When she turned back to Kingston, her face had taken on a serious air. Not pensive or the wrinkled-brow sort but the kind of expression that fore-shadows a statement of some consequence. He'd seen it before.

'Lawrence,' she said, sitting down to face him. 'I won't beat around the bush. I've decided that all this business of yours digging into Ryder's past has got to stop.'

'But, Jamie –'

She raised a hand, palm facing him. 'Let me just finish, please. When you and I talked earlier, I told you how I felt about your prying into the past and how it was starting to affect me. I know at the time I agreed to your meeting with Loftus mostly because it was a done deal on your part. But to tell the truth, I thought – hoped, rather – that it would lead to a dead end. That it would all eventually go away. But by the looks of it, it clearly hasn't.'

Kingston listened, like a schoolboy having his privileges withdrawn. He knew when silence was well advised.

'First, the body in the well, then the theft, and now this hang-up of yours about Ryder. I realize that these events are not necessarily connected in any way, much as *you* might want them to be, but they're all very serious, scary, in fact. I have this horrible feeling that if we – you, that is – keep digging deeper and deeper, we might uncover things that are best left alone, things that we will come to regret.'

It was the first time Kingston had seen Jamie lose her composure. Biting her lip, she looked away from him. He thought it best, for a moment anyway, to hold his tongue.

At last, she looked back at him, the resentfulness gone, her eyes wistful. 'What I'm trying to say, Lawrence, is that we are creating something very special here and I want it to continue that way. When you decide that the gardens are ready, it's my plan to open them to the public, like all the big gardens. Not so much for the money – although I hope that they eventually become self-sufficient – but purely to provide pleasure. I think that gardens should be treated like the paintings that hang in museums. Everyone should be able to see and enjoy them, preferably for free. Gardens even more so than paintings because gardens are a true gift of nature.' She cast her eyes to her lap, gently kneading her hands. 'Lawrence, I want you to understand where I'm coming from. If, for whatever reason, I were to lose all this, I'd be sad and disappointed for one reason only, and that is not being able to finish what we're doing here.' She made an attempt at a chuckle, looking up at him again. 'It's funny, I don't think I'll really miss being filthy rich. You've come to know me, at least a little, and I'm sure you must have concluded by now that it's not money that motivates me.' She gave barest hint of a smile. 'I'm sorry to have to ask you to give up your deerstalker, Lawrence, but from now on you're going to have leave all that stuff to Chief Inspector Chadwick.'

While he had been listening Kingston had also been trying to come up with some kind of response. He knew, of course, that he had little or no choice in the matter. In retrospect, perhaps he *had* stepped a few paces over the boundaries of acceptable behaviour, given that he was, after all, being paid to do a job. But he was also ready to give himself the benefit of the doubt inasmuch that his principal concern all along – allowing for his admitted propensity for meddling, trying to solve other people's problems – had been for Jamie's interests. He certainly didn't want to let his disappointment show. If he were to admit the truth, though, he wasn't really getting very far with his investigations anyway – with the exception of Ferguson's recent information. He had planned to tell Jamie about that conversation today but it hardly seemed prudent to bring it up now.

Kingston regarded her, as she sat down and took another sip of water. Her face showed no signs of emotion. After the long silence, he spoke. 'Jamie, I understand fully and I'm sorry. I suppose it was insensitive of me in the first place to get involved with your personal affairs but you must know that it was all done for your sake. But I can see the down side and agree with you.' He looked past her, out of the tall windows at the failing light. 'I agree that there is the possibility – though slim, I would think – that further examination of Ryder's background could result in dredging up something that we least expect, as you say, something we might regret. And if that were to affect you adversely, I would never forgive myself.' Kingston turned back to her, got up and smiled. 'So, that said, I promise to hand the case over to Detective Chief Inspector Chadwick from now on and turn my full attention to the gardens.' He scratched his chin, thinking. 'I should go and return Loftus's call though, purely as a courtesy, of course.'

Jamie responded with a faint smile, nodded and watched as he left the room.

In the cottage, ten minutes later, Kingston reached Loftus.

'Nice to hear from you, doctor,' he said, his tinny voice sounding even worse on the bad line.

'How do you like Nottingham?' Kingston asked, immediately regretting it. He hoped the innocent question wouldn't set Loftus off on a five-minute dissertation on his sister's medical history.

Luckily Loftus wasn't in one of his talkative moods. 'Very nice,' he replied. 'Don't miss the Smoke one bit.'

'Jamie said you wanted to talk to me.'

'Right. I came across something you might be interested in. Gladys, me sister, bought me some new scrapbooks and I've been sortin' through all my photos. Anyway, I came across one of Sergeant Kershaw with his arm round that young soldier friend of his. The one whose name I couldn't remember. Wondered if you'd like it.'

'I would,' said Kingston. 'Very much.'

'Right then, I'll pop it in the post.'

They chatted for a bit, said their goodbyes and Kingston put down the phone.

Two days later he received Loftus's photo and a scribbled note. He put the note, which was almost indecipherable, aside for a moment and studied the two-by-four photo then flipped it over. On the yellowing back, in scratchy pencil, were the words, *Jeremy and Kit – July 22nd 1944*. Turning it over he looked at the photo again. The two smiling soldiers were in an off-duty moment, with rolled-up shirtsleeves, braces and wearing no hats. From Loftus's description, it was immediately apparent which one was Kit. Shorter by several inches, he had close-cropped hair and next to Kershaw, whose face looked fit and tanned, Kit's face looked a ghostly white, his eyes dark and sunken. Kingston put the photo down and continued to stare at it, Kit's eyes staring back at him. His mind was a blank. It was another dead end. Now he knew what Kit looked like but that wasn't of much help. Recalling his promise to Jamie, he put the photo back in its envelope and, with considerable difficulty, deciphered the note.

Dear Doc,
It was a treat chatting with you. Hope we can meet again some day. Sorry I still can't remember Kit's last name. If you're up in Nottingham any time, give me a jingle.
Yours truly, Art Loftus.

Underneath was a PS.

For what it's worth, I did remember one other thing. Just before we surrendered Kershaw took a Jerry bullet. It was nasty but as you know, he eventually pulled through okay.

Chapter Thirteen

The planning, logistics, cataloguing and physical demands of recreating the gardens at Wickersham were now reaching a feverish pitch. Every day there were a hundred decisions to be weighed and made. Every week, more purchasing, research, experimentation, meetings to be attended and new permits to be filed, not to mention the demanding physical labour expected of everybody – Kingston included, every once in a while. Then there were the mistakes and minor disasters. Not many but each cost valuable time and manpower.

The vegetable garden alone, a one-acre partially walled plot, had taken much longer to establish than any of them had anticipated. Eric Newsome, an estate gardener with four decades of experience, was brought in to finalize the layout, select the seeds and plant the garden. The original network of paths, irrigation pipes and drainage runs had been traced during the clearing and re-established. The paths divided the area into four huge squares, allowing planting on a four-year crop rotation, each square representing one year of the rotation. Eric had amassed a collection of seed catalogues and was ordering from sources all over the country. Not only vegetables but fruits, too. A bed along one side of the interior wall was double-dug with manure and ready to plant the apple and pear trees that would be espaliered along its fifty-foot length. Cages were ready for the soft fruit planting.

Having no seed or plant lists, other than the scant in-

formation provided in Ferguson's books, it was not possible to stay true to historical precedents where vegetable
and fruit varieties were concerned. Nevertheless, if the
vegetable garden was to be a productive garden, cultivated
for the quality and taste of its edibles, and not simply a
token showpiece, then it was imperative that older varieties, with their much more distinctive flavour, would be
grown exclusively.

Bed after bed, some half the length of a football field,
were double-dug and a mountain of manure and amendments worked in to enrich the soil. Soon regimental rows
of raised mounds, frames for climbing beans and peas
would transform the space ready for intensive cultivation.
In some rows, allowances had been made for companion
planting. These wide swaths of flowers and herbs would
add a welcome jumble of colour to the otherwise uniform
green ranks, some helping to ward off pests. Sweet William, marigolds, cosmos, chrysanthemum, comfrey and
borage were among those already picked out.

Kingston's aim was to make the vegetable, fruit and
flower garden the same model of self-sufficiency and
responsible environmental and ecological agricultural
practices as had been the case with the original gardens.

Kingston sat in the reception area of the police station at
Upper High Street in Shuttern, leafing through a six-
month-old copy of *Top Gear*. He was waiting to see Detective Chief Inspector Chadwick. Three days earlier he had
called the inspector, saying that he would be in Taunton
today and asking if he could stop by for a brief visit.
Without asking what it was about, Chadwick had readily
agreed to see him.

With Jamie's recent dictum, Kingston had reluctantly
decided to tell Chadwick about his aborted investigation
into Ryder's past and of Loftus's revelations. He was still
perplexed as to whether the events of that day almost sixty

131

years ago had any bearing on Jamie's inheritance but had a gut feeling that they were connected in some way.

Sitting waiting for Chadwick, he was beginning to think his visit might be a bit premature, that he should have waited until he had more solid information linking Ryder to Jamie. It was too late for that now, though. All he could hope for was that Chadwick wouldn't think of his investigative efforts as being frivolous and send him on his way with an indulgent pat on the back. The more he thought about it the more he realized that he had little or no case. An experienced police officer would see that right away. As the thought was crossing his mind, the desk sergeant called his name.

In casual clothes, with his sleeves rolled up, Chadwick looked as if he had just come in from mowing the lawn. Mid-fifties, Kingston guessed. He had a high shiny forehead that sloped up to a receding hairline, kindly but tired grey eyes with dark bags that could be the result of lots of late night reading or off-hours spent in the company of Johnnie Walker. He looked more like a teacher than a copper.

'So, how's it going up at Wickersham, doctor?' The swivel chair squeaked as Chadwick leaned back in it. 'Haven't dug up any more bones, I hope.'

'Slower than we'd all like, but very well, thanks,' Kingston answered with a smile. 'No more bones, thank goodness.'

'Did those stolen books and papers ever show up? Eldridge told me about them.'

'No. I think we can kiss those goodbye.'

'Can't imagine what use they could be to anyone. That's the odd thing.'

The phone on the cluttered desk rang. Chadwick picked it up and had a brief conversation, then hung up. 'Anything more on Ryder?' he asked.

'Well, yes, in a way. That's why I'm here, in fact.' Chadwick appeared content to sit back and listen, so Kingston went on. 'This may sound a little Holmesian, but I've been conducting an investigation of sorts into Major Ryder's background.'

'Really? Can I ask why?'

'I should say *was*. I was doing it for Jamie Gibson's benefit, thinking she would be curious to know why Ryder left her his estate – what the connection was. But it appears that she's opposed to resurrecting the past and has asked me, in no uncertain terms, to knock it off.'

'What have you found out so far, then?'

For the next five minutes Kingston proceeded to tell Chadwick of his correspondence with the Army Personnel Centre and his meeting with Loftus and about the incident with Kershaw and the young deserting soldier. When he was finished, Chadwick studied him, taking his time, thinking.

'So,' he said, at length, 'have you come to any conclusions on all this?'

'Nothing definitive, no. I thought the logical next step would be to find out more about the sergeant, Kershaw, discover what happened to him when he was released from prison, see where that led, but I'm afraid that's out of the question now – well, for me, that is.'

'No wild guesses?'

'Well, for what it's worth, my first take – and mind you, this is all predicated on Loftus's account – was that Kershaw, having been unjustly incarcerated for twenty years because Ryder lied at the court martial, plans revenge. After serving out his term he tracks Ryder down and – by design or accident – kills him and dumps the body down the well.'

Chadwick's answer was forthright but friendly. 'Quite a few problems there, old chap.'

'I know,' Kingston replied. 'I did say it was my first theory. But you're right, the biggest problem being that if those bones are indeed Ryder's, it means that Kershaw, or

133

someone else, managed to pull off the identity switch of all time, continuing to live at Wickersham posing as Ryder.'

'It's asking a lot,' said Chadwick. 'Housekeeper, gardener probably, tradespeople, his lawyer, doctor, dentist – they would all have to be hoodwinked. Then there's the time frame. When did Kershaw get out of prison?'

'Most likely sometime in the early to mid-sixties.'

'That would mean the phony Ryder would have had to pull off the charade for over thirty years. Highly unlikely, wouldn't you think?'

Kingston nodded.

'Though similar cases have been known,' Chadwick added. 'Pity we don't have some DNA to compare.'

A pause followed while Chadwick scribbled a note on his desk pad, then he turned his attention back to Kingston.

'The other scenario I came up with,' said Kingston, 'was that it could have been Kershaw who was killed and the bones in the well are his. From what Loftus remembers, he and Ryder were about the same height and were close in age.'

Chadwick's expression was stolid.

Sensing that there was nothing more to be said by either of them, Kingston gestured with open hands. 'Well, that's about it,' he said. What he really wanted to say was that he was disappointed in Chadwick's seeming lack of enthusiasm for what Kingston thought was diligent work on his part. At least some acknowledgement for his time and effort would have been appreciated.

'Sorry,' said Chadwick, with a slight shake of the head, as if reading Kingston's mind. 'Your theory about the body being Kershaw's is certainly admissible but we have a new piece of evidence that would suggest that that's not the case.'

'A new piece of evidence?'

'Yes. It was found after the remains were analysed at the lab. Tangled up in some of the debris and sludge that came up with the bones there was a wristwatch. We found a leather belt at the site but the watch wasn't discovered till later.'

'How does the watch corroborate that it's not Ryder's or Kershaw's body?'

'Because it had initials engraved on the back. CMA. Not anyone you know, by chance?'

Kingston was thrown off balance. This was not what he wanted to hear. For a moment he said nothing. He was subconsciously rubbing his chin, thinking hard, looking away, to avoid Chadwick's gaze. Then he looked up. 'CMA. No, nobody I can think of.'

Chadwick leaned back in his swivel chair. 'Unfortunately, it doesn't look like it's going to help us much.'

'The watch. Obviously you know the make?'

'It was a Hamilton. A tank watch, I think it's called.'

'Hamilton? That's American, isn't it?'

'You're right, it is.'

'Hmm. Any idea when it was made?'

'Late thirties, as best I recall.'

'Meaning, it could have been purchased several years later.'

'Exactly.'

'So we know that the body couldn't have been in the well prior to 1937 or thereabouts?'

'But any time after. Up to today as a matter of fact because that particular watch is now a collector's item. Worth quite a few bob, I'm told.'

'But American made?'

'Yes, but we know they were exported to Britain, if that's what you're thinking, so it doesn't tell us much.'

Kingston looked up at the ceiling. 'CMA,' he said shaking his head. 'I've no idea. Unless it was bought as used.' He got up from his chair. 'Well, inspector, thanks for taking the time to see me. I trust that if you learn any more you'll let Jamie or me know. That would be appreciated.'

Chadwick rose. 'Unfortunately, none of this sheds any more light on why Ryder left his estate to Miss Gibson.

135

Which, I believe you said, is what motivated you in the first place.' He walked around the desk. 'Not unless you can connect CMA with Jamie in any way.'

'I'll ask her, of course, but I would seriously doubt it.'

'Good,' Chadwick said with a smile. 'Let me know. Meanwhile tell Jamie that the case is by no means closed but given everything we know at this point – which I'm afraid is not much – we may never discover whose bones they are and how they came to end up in the well.'

Kingston paused, one hand gripping the back of the chair. 'I have one more question, inspector,' he said. 'You had a phone conversation with Jamie shortly after the skeleton was found.'

'Yes, I remember. We'd just got the results back from pathology.'

'The victim was a male, roughly sixty years old, about five eleven. Been down there a long time, I believe you said?'

'Sounds right.'

'She said there was more but it was a bit over her head. You know, medical terminology.'

Chadwick gave the question frowning thought. 'As I recall, there really wasn't much more. I'd have to go back and look at the pathologist's report.'

'If it's not asking too much, could you do that?'

'It's frowned upon to provide information to any outside source on an active case but in this case I don't see why not. I'm curious, what do you expect to find?'

'I'm not sure. Just grasping at straws, I suppose.'

Chadwick shrugged and got up from his chair. 'It might take a couple of days. I'll call you when I have it.'

They shook hands and Kingston departed.

Two days later, at eight o'clock in the morning, the phone rang in Kingston's cottage. It was Chadwick.

'I've just finished reading the pathologist's report again,' he said. 'I've got it in front of me.'

'Does it mention injuries of any kind?'

'As a matter of fact, it does. Now I think of it, I believe I did mention it to Jamie at the time.'

'What does it say?'

'That there was evidence of past trauma and reconstructive surgery to the left patella and left upper tibia.'

'Hmm. Any idea what caused the damage?'

'Nothing definitive, no. Why?'

'Just curious, that's all.'

There was a momentary gap in the conversation.

'Did you ask Jamie about the watch?'

'Damn. Stupid of me, I forgot to tell her.'

'Well, let me know when you do.'

Shortly thereafter, the conversation ended. Kingston stood by the phone for a few moments, pulling on his earlobe, thinking.

Chapter Fourteen

No more than a minute after his conversation with Chadwick, Kingston dialled Loftus's number in Nottingham. His sister answered, clearly distraught. Her brother had suffered a mild stroke and was in hospital, she said. He had lost some movement on his right side but his speech wasn't impaired. The doctor was confident that, given time and with therapy, he would make a complete recovery.

Kingston had been hoping that Loftus might be able to clarify something. He remembered the old man saying that, in the struggle for Ryder's pistol, Ryder had been shot. But he hadn't said where on his body. In his note, he had said that Kershaw was wounded, too. Kingston was going to have to wait for a while to get the answers now.

Over the summer, Kingston had developed the habit of winding up the day with Jamie at the office or sometimes at the house where he would bring her up to date on recent work and they could discuss the events of the day over a glass of wine. At first it was all business, mostly dealing with the gardens, but as their get-togethers became more frequent and drawn-out, they began to talk more and more about other things. It had reached the point now where Kingston looked upon her as much as a friend as an employer. He was glad that she'd given no signs of discouraging what he wanted to believe was an easygoing and symbiotic relationship.

At first, it was just one glass of wine each evening. But lately their discussions invariably featured a special bottle of wine, often an unusual varietal. The tasting of *le vin de soir* as Kingston had come to call it became a much looked forward to ritual and the bottle was nearly always consumed by the time they parted. As the days progressed, he was quickly broadening his already respectable knowledge of wine and winemaking, which pleased him no end.

Over the years, Kingston had visited quite a few wineries in France, Italy, Spain and England and had inched along with the camera-toting shuffle of visitors through many a winery tour. Now, after many hours of listening to Jamie talk about the subject, he had come to realize how minuscule a picture those tours presented and how little he really knew about the complex business of producing great wines.

The long journey from the day the first furrow is ploughed to the moment the precious liquid is poured into a glass can take five years or more. And along the way there are innumerable decisions to be made and no guarantees. Jamie quoted a writer who said that 'there is nothing so irascibly difficult as making a truly fine wine, given a thousand unpredictable variables'.

During one of their earlier chats, when they had tasted a particularly nice 1995 Musigny Burgundy wine, Kingston asked an innocent question about *terroir*, a French word that has no English equivalent. It attempts to describe all of the natural conditions in a vineyard as relate to the growing of grapes: the land, soil, slope, elevation, orientation to the sun, rainfall, wind, fog and so on.

'There's an industry cliché,' said Jamie, 'that wines are made in the vineyard. And I agree with that. If you screw up great grapes, you'll never get a great wine.' She held up a hand, fingers splayed. 'It's a bit embarrassing, you being a professor of botany and me spouting off about growing grapes. It's more than just agriculture, though.'

'Don't you worry one bit, growing grapes was hardly a

hot topic in my teaching days. I'm learning a lot, believe me.' He paused to take a sip of the silky wine. 'You were saying that it's not necessarily a form of agriculture, right?'

'Exactly. Most people assume that viticulture is a subset of agriculture but philosophically and in practice they are quite different. With conventional farming, the goal is usually to achieve standardization, uniformity, high yield and consistency on a large scale. Growing grapes for the purpose of making wines is much more a matter of individuality – manipulating the fruit in a lot of different ways, not to produce the biggest and meatiest grape but one that will make the kind of wine the winemaker is aiming for – often with low yield as opposed to high. The business of growing grapes and making wine is really all about balance. It's one great year-long balancing act.'

'You want the grape to conform to your ideal standard, is that it?'

'Yes. And to reach that goal you have to thread your way through a minefield of variables. I'll give you a few. To start, you have to regulate your soil and sub-soil, fertilizing it and maintaining the right pH levels, You have to figure out the water and drainage, exactly where in the vineyard you choose to plant, what rootstock to use, what clones, how far apart to plan the rows, which direction the rows will run, what kind of trellis to use, how you're going to irrigate.' She paused. 'That's just the beginning. And no matter how hard you try sometimes grapes have a mind of their own. We've taken identical clones, grafted on the same rootstock, exposed them to the same weather conditions and irrigated them identically and yet these presumably same vines, planted only a few feet apart, developed differently and bore grapes with totally different tastes. Go figure?'

'That's extraordinary,' said Kingston.

Jamie shook her head. 'Sometimes it's downright exasperating. Once the grapes start growing they're sitting targets for all kinds of problems. The vagaries of the weather are the most difficult to deal with and the most crucial. Frosts and too much early rain can play havoc with the crop. Rain absorption dilutes sugar levels, one of the most important things to keep an eye on as the berries begin to develop. Not enough sun, too much sun, the angle of the sun, all can make a huge difference. The more sunlight that strikes the grape clusters, the sweeter they'll be but the goal is not to grow the sweetest fruit. Sweetness or the sugar level is something that you have to monitor on a daily basis once the grapes reach a certain stage in their development. Grapes are harvested when they reach the Brix level that you're shooting for and the flavours have matured to where you want them.'

'Yes, Brix, I remember learning about that in France.'

'It's the scale used to measure the concentration of sugar in the grapes. It's measured right in the vineyard with a small gadget called a refractometer.'

'So how are you able to control the sugar content?'

'Pruning, thinning, fertilization, irrigation – they all affect the ripening process including sugar accumulation. For example, thinning out the canopy can open it up to allow more sunlight and air circulation. It can be quite a guessing game because once you've removed leaves you can't put them back on again.'

'How about pruning?'

'How you prune the vines at the very beginning of the year is another make-or-break operation. Good pruning hands are worth their weight in gold. Not only for how well and properly they can prune but also how fast. We have an annual pruning contest in Sonoma, pretty good prize money, too.' She stopped for a moment to pour the remainder of the Burgundy in their glasses, taking a sip before she picked up where she left off.

'The other consideration that helps maintain balanced sugar levels is to plant rows from east to west. In doing so, both sides of the vines get an equal share of sunlight

141

through the day, whereas if you plant north to south, one side gets milder morning sun and the other side, the longer, much hotter afternoon sun.'

'It makes so much sense,' said Kingston. 'You know, you would make a great teacher.'

'Thank you,' she said with a quick smile. 'Anyway, you can see already that just the growing part alone is an art unto itself. And I haven't even mentioned some of the other little tricks that Mother Nature sometimes springs on us, like botrytis mould, the dreaded phylloxera and insects such as the blue-green sharpshooter and the voracious glassy-winged sharpshooter, which can wipe out a vineyard in no time. When those show up it means deciding what to spray with and when to spray. If it's phylloxera, forget it. All you can do is to rip all the vines out and replant.' She offered a thin smile. 'I don't want to disillusion you but the entire farming year is non-stop pruning, monitoring, thinning, measuring, spraying, hoping and praying until you drop the crop and take it to the winery to turn the grapes into wine. And that's where another thousand things can go wrong.' She paused then smiled. 'Still want to grow grapes?'

Back at the cottage, stretched out on the sofa, reading, after another of their evening chats, Kingston became aware of subconsciously rereading the same sentence. Soon, he found it impossible to concentrate. His mind kept coming back to Jamie. Clasping his hands behind his head, he lay back, head on the plumped-up cushion, and stared up at the plaster rose that graced the ceiling above the tasselled lampshade. He thought back to his very first real conversation with her, that first day of theirs in Somerset. How he'd felt at the time, about his uncertainty, his apprehension regarding her lofty ambitions for Wickersham, his teetering between curiosity and indifference. It was extraordinary what had happened in the relatively short time since he'd arrived here. Not for the first time, he wondered how she regarded him. He smiled to himself. Most likely as a father figure, a sort of elder statesman-cum-horticultural sage, an inquisitive academic. Thinking more about it, any one or all three would not be far off the mark.

Over the years Kingston had got to know a number of Americans, a few of whom had become more than nodding acquaintances. Jamie was certainly not a 'wear your heart on your sleeve' type, who thinks nothing of reciting her entire life and medical history the very moment one's introduced. She was the opposite. But over the last weeks there had been a noticeable shift in her reticence: her candour in telling him about her job and her garden, confiding in him about her parents that night at dinner, and the education she was giving him about winegrowing.

Every now and then, he detected what he thought was a flicker of mutual attraction. It struck him as curious, too, that a woman as attractive and intelligent as Jamie should not have a boyfriend. Surely that couldn't be the case? There was the chap she worked with – the one that was coming over – what was his name? Matthew. But from what little she had said, that was strictly an office relationship. Of course, there could be any number of explanations. For no particular reasons, he guessed that she'd never been married. If she had she would surely have mentioned it by now. And if it were recently ended, she would probably still be wearing a wedding ring. Women did that, he'd noticed. Maybe she had just had a bitter break-up with a boyfriend, a broken engagement? That would certainly explain why it was not so hard for her to drop everything and travel halfway around the world to start a new life.

Why was he so concerned about her personal life? Why didn't he just do what he came down to do? He knew the answer but wasn't prepared to dwell on it. In his mind he wasn't willing to accept the simple truth that he was growing very fond of Jamie – perhaps too fond.

He picked up the book. 'Christ,' he muttered under his breath. 'What *are* you thinking of?'

Chapter Fifteen

'That's very disturbing news,' said Kingston, a sombre look on his face, the hard lines around his jaw accentuated by the shafts of sunlight deflecting through the nearby window. Jamie said nothing, her face, too, registering concern and noticeably drained of colour.

Minutes earlier, a breathless Dot had found Kingston in the vegetable garden saying that Jamie wanted him up at the house right away.

Facing Jamie and Kingston, Detective Chief Inspector Chadwick, in a dark grey pinstripe suit, sat leaning back into the sofa, his arm stretched casually along the back. 'We're not treating it as a homicide yet,' he said. 'But there're sufficient reasons for us not to rule it out entirely.' He had just informed Jamie and Kingston that, late the previous afternoon, Jack Harris had been discovered face down on the kitchen linoleum of his rented house, dead. His landlady had called the police after several unsuccessful attempts to serve him final notice on his rent that was two months in arrears.

'What was the cause of death?' Kingston asked.

'Don't know yet,' Chadwick replied. 'There were a number of contusions around the head and on the hands and wrists, suggesting that he was warding off an assault of some kind, but according to the medical examiner some of those were caused earlier.'

Kingston nodded. 'Yes, he had bruises on his face the

other week. Swore he'd got them falling off his motorbike. I'd give you even money he was lying, though.'

Chadwick leaned forward. 'When was that, doctor?'

Kingston told Chadwick about Jack not showing up for work and his visit to Jack's house. 'He did return to work the following Monday, though,' said Kingston. 'I know he was here last Friday. He took off early as a matter of fact.'

Chadwick got up from the sofa. 'Anything else?'

'There was, actually,' said Jamie, giving Kingston a sideways glance first. 'He wanted me to loan him some money. Said he was strung out on his credit cards.'

'How much?'

'Two thousand pounds.'

'Hmm – not exactly small change. We'll soon find out, though, if that's the real reason why he wanted the money.'

Chadwick didn't stay long. He asked again about the stolen books and papers, Kingston telling him that none had turned up. Standing in the courtyard, the talk was mostly about progress on the restoration project. Kingston dutifully answered a question from the inspector about using Epsom salts to feed roses. Before getting in his car, Chadwick cautioned them to make sure that their security devices were all in good order and to be vigilant. They were experiencing a higher than usual incidence of burglary and break-ins, he said. Kingston's mind flashed to the hooded figure then to his ransacked cottage. 'Now he tells us,' Kingston said aside to Jamie as Chadwick was closing the car door.

Back in the living room, ensconced in his favourite wingback, Kingston shook his head and scoffed, 'Security devices? I suppose that's police talk for locks and bolts.'

'Phew! Poor Jack,' Jamie exclaimed. 'What a horrible thing to happen.' She faked a shiver. 'I hope to God it wasn't murder.'

'Me, too, but from what Chadwick was saying, it doesn't sound as if he's ruling it out.'

'But why?'

'Who knows? You said that he was badly in debt. Maybe they were gambling debts, not credit cards.'

Kingston crossed his legs and looked in Jamie's direction but not at her. 'There could be another explanation,' he said, talking to himself. 'But the question is, how?'

'What are you trying to say, Lawrence? That there might be another explanation for Jack's death?'

'Possibly. You know, more and more I get the feeling that all these strange goings on here are connected in some way.'

'What, you mean the theft and the skeleton?'

'Ryder too – even the paintings. I grant you it's hard to see any connections and I know we've been over all this before but – '

'Come on, Lawrence, certainly not between Ryder and Jack. There's no *way* they could have known each other, is there?'

'I suppose not.'

'Anyway, it's all in Chadwick's hands now – isn't it?'

'Yes,' he nodded.

'Then there's not much point in our losing sleep over it.'

Kingston sat with his chin resting on his fist, looking off into space. After a few moments, he looked back at Jamie, tapping his fingers on his forehead. 'I keep forgetting to tell you about the damned watch. I must be losing it.'

'What watch?'

'Chadwick told me about it when I saw him at the station. I told you I'd been there. They found a watch in the debris that came up from the well.'

'Bit late telling you now, isn't it?'

'That was my reaction but it doesn't make any difference anyway. It turns out the watch belonged to a stranger. Nobody we know, that is.'

147

'How do you know that?'

'It had the initials CMA on the back.'

Jamie was about to say something, then changed her mind and simply shrugged.

'I suppose you don't happen to know anyone with those initials, do you?'

She thought for a long moment then shook her head. 'Nobody comes to mind right away. I'll have to think about it.'

'It was quite an old watch, so there is the possibility that it could have been purchased second hand.'

'If it was, then the initials would have no connection whatsoever to the wearer.'

'That's right. Anyway, it was American, a Hamilton. So Chadwick is probably right. He doesn't think it's going to tell us anything.'

A lengthy silence followed, then Kingston got up from his chair. 'About the paintings. I meant to ask you, Jamie. Did you hear any more from that chap?'

'No, I didn't. I wasn't really expecting to.'

'You still don't believe him, then?'

'I don't follow you.'

'You told me the man was convinced that the paintings were here, somewhere, didn't you? Isn't that why I turned this place upside down?'

'Yes, Lawrence,' she said, clearly trying to hold back a smile, 'but that was all your idea, not mine. I told you so at the time.'

'Don't remind me.'

'I grant you it's possible that they could have been here at one time, way back when Ryder was still involved with the dealer in Paris, but I'll bet you anything that those paintings are long gone. Besides, if whatever his name –'

'Fox or the Frenchman?'

'Both of them. If they knew the paintings were here, and if they're as valuable as Fox claims, don't you think he'd have been calling us night and day, trying to obtain a

148

search warrant, threatening us with a lawsuit? He would have been doing everything he possibly could to find those pictures. In any case, the first person he would call would be Latimer, surely. And why hasn't he gone to the police? None of it makes sense.'

'I know it doesn't, Jamie. That's the problem.'

'By the way, David agrees with me. He says not to worry about it unless the man makes contact again, which he thinks rather unlikely. If Fox does call again or write, David wants to know right away.'

With her words hanging in the air, Kingston was getting a strong message that next she would tell him that she didn't want to hear anything more about the paintings. That, like Ryder, the subject was about to become a closed book. 'Jamie,' he said at length, 'you're probably right but listen to me, just for a moment. There *could* be an explanation – a good reason why Fox hasn't got back to you.'

Jamie mustered the slightest of smiles. 'Somehow I knew you might have one, Lawrence,' she said, shaking her head slowly from side to side. 'Okay, what's the reason?'

'Well, we know that Ryder *was* in Paris after the war, which squares with Fox's story about Girard working with Ryder, the two of them dealing in art. And anyone with an interest in art – paintings particularly – knows that prior to and during the war years, the Nazis misappropriated – looted might be a better word – vast numbers of paintings and works of art from individuals and private collections.'

Jamie was looking at him like a blasé student at a required lecture. At least she hadn't interrupted. Not wanting to give her the chance, he quickly followed up.

'There came a time, towards the end and after the war, when the fleeing Nazis started to unload a lot of these paintings. Possession meant culpability and the works of art could become a liability. As a result, many of them were sold to dealers and were put back on the market, in Paris, Zurich and other European cities.' Kingston was up and pacing now, clearly back in the old professorial groove. 'In short, Jamie, what I'm suggesting is that the paintings that Girard is trying to locate could be stolen. That would explain why Fox was vague about them. He had to be. Surely, Girard would know the paintings intimately. He would know the artist, the subject, the size – all of that. No. Fox didn't tell you all this because he didn't want you to know how valuable the paintings really are. It wouldn't surprise me if they were French Impressionist paintings. If that's the case, they could be worth a bloody fortune. And that's why you haven't heard from him. But I have a feeling you will.'

Already, Jamie was shaking her head and smiling. 'You make it all sound like a movie, Lawrence. Look, I don't want to be the one to pick holes in your thesis. And maybe there aren't any but you seem to find the most illogical and convoluted answers to all these things. I know this whole paintings business sounds fishy but you have to admit that there might be perfectly normal explanations for all of these happenings. The man could be telling the truth. Or what he thinks is the truth. After all, he's learned it all second hand from the Frenchman. If I were you, I'd forget all about it. If you want my opinion, I'd say we've seen the last of Fox.'

Kingston returned to his chair trying not to look too crestfallen. The jury had given its verdict before he could finish his summing-up. He knew that there would never be a better time to tell her than now. He tried to sound as detached as possible. 'Jamie, I had a brief conversation with a lady from an organization called the Art Loss Register a while back. They have a large database of stolen art and I would imagine other records concerning specific paintings and the names of dealers and galleries involved in the exchange of artworks in the late forties and after.'

'And?'

'I'd like to meet her and ask a few questions. Just to

satisfy my own curiosity, of course. It's a subject that fascinates me.'

Jamie was smiling again. 'If I didn't know better, I'd say that you want to find out if Ryder was dealing in stolen art? Right?'

'No, not necessarily. I want to find out if Ryder was, indeed, the guardian of those paintings that Fox is so interested in and, if so, whether they could still be here. At the least, it might corroborate the fact that the paintings in question are a lot more valuable than he would have us believe.'

Jamie got up from her chair and made to leave. 'If it makes you happy, go ahead, Lawrence.' At the door, she paused and looked at him over her shoulder. 'I don't think I'll ever get to understand you Englishmen,' she said, with an indulgent smile. With that, she left the room.

Kingston sat staring at the polished surface of the end table. The best part was that she hadn't said no. Nevertheless, he knew that, as far as his detective work was concerned, this was doubtless the last concession she was going to make. Anything much beyond this would be to risk alienating her and that was the very last thing he intended to do. He very much wanted her as a partner and even more, as a friend.

He got up and headed for the kitchen to look for Jamie to tell her he was going back to the cottage. When he entered, she had her nose in a cookbook.

'Well, I'm off,' he said.

She looked up. 'All right. I'll see you in the morning.' She turned away for a second. 'I still can't get over Jack.'

'Try to forget it, Jamie. Think about roses instead. Tomorrow, we can go over my ideas for the rose garden, if you like.'

'I'd like that,' she said, returning to the book. 'Thought I'd take a stab at making Cioppino tomorrow night.'

'Really?' asked Kingston, his hand on the brass door-knob. 'What's that? Sounds Italian.'

'American, actually. It's kind of a fish and shellfish stew.'

'Sounds like bouillabaisse.'

'It's similar. Cioppino's a true San Francisco dish. It came from the old American-Italian fishermen. My dad loved it.'

'Why don't you have Dot make it?'

'I could. But I enjoy cooking once in a while. It satisfies my creative urges. I did it all the time at home.'

'Maybe I can come up with a good red. Anything you might suggest?'

'A nice Burgundy would work – and some French bread. I don't suppose you can get a good sourdough here, can you?'

'I doubt it. In London, but not down here – at least, I wouldn't think so. I'll call around, though.'

Kingston said goodnight and left for the cottage. Entering the small living room he could see the red light flashing on the answering machine. He walked over and pressed the Message button.

'It's Andrew, Lawrence. I've got some bad news. Your flat's been broken into. Bit of a mess, I'm afraid. I called the police and they came over right away. But obviously we can't tell if anything's been stolen. Good news is that, as far as I can tell, they didn't take any of your rugs or the new telly or any of the paintings. By the way everything was turned upside down, the police think they were looking for money, jewellery, that sort of thing. You'd better come as soon as you can, though. I'll keep an eye on things till you get here. Call me – cheers.'

Kingston sat down on the sofa. 'Jesus, what next,' he said under his breath. He picked up the phone and dialled Jamie's number.

'You'd better hold off on the Cioppino, Jamie – for me anyway,' he said, when she answered. Then he told her what had happened.

Chapter Sixteen

With Andrew's help, Kingston spent the next two days sorting through his flat. Andrew's 'bit of a mess' was the understatement of the year. A cyclone passing through might have wreaked less havoc. As he went about picking up the pieces and returning them to their rightful places, throwing away the few things that were broken beyond repair, he began to realize that, as yet, he hadn't noticed anything missing. He couldn't be sure, of course, but all the items of value appeared to be intact. He never left money lying around the house and had little or no jewellery to speak of.

By the middle of the second day, order was more or less restored. A locksmith had replaced the front door lock and Kingston had phoned the police to report that, as far as he could tell, nothing had been stolen. While he was relieved, he still thought that a burglary with nothing burgled was a bit out of the ordinary. But the policewoman on the phone assured him it wasn't. Kids looking mostly for money, an interrupted burglary, there could be several explanations. They got hundreds of burglary calls a day, she said.

Kingston had just put the phone down on Jamie after bringing her up to speed on the situation and telling her that he would be coming back down the next day. He heard the doorbell ring and glanced at the carriage clock on the mantel. Andrew was his usual punctual self. Also a bachelor, Andrew was about ten years younger than Kingston and lived mainly for two things – the racetrack and good food. He had made a lunch reservation for the two of them at one o'clock, at Bibendum on the Fulham Road.

In the living room, Andrew handed Kingston a small brown paper-wrapped package. 'Here,' he said with a grin.

Knowing Andrew's twisted sense of humour and expecting the worst, Kingston opened the package. Inside was a box with a picture of a snarling German Shepherd on it. Above the dog's head was the name Rex.

'What is it?' Kingston asked.

Andrew continued grinning. 'It's a barking dog alarm. It's really nifty. It can actually see through walls. The minute it detects a movement it starts barking. It's radar activated.'

Kingston laughed, then studied the label. 'Where on earth do you find these things?'

Andrew shrugged.

'Well, thanks, you clever old thing. I'll plug old Rex in before I leave tomorrow.' He placed the box decorously on the table, rolled the brown paper wrapping into a tight ball, then looked up at the ceiling. 'You'd better remind me to forewarn Mrs Badger upstairs, she'll have a conniption if she thinks I've got a dog down here.'

'Oh, and it can make the sound of a siren, if you want,' said Andrew, looking as pleased as Punch.

'Heaven forbid,' said Kingston.

Bibendum, in the proto-art-deco Michelin building on the Fulham Road, had its usual high-energy lunchtime buzz. Tables of wine-sipping, well-dressed business types competed with the chirp and chatter from isolated drifts of tourists, cranking up a decibel level that was red needling. Settled in at their table, each with a glass of wine, Andrew and Kingston had just finished studying the menu.

'So, what's this place you're going to this afternoon?'

said Andrew, sliding the two menus to the edge of the table.

'The Art Loss Register. It's been in operation for about fourteen years. They have offices in several cities around the world now.'

'And they track down stolen art?'

'That's a big part of what they do. Their main function is to locate and return to the rightful owners works of art that were lost or looted during and after the Second World War. I looked them up on the Internet. They have a database of over 150,000 items, all stolen or missing.'

'That's a lot of loot!'

'I know. It's been called the most systematic government-supported art robbery in history. The strange thing about it is that many of the stolen items were well documented. Not only was there no attempt to conceal their activities, the Nazis actually kept track of their entire haul on – if you can believe it – index cards that meticulously described each work.'

'That doesn't sound too bright,' said Andrew, trying to catch the waiter's eye.

Kingston shrugged. 'I suppose it didn't occur to them that they might lose the war and have to give them back one day.'

The waiter finally arrived and took their orders.

'Where were we?' asked Kingston, after the waiter had left.

'Keeping records.'

'Right. I read that a typical card of one of the major SS art-plundering outfits would list the name of the piece, its dimensions, the artist's name, scholarly notes on the significance of the work and sometimes – believe it or not – where and from whom it was stolen. They had lists of paintings from all over Europe and knew exactly where they were, and which ones they wanted.'

'That's unbelievable. I take it a lot of the art belonged to victims of the Holocaust?'

'Absolutely. From private collections and from pre-war victims of Hitler's Third Reich.'

'Are we talking about masterpieces?'

'Most definitely. Da Vinci, Botticelli, Titian, you name it. A lot of the French Impressionists, too. All museum quality stuff.' Kingston paused for a moment. 'As a matter of fact, sad to say, many of the finest and most reputable art collections around the world are filled with stolen artwork. Hard to believe, isn't it?'

'It is.' Andrew smiled. 'So what's going on, Lawrence? Have you turned up a missing masterpiece?'

'No, not exactly. But I may be on to something down in Somerset and before I start shaking the trees I want to see if the Art Loss people can dig up some information for me on a French art dealer who was a partner of this Major Ryder chap I told you about, the one who left Jamie Gibson his estate.'

Andrew raised his eyebrows. 'Quite mysterious!'

'In a way it is, Andrew. During the war and afterwards a lot of artwork was smuggled out of Europe through neutral countries like Spain and Portugal and cities like Buenos Aires and Havana. I have a strong hunch that Ryder was involved in selling looted art but I need more information. I'll let you know how it turns out.'

Andrew was smiling again. 'How come you always manage to get yourself involved in these crazy situations, Lawrence?'

Before Kingston could reply, the waiter arrived with their dishes.

The meal lasted another hour, finished off with pear sorbet and lattes.

Outside Bibendum, facing a curtain of grey drizzle blurred with crimson from the passing rumble of buses, they parted company and Kingston got a cab to the Art Loss Register offices, off Blackfriars Road.

As they shook hands, the crown of Jennifer Ingels' shoulder-length blonde hair came barely level with Kingston's chin. She was model-slender with a soap-commercial English complexion and a disarming smile; the blush in her cheeks definitely not from a brush. Expecting an older lady in a suit or a blouse and skirt, Kingston was at first taken aback at the trendy jacket over black turtle-neck shirt and trousers. Somehow it belied her position of Public Affairs Director.

When Kingston had phoned, he had been careful how he phrased the reason for his visit. To come right out and say that several stolen French Impressionists might be hidden somewhere on an estate in Somerset could send off all kinds of alarms and if the press ever got wind of such a story all hell could break loose at Wickersham. It would undoubtedly mark an ignominious end to his employment and his relationship with Jamie would be damaged beyond repair. On the phone he had resorted to a couple of white lies and a salting of charm to gain this interview.

'So, doctor.' Jennifer Ingels leaned back, arms folded, in the black leather chair. 'You have information about some stolen paintings.'

'Possibly, yes.'

'Tell me again, how did you learn about them?'

'A friend of mine who used to live in Paris made the acquaintance of a French art dealer immediately after the war. He seems to think that the dealer, a man by the name of Girard – I don't know his first name – could have gone into business with another person, an Englishman. I'm trying to find out who that person was and locate him. It has to do with an estate in the West Country that was recently inherited by an associate of mine.'

'Do you have reason to believe that either of them was dealing in stolen art?'

'I really can't say. But if I can find this man, he might be able to answer that question for you.' Kingston then gave her the bait. 'If you want an educated guess, I believe he could, at the very least, provide valuable information on a number of art transactions that took place in the months and years right after the war. Whether these were all above board, who knows.'

'So, what is it specifically that you're asking me to do?'

'Two things. One, to provide all the information you might have on the French dealer, Girard. And two, I'd like to get a list – if one exists, that is – of all the people in Paris, the dealers, the galleries, and anyone else who was buying and selling art from 1945 on.'

'Just Paris.'

'That's right.'

She unfolded her arms and pulled herself close to her desk, picking up a pen. Ready to write, she eyed Kingston momentarily, then said, 'I'll see what I can do. First, why don't you give me your full name and an address where you can be reached, fax number, e-mail – all that stuff.'

Kingston complied, as Jennifer Ingels wrote the information on the blue-lined notepad in front of her.

At six thirty the next morning, Kingston locked the door to his flat with the shiny new key and walked to the garage. The drive back to Somerset would give him plenty of time to think about the string of things that had happened since he had first joined Jamie at Wickersham. It would be the first time in quite a while that he would have the luxury of several hours' quiet uninterrupted thought.

He was still convinced that most, if not all, of the events were in some way connected. It would defy all odds if they weren't. The burglaries in particular perplexed him. It seemed to be just too much of a coincidence that his flat and the cottage had been broken into within the span of a few weeks. But if the two *were* connected, perpetrated by the same person or persons, what on earth were they looking for at the flat? Certainly not missing French paintings.

As the traffic started to back up approaching the exits to

Heathrow he gave up thinking about it. Andrew was probably right, he concluded. It was just one of those bizarre coincidences.

Pulling into the courtyard at Wickersham, Kingston saw Dot standing on the doorstep wringing her hands, the door open behind her. It was as if she had been watching and waiting for him. He pulled up and got out of the car, legs a little unsteady. As she approached he could see that she looked even grimmer than her customary stone-faced demeanour.

'Mr Kingston. I'm so glad you're back. Jamie's been in an accident.'

Chapter Seventeen

With an economy of words – this was one time when Kingston appreciated her laconicism – Dot told him that Jamie's car had run off the road into a ditch. She wasn't seriously hurt and was being kept in the hospital in Taunton for X-rays and observation. Anticipating his reaction she handed him a note that gave the hospital address and precise directions.

Twenty-five minutes later, at three o'clock, Kingston was at Jamie's bedside.

With the exception of a gash on her forehead and an ugly bruise on the cheekbone, she didn't look too much the worse for wear. Her wincing at the slightest movement told him that she was in pain in spite of her reassurances of feeling all right. 'Mostly aches and bruises, according to the nurse,' she said, forcing a smile.

Jamie told him what had happened. The good news, she said, was that she wasn't going very fast. Three or four miles after leaving the house she started to notice that the steering didn't seem right. Her immediate thought was that one of the front tyres was going flat. She slowed down with the idea of limping to the nearest turn-off where she could pull over and take a look. Approaching a sharp curve she had to correct the steering. As she did so she heard a loud metallic noise, as if something had sheared or broken. The steering wheel now spun freely in her hands and the car was out of control. Seeing that the car was heading straight for the verge and a shallow dip in the grass beyond, she curled up into a ball, scrunching as far below the windshield as the seatbelt would allow. When the car finally bounced to a rest and she saw blood on her hands and on the dashboard her heart was beating a mile to the minute, she said.

Immediately a passing motorist came to her aid. He called 999 and within five minutes a police car was at the scene. Ten minutes after that an ambulance and a tow-truck arrived.

Kingston spent the next half-hour telling Jamie about what had happened at the flat, including Andrew's canine gift. At least that made her smile. Kingston left, assuring her that he would pick her up the minute she was discharged. In the meantime, he would find out where they had taken her Volvo, and see if he could find out more about the failed steering. He left buoyed with a huge sense of relief, knowing that Jamie wasn't seriously hurt but also with a sense of foreboding, praying that this was not another calculated incident meant to harm.

Back at Wickersham Kingston stopped by the cottage to change his clothes. In the living room, the answering machine light was flashing. The message – a brief one – was from Loftus. Considering the stroke, Kingston thought he sounded remarkably well – even chipper. In a minute or so Kingston had him on the line. Loftus's health took up the first minute or so of the conversation. He was taking physiotherapy and was back at his sister's and doing 'quite well thank you.'

'Well, I'm delighted to hear you're making such a good recovery. If you weren't so far away I'd come and pay you another visit.'

'I'd enjoy that,' Art replied.

'I have a question to ask you, Art. This is going to test your memory.'

'What's left of it.'

'You said in your note – the one you sent me with the picture of Jeremy and Kit – that Jeremy was shot.'

'Yeah, I remember that.'

'This could be important. Do you remember where he was shot?'

Before Kingston had a chance to finish his question, Art replied.

'Sure, I told you, it was in that Dutch town.'

Kingston smiled to himself. 'I know that, Art. I should have phrased it better. I meant where on his body?'

'Crikey – well, let me think a moment.'

While he waited, Kingston looked around the room. Seeing an empty vase on one of the window ledges, he made a mental note to buy some flowers for Jamie. Loftus came back on the line.

'You know, I do remember, because his bandages were such a mess. Our medics had been killed and we were all pitchin' in trying to take care of the wounded. Jeremy was one of them that couldn't walk –'

'Where was he wounded, Art?'

'In the leg.'

'Where was the bandage? Was it around his knee by any chance?'

Loftus mumbled something that Kingston couldn't quite get, then said, 'I wouldn't swear to it but I think that's where it was. Yeah, I think you're right.'

'Good man.'

'Why is it so important, doctor?'

'It's too long a story to tell you on the phone but I promise you, Art, if I get to the bottom of it, I'll come up to Nottingham and tell you all about it. If it's what I think it is, you're going to be very surprised.'

Kingston went to the bedroom and changed into more comfortable clothes: corduroy trousers, tattersall flannel shirt and an old cardigan that, over the years, had stretched up two sizes from the one on the label. Whenever he was in London – though he knew it was unnecessary in this

162

day and age – he still felt obliged to wear more dressy clothes. He was half of a mind to take a nap before setting off for the village and a light supper at the Griffin. Instead, knowing he might well doze off for several hours, he decided to go up to the house to see if there was any mail and tell Dot about his visit to Jamie. Then he could get an early night.

Opening the cottage front door, he was almost face-on with the key rack on the wall. It wasn't until a few seconds later, after he'd stepped through the door, that he realized something was wrong. The iron key to the chapel was on the wrong hook. There was no question about it. It always hung on the last hook. Now it was two hooks over. He took the key, put it in his trouser pocket, closed the door and walked up to the house.

He found Dot in the kitchen, ironing sheets.

'How is Jamie?' she asked, standing the iron on its end.

He dragged a chair out from the pine table and sat down. 'She seems to be fine, thank God. A bit bruised and a nasty gash on her head but nothing's broken. They're going to keep her in overnight but she's going to be okay. She's in good spirits '

'How did it happen – the accident?'

'The steering on her car went out.'

'I'm surprised. That's a brand new car.'

'I know. It's almost unheard of. She was very lucky. It could have been much worse.'

'When can she come home?'

'I'm hoping, tomorrow.'

Dot had gone back to ironing. It was rare for her to carry on this much of a conversation.

Kingston plucked a handful of grapes from the bowl on the table. Popping one in his mouth, he went on – although she didn't ask – telling her about the break-in at his flat.

Dot listened, occasionally looking up from her ironing.

'Well, I'm glad that nothing was stolen,' she said when

he was finished. 'Jamie told me why you'd gone, by the way. Would you like me to make you some tea?'

'No thanks,' he answered, getting up. 'I'm going up to the Griffin in a while. I'll give Jamie a call in the morning, let you know when she's coming home.' Near the door, he turned and looked at her. 'Anybody here today, Dot?' he asked. 'Other than the workmen and China, I mean. Any visitors?'

'No, sir,' she replied, continuing to iron, glancing up at him.

'By any chance were you in the cottage, cleaning?'

She had stopped ironing and was taking her time folding the sheet. 'No, I wasn't. I couldn't get round to it. I'll see to it that it gets done tomorrow, doctor.'

'Fine,' he said, opening the door and leaving.

Kingston looked at his watch. Nearly six, all the workmen would have left by now. He walked along the side of the house, across the lawns, on to the path leading to the Wedgwoods' cottage. Prettier than his, the narrow garden in front of the geranium red door was a cheerful jumble of perennials, climbing roses and honeysuckle. He lifted the polished brass knocker and rapped twice.

China opened the door, holding a napkin in his hands. 'Oh – 'ello, doctor.' He paused, surreptitiously hiding the napkin behind him. 'Well, come on in,' he said.

'No thanks, Stanley, I'm interrupting your meal. I just wanted to let you know that Jamie's fine. By the looks of it she'll probably be home tomorrow.'

'That is good news. We've been worried sick since Dot told us about it. Gwyneth's going to be so relieved.'

'Well, sorry again to interrupt your dinner, China. Oh – there was one more thing. Were there any visitors today? Did anyone show up, asking for me or Jamie?'

China thought for a moment then shook his head. 'No, I didn't see anyone.'

'Well, thanks. Say hello to Gwyneth for me, will you.'

China closed the door and Kingston starting walking in

the direction of the chapel. He hadn't gone too far when he heard China calling him. He turned and walked back till he was within earshot.

China reached the gate where he stopped. 'Gwyneth said there was a man asking for you today. She forgot to tell me. She's like that a lot nowadays, poor thing. Seems with nobody at the big house – Dot must have been outside or something – he came down here and knocked on the door. An older man, grey hair – she said 'e was very polite. She told him you'd gone up to see Jamie in the hospital. When she asked if there was any message, he said no, and that he would call you. That's about it, doc.'

Kingston thanked him, adding that he thought he knew who the man might be, and said goodbye for a second time.

The only person Kingston could think of that answered Gwyneth's vague description was Ferguson. It was possible that he'd just stopped by without calling first. He'd done that on his first visit. Somehow, though – even knowing how badly Ferguson wanted to see the chapel – he just couldn't picture him going to the cottage, taking the key and opening up the chapel. That was too hard to swallow. Tomorrow, Kingston would phone and ask if he *was* at Wickersham.

First, he pulled on the chapel door handle to make sure it was locked. Then he unlocked the door and entered. He walked down the centre aisle to the pulpit and flicked on the floodlights. They had been left in place since that first day. Sitting in the front pew, he gazed around the room. Since Ferguson's revelation, he'd given a lot more thought to the chapel and the coins. *If* there was another way into the chapel, it could only be from the floor or the back section where it had been built into the wall. One of his theories was sparked by a long-ago visit to the Hell-Fire caves in West Wycombe, Buckinghamshire. There, in the 1750s, former Postmaster General and wealthy landowner, Sir Francis Dashwood excavated a labyrinthine series of tunnels, chambers and banqueting rooms deep into the chalk hills, creating a meeting and partying place for the part mythical Hell-Fire Club – the Knights of St Francis. So Kingston had hypothesized that, at one time, there could have been a cave in the wall that had led to the underground rooms at Wickersham. And when the chapel was built – or more likely, long before – it was purposely concealed or permanently sealed. Several times he'd gone over the walls in that area with a fine-tooth comb and had concluded that the latter must be the case. That left the floor.

The entire floor was composed of flagstones, each exactly sixteen inches square. He had closely examined it on his hands and knees to see if there were any places where the floor didn't conform to the overall pattern or appeared irregular. He had also painstakingly traced the grout lines of cement to see if a section had been disturbed or was of a different colour or texture. His efforts had revealed nothing.

With its virginal white walls, Spartan trappings and cool silence, as intended the space was conducive to prayer and contemplation. He sat thinking of Jamie, contemplating the accident. All along, he had been prepared to give her the benefit of the doubt inasmuch as there were credible explanations for all the unaccountable things that had taken place at Wickersham since he'd arrived. But now, with the accident – the first event to actually involve Jamie physically – he was more certain than ever that *he* was right. This had changed everything and the thought hadn't escaped him that he could be vulnerable, too. While it was reassuring to know that Chadwick and his people were now actively involved, Kingston was keenly aware that it was also very much up to him to keep a close eye on Jamie and everything that happened on the estate. He was also determined, whether Jamie approved or not, to keep up his search for the paintings and find out what was really behind all the many mysteries shrouding Wickersham Priory.

He sighed and got up, taking one last look around. As of now, it looked very much as if his exploration of the chapel was ended. He walked up the aisle, locked the door behind him and headed in the direction of the courtyard of the big house where his TR4 was parked. He was looking forward to a medium rare entrecote steak and a couple of glasses of Burgundy.

In the morning, he waited until eight thirty before calling the hospital. After several minutes, first being transferred then put on hold, he was informed that Jamie would be discharged sometime after two o'clock, and he should call again, closer to that time, just to make sure. Next, he called the police station in Taunton to find out where Jamie's car had been towed. Spinning a convincing story about wanting to retrieve some items from the car, whose owner was in hospital, he was told that the Volvo had been towed to Larkin's garage on William Street, a repair and storage facility under contract to the Taunton police force. Before picking up Jamie, he planned to call at Larkin's and afterwards buy her some flowers.

He found Larkin's with no trouble, parking in a huge yard that was surrounded by a high metal fence with security warning signs posted every twenty feet or so. Walking past rows of parked cars, many whose rubber would never see a road again, he entered the hangar-like garage. Inside, a number of cars were being worked on. Hip-hop music blared around the cavernous space. Off to his right, he saw a glass-fronted office, walked over, knocked on the door and entered.

A thin balding man, fiftyish, gestured for Kingston to sit down. The name Sean was stitched on to the chest of his oily overalls. The metal desk between them was cluttered with messages, bulging folders, stacks of papers with metal car parts as paperweights, and clipboards laid out in a shingle pattern, the work orders for the day, by the looks of it. Kingston explained why he was there.

'The silver Volvo, right.' Sean sniffed and continued. 'Yeah, we did get a chance to take a quick look at it when it came in,' he said, shaking his head. His expression telegraphed what was going to be bad news. 'I'm afraid I can't tell you too much until we've taken another look at it and filed a report with the police, but I can tell you one thing – it was no accident, mate.'

Chapter Eighteen

Grim-faced and shaken, Kingston left Sean and crossed Larkin's yard. Numbed by what he had just heard, he walked right past his car without realizing. He would have called Chadwick right there and then but he'd left the damned mobile on charge at the cottage. Getting into the TR4 he glanced at the clock: it was almost one fifteen. Barely enough time to buy the flowers and be at the hospital by two to pick up Jamie. How was he going to break the news to her? There was no way to do it without avoiding the terrible truth. Someone had wanted to harm or kill her.

While he waited at a traffic signal, tapping his fingers on the steering wheel, another thought crossed his mind. On the drive back from London, it had occurred to him that the burglary might have been carried out for no other reason than to get him away from Wickersham. At the time he had dismissed this idea as being a bit too far-fetched. But now, with Jamie's accident, he wasn't quite so sure. If that *were* the case there wouldn't be much point if it were just he that were absent. But with Jamie gone, too, it would be much easier for someone to snoop around – to go over the inside of the chapel for starters. Pursuing this line of reasoning led to more questions. It would also mean that the person responsible must know about the chapel and the fact that it might hold a secret: a means of entry to the underground rooms – if, indeed, they existed. Another thing, how would they know where the key to the chapel was? It all suggested prior knowledge.

He arrived at the florist's shop just as a Rover was pulling out of a parking spot. In the space of five minutes, he and the young florist had assembled a large bouquet. When it came to selecting flowers, Kingston didn't waste any time. He not only knew exactly what every single flower was, by common and Latin name, but could also tell right off what was going to last and what was likely to go into terminal shock the minute it left the shop. The bouquet was made up of a dozen white old garden roses, pale peach oriental lilies, tuberose for their fragrance and ferns and salal leaves as filler. Laying the flowers carefully in the boot, he took off for the hospital.

Jamie was waiting at the front door when he arrived, the hospital bracelet still on her wrist. Pulling out of the hospital parking area, Kingston told her about his conversation with Sean. There was no point in saving it for later. She took it remarkably well. Not the reaction that he'd expected. But then again, she had had a lot of time to think about it and must have come to grips with the possibility, no matter how much she wanted to disbelieve it, that someone had purposely sabotaged her car.

'Are they absolutely sure about the steering, Lawrence? I mean – it seems so – so inconceivable. It doesn't make any sense. Who would do something like that – and why?'

Kingston took his eyes off the road and glanced at her. 'There's no question about it, I'm afraid. The chap at the garage was positive.'

'God! I could easily have been killed.' She closed her eyes and rubbed her forehead. 'Or someone else could have been killed.'

'I know. Whoever did it is obviously prepared to go to any lengths to get what they want.'

Jamie leaned back in her seat. 'So, you think this has something to do with – *what*?'

170

'I'm not sure. I've got one theory that makes sense but it doesn't really explain much.'

'What's that?'

'That your accident and my flat being burgled were done by the same person. To get us off the estate, away from Wickersham.'

She frowned. 'For what purpose?'

'So that whoever was responsible could take his or her time having a close look at the chapel.'

'Her? Surely you don't think Dot had anything to do with it, or poor old Gwyneth, do you?'

'I don't. No. But at the risk of sounding like a cracked record, I'm more convinced than ever that all these things that have been going on are not random incidents. They're connected.'

'I know, Lawrence, you've told me before, a hundred times – connected to Ryder. You have this fixation that he's at the bottom of all this – a dead man, mind you – but who is actually doing all this stuff? Who in hell would have purposely wrecked my car? I mean it's not as though we have a long list of suspects, do we? People ready to run the risk of attempted murder to get what they want – whatever *that* is.'

Kingston kept his eyes on the road. He was about to respond when she raised the question that had been on his mind. He had expected it sooner.

'God,' she said, shaking her head from side to side. 'I'm beginning to wonder about Jack now. Maybe you're right after all, and he wasn't killed because of his debts.'

'Right. It's beginning to look more and more likely that that wasn't the case. You haven't heard from Chadwick, have you?'

'No.'

'I'm not surprised, really. He's probably getting a little tired of listening to my crackpot ideas. I wonder if he knows about your accident yet?'

171

'He must have got a report from the garage by now, don't you think?'

'Probably. I think I'd better call him, anyway, when we get back.'

The conversation petered out. Jamie, clearly brooding over the accident, stared out of the window at the countryside.

'Perhaps you're right, Lawrence,' she said eventually. 'Maybe we *should* have somebody come in and take a look at the chapel – a contractor – whoever. One way or another, maybe we can get to the bottom of all this.'

'I think we should.'

Another gap in the conversation, then Kingston spoke. 'I might as well ask the question, Jamie, because I would imagine Chadwick's going to, anyway.'

'What's that?'

'Before you came to England, back home, did you have any enemies there? Well, not enemies per se but anybody you can think of that might want to harm you – get their own back – that sort of thing?'

She didn't reply right away. Then she sighed. 'I've asked myself the same question and the answer is no.' She gave him a quick glance. 'Well – there was one thing. It's taken me all this time to forget it but I suppose there's no harm done in telling you,' she said softly. 'Several weeks before I got news of the inheritance, I broke up with a man who wanted to marry me. His name was Dominic. He was quite a few years older than me but that was fine. He was an architect, good-looking, fairly well off. We'd been going out for six months or so and it looked like the real thing, so we got engaged.' She paused. 'Then things started to go wrong. I won't go into detail, but suddenly he became overly possessive and controlling, constantly pressing to get married. I told him I wanted more time to think about it. He didn't like that. Then I found out he was following me. It started to get very ugly and I wanted out but he wouldn't take no for an answer.' She took her eyes off the road to glance at Kingston. 'You sure you want to hear all this?'

'Only if you want to tell me, Jamie.'

She focused on the road again. 'Well, finally, one night at dinner in a restaurant, I told him I wasn't going to marry him and that our relationship was over. I expected him to go ballistic but he didn't. In fact, he hardly said a word. It turns out he'd saved it all up for the next morning when he showed up at the place where I work. He was waiting there for me, in the parking lot, when I arrived. I won't try to describe what happened, but I couldn't believe how someone who was supposed to love me could be so vicious. It was frightening. At one point, I was sure he was going to attack me physically. The garbage that came out of his mouth was –'

A quick glance and Kingston could see that she was clearly unsettled as the memory of it all rushed back. 'Jamie, you don't have to go on,' he said.

Straightening up, she gave him a tight-lipped smile. 'It's okay.' She paused, then gave an apathetic shrug. 'That was the last time I saw him.'

'By the sounds of it, you should consider yourself lucky. From everything you've said, the man was clearly psychotic.'

'Unfortunately, it didn't end there, Lawrence.'

'You said that was the last time you saw him?'

'It was, but the next day I got a phone call from his partner saying that Dominic's car had gone off the road – off a cliff on a treacherous stretch of coast road above Bodega Bay. His Mercedes ended up on a small beach. When the paramedics eventually got down there, there was no one in the car and no sign of a body. The seatbelt was undone, too.'

'A suicide?'

'It looked that way because there were no skid marks.'

'Was there an inquest?'

'You know, I'm not sure. The police questioned me about

173

our relationship and I told them everything, of course. Some time later, Dominic's partner told me that the police were keeping the case open but until they had further leads, they were listing it as a suicide.'

'From what you've said, I'd say the odds are it *was* a suicide,' Kingston said. But he was thinking of the American watch.

They arrived at Wickersham mid-afternoon, just as it started to rain. Dot had lit a fire and had tea on the go when they stepped into the house. No sooner had Jamie stretched out on the sofa with a blanket and Kingston was lodged in *his* chair, than the phone rang. Kingston walked over and picked it up. It was Inspector Chadwick. He had read a copy of the accident report, he said. The officer in charge had followed up with calls to the hospital and to Larkin's, who confirmed what Sean had told Kingston. Chadwick's demeanour was markedly changed from their last conversation at the police station. It was as if Jamie's accident had sparked a much greater interest in his investigation of Wickersham. In the past he had been politely tolerant of Kingston's theories but now he was much more solicitous.

'Lawrence,' he said – it was the first time in Kingston's recollection that Chadwick hadn't addressed him as 'doctor' – 'I'd like to get together with you and Jamie. Tomorrow, if it's not inconvenient – ask you a few questions related to her accident. But while we're at it, I'd like to revisit everything that's happened at Wickersham since Jamie moved in. I know you've already told me most of it, but I want to make sure I'm not missing anything.'

Kingston cupped the phone while he told Jamie about Chadwick's request, asking her what time would work best for her. In a few seconds he was back to Chadwick. 'How's three o'clock tomorrow afternoon?' he asked. Chadwick agreed and the conversation ended.

Kingston returned to his chair, picked up the gold-rimmed china cup and took a sip of tea. 'Chadwick wants a full report on everything that's happened since you arrived here,' he said.

'There's not much that Chadwick doesn't already know, is there? You said that you'd told him all about your investigations, didn't you?'

'I did, yes. But only things concerning Ryder and what Loftus had told me.' Kingston frowned. 'I don't think he knows about Mainwaring.'

'What about Fox? Chadwick should be told about him, too. Though I can't imagine how he would be implicated.'

'You never know. I would imagine that Chadwick's going to want to know everything about everybody who's set foot here from day one.'

'Your friend, Ferguson. He's another.'

Kingston nodded. 'I have to call him. I think he might have been here yesterday, when I was with you at the hospital. From Gwyneth's description, it sounded like him. I'm feeling a little guilty about him. He can't wait to see the chapel.' He thought for a moment, deciding that now was not a good time to tell Jamie about the key.

They talked more over tea, then Jamie announced that she was tired and was going to rest for a couple of hours, then take it easy for the remainder of the evening. It was Kingston's cue to leave, which was fine by him. It had been a trying day all round. A day that may well have marked a turning point in the mysteries surrounding Wickersham.

Chapter Nineteen

Kingston woke at seven thirty with a headache, unusual for him. After leaving Jamie the evening before, he'd gone back to the cottage and fixed himself a light supper: fettuccine with mushrooms and a spicy Italian sausage that was left over from a dinner three or four nights ago. With a Cleo Laine tape playing, he went about the business of sautéing the mushrooms and boiling the salted water. By the time he sat down to eat, half the bottle of Sangiovese was gone.

He was feeling good. It was just like the old days, up in London, at his flat. Experimenting with new recipes, matching wines with the food. Picking out a CD from his eclectic collection, close to five hundred discs from Poulenc to Pink Floyd, and listening to it with the volume turned up. Yes, it would be nice to have company sometimes; someone to clink glasses with when everything arrived at the table. But he had long ago come to grips with the single life. The times he spent with Jamie over the last months had given him pause to think about the pluses of a steady relationship. But as attractive as it sometimes seemed, he knew that it wouldn't work. He'd been alone for too long now. He had become married to being single.

For Kingston, one of the most unsatisfying things about eating alone wasn't so much the absence of company as the fact that the meal lasted such a short time. It was not unusual for a meal in a restaurant, with a companion, to go on for two hours. Yet the same meal served at home to just one person would probably be consumed in less than fifteen minutes. Somebody, somewhere, he mused, had doubtlessly done a study on it. Invariably, he did the crossword puzzle while he ate. At least it helped pace the meal.

Kingston cleared the table and took plate and wineglass into the kitchen to wash them up. He never left dishes in the sink overnight. After another fifteen minutes on the crossword, finally getting 14 across: *A king in the ring* (5), he pencilled in LOUIS, and then put the puzzle aside for the morning when his head would be much clearer. He read for the rest of the evening, finally dozing off with the book in his lap.

By quarter past nine the next morning, after a cup of tea, two slices of buttered toast slathered with marmalade, and two aspirin, the headache was almost gone. He picked up the phone and dialled Ferguson's number. To his surprise, Ferguson answered after the second ring.

'Morning Roger, it's Lawrence.'

'Good to hear from you, doctor. How's it going up there?'

'Everything's fine.' Kingston wondered if he should tell him about Jamie. He decided it served no purpose. 'Sorry it took a while getting back to you,' he said. 'I was taking care of things up in London for a few days and it's been frightfully hectic since I got back.'

'No problem. I've been away from the office myself for a few days anyway, so your timing's good.'

Kingston wondered why he hadn't mentioned being at Wickersham right off the bat. Maybe it wasn't Ferguson after all. Gwyneth's description had been vague. No harm in asking, though.

'By chance, were you up at the house recently?'

There was a pause before Ferguson answered. 'Oh, yes, I was, as a matter of fact – a couple of days ago. I was about to tell you. I happened to be up in your neck of the woods that day, visiting an historian who lives in Watchet.

177

I tried the house but there was nobody there, so I just turned around and left.' He hesitated again. 'Actually, I was hoping I could take a look at the chapel.'

'That was the reason for my call. I'd like to show it to you. See what you think.'

'Absolutely. Can you hold on a minute?' After checking his diary, they arranged to meet the coming Monday at noon.

As Kingston tidied up the kitchen, he was thinking about Chadwick's visit that afternoon. It was going to be interesting to listen to what he had to say. Somehow he doubted that Chadwick would have come by any more information concerning Jamie's accident – or, for that matter, Jack's death. He also pondered the question of how much he should tell Chadwick about the chapel and Ferguson's assertion that, at one time, underground rooms existed below Wickersham – or if he should mention it at all. He decided to wait and see how the meeting went, what kind of questions Chadwick would ask. Given all the ground to cover, it promised to be a long one.

Still, it looked like a nice day for a change. The unseasonable heavy rain and cold winds had slowed down outdoor work on the gardens over the last couple of days. He put on his wellies, leather waistcoat and cap and patted his pocket, making sure he had his keys. He now locked the cottage when he was gone. The key to the chapel no longer hung on the hook in the hall. For safekeeping, it was in a zip-lock bag in the refrigerator. He glanced around the kitchen one more time, walked through the living room, closed the cottage door behind him, and started up the path to the house. Before going up to join the workmen and gardeners, he would see how Jamie was faring.

At two forty-five, Jamie cast her eyes around the living room. Thanks to China, it looked clean and respectable.

There had been a flap earlier when Dot failed to show up for work. It was unexpected because she had told Jamie yesterday that she would be in early, on account of the meeting, to get the place cleaned up and do some baking. It had happened a couple of times before, and on those occasions Dot had eventually phoned, so Jamie wasn't unduly concerned. China had filled in and done a presentable job, taking it upon himself to clean the kitchen, too.

Kingston made an appearance just as Jamie was about to leave the room. She told him about Dot, saying she had to go and check on things in the kitchen. After she left, knowing that it was going to be a long session, he commandeered the wingback chair before Chadwick or his sergeant could get it and picked up a copy of *Country Life* from the pile of magazines on the coffee table. He enjoyed it as much for the property listings in the front pages as anything else. Every time he read them, he found himself gasping at the prices.

Inspector Chadwick and an attractive redhead he introduced as Detective Sergeant Wendy Lawson, who was taking DS Eldridge's place, arrived a few minutes before three. Because they had just come from lunch at the Griffin, they declined Jamie's offer of tea or coffee.

Chadwick looked as if he had dressed for a dinner date, right down to the polka dot hanky in his breast pocket. Kingston smiled inwardly; it was for Wendy's benefit, he was thinking. The four of them sat in a circle of sorts, separated by the coffee table, which Jamie had cleared of magazines and other decorative bits. The DS had a notebook open on her lap.

'So,' said Chadwick. 'I've brought Wendy up to speed on most of what's been going on up here, including the thoughts you expressed the last time we met, Lawrence.' He sniffed, rubbing his nose between thumb and forefinger. 'So, to start with, why don't we go back to the very beginning and work from there. That way, hopefully we won't miss anything.'

179

The DS sat motionless and expressionless, pen at the ready.

'Makes sense,' said Kingston, more to fill the pause than anything.

Chadwick crossed his legs, carefully adjusting the crease in his trousers. 'First, the skeleton in the well,' he said. 'Not much to report there, I'm afraid. As you both know, the bones are those of a white male in his mid to late forties, approximately five-eleven, indications of healed trauma to the knee and upper tibia. Impossible to tell how long the body was down there. No soft tissue, ligaments, scraps of clothing, jewellery or any other means of identification.' He nodded towards Kingston. 'Other than the watch, that is, which I told you about, Lawrence. The body could've been there many years according to the pathologist.'

'But no more than sixty-odd years?' said Kingston.

'Right,' Chadwick nodded. 'Not before 1936, the year the watch was made.'

Kingston had decided to let Chadwick rattle on a bit before he told him what Loftus had said about the injury to Kershaw's knee.

Jamie shot Kingston a glance. 'What about dental records, inspector?'

'We've been checking all the dentists in a fifty-mile radius. If the body has been down there for, say, less than thirty or so years, the odds are much greater of the forensic odontologist finding a match – if the man was from this area, that is. But so far, nothing.'

'I know this is far-fetched,' said Jamie, 'but it's been suggested that the body may be that of Major Ryder.'

'Yes, Lawrence discussed that possibility with me. Given the enormity of the cover-up – that someone would have to have posed as Ryder for as long as that body's been down the well – it is highly unlikely.' He glanced at Kingston. 'As I recall, I think you had given up on that idea, too, hadn't you?'

'Yes. It's just not possible.'

180

'You thought it was more likely the other chap – the other soldier, Kershaw, I believe?'

Jamie looked puzzled. Kingston knew that this was new ground as far as she was concerned. Earlier, he had told her everything he'd learned from Loftus, but hadn't mentioned his more recent conversation that reinforced his supposition that the bones in the well were those of Sergeant Kershaw. That is, until he'd learned about the watch. But that by no means squelched his theory entirely.

Kingston nodded. 'That's right,' he said. 'As a matter of fact, I learned something very recently that tends to reinforce that supposition.'

'Really?' said Chadwick. 'What's that?'

'Before his company was captured Kershaw was wounded.'

'And?'

'He was shot in the knee.'

'Hence the trauma.'

'Exactly.'

'When did you find this out?'

'The day before yesterday.'

Jamie interrupted. She was frowning and clearly bewildered. 'What's all this about, Lawrence? Who is this Kershaw man?'

'He was a soldier who fought with Ryder in the war. Loftus told me about him. A day or so before the surviving soldiers were captured by the Germans, Ryder and Kershaw got into a fight and Ryder ended up getting shot by his own gun. Kershaw got twenty years in prison for it.' He paused, choosing his words. Right now, he didn't want to get into a long explanation.

Jamie looked disturbed but said nothing.

'It's a bit more complicated than just that, I'm afraid,' said Kingston. 'Perhaps it might be best, to save the inspector's time, if I tell you the whole story later, Jamie.'

'That's fine. I'm just wondering why you didn't tell me about all this before, Lawrence?'

'I would have done. In fact, I was planning to but that was about the time you told me you didn't want me digging any further into Ryder's past. I thought it best to forget the whole thing.' He nodded in Chadwick's direction. 'That's when I went to see the inspector – to tell him about my suspicions – what I'd found out from Loftus.' He looked from Jamie to Chadwick and gestured with open palms. 'I still don't know if this has any bearing on what's been going on here. It's *all* speculation, you know.'

Jamie shrugged. 'Let's continue, then,' she said, clearly still confused.

Chadwick looked distracted and was thinking hard. Kingston's news about Kershaw's injury had obviously taken the wind out of his sails. Then he launched into the subject of Jack's death. There was little to report that they didn't know already, he said. They had now run out of leads, but still they had no idea as to who might have killed him. Items found at the house proved that he was in serious debt, some of it credit card loans. Other evidence indicated that gambling and drugs were involved. He went on to quiz Kingston and Jamie about Jack's work habits. What he did in his spare time, which pub he frequented, whether he had friends, relatives, anybody who had visited Wickersham, whether he had quarrelled with any of his workers. After several minutes of questioning, nothing came to light. It was looking as if Jack's death had nothing to do with Wickersham.

Next, Chadwick introduced the burglary of Kingston's London flat.

'I understand nothing was stolen. Is that correct?'

'Yes. And there's quite a lot of valuable stuff lying around, I might add.'

'So, you think there could have been another reason?'

'I do, despite the fact that the London police didn't think it so unusual. They gave me several possible reasons why nothing was taken. But I'm more convinced than ever that it was done to get me away from here.'

Chadwick frowned. 'Plausible, I suppose,' he said. 'But why would someone want you off the estate?'

Kingston saw the question coming. 'That's what baffles me, inspector. I've no idea.'

Eventually Chadwick came around to the subject of Jamie's accident.

The answer to his first question, whether she knew anyone who might want to harm her, was a quick and emphatic, 'No.'

Questions about Jamie's staff followed. Then, Kingston and Jamie took turns telling Chadwick everything they knew about Mainwaring, Fox and Ferguson – the only people they knew, other than the workers and gardeners, who had any direct connection with Wickersham. As Chadwick questioned them about the three men, the DS was busy, head down, scribbling away.

A couple of minutes after the hall clock chimed five, Chadwick posed his last question: 'Anybody you might know back home who could have done it?'

Kingston shot an 'I told you so' look at Jamie, who simply shrugged. Then she gave an account of her broken engagement. Soon after that the meeting ended.

'Well, what do you think?' asked Jamie after Chadwick and his DS had departed. The two of them were in the kitchen.

'About what I figured,' said Kingston, taking a bite out of one of Jamie's cookies. 'Mmm, these *are* good.'

'We don't seem to be much further ahead.'

'It looks that way but then Chadwick's not going to tell us everything that's going on. With an ongoing investigation there're bound to be certain things that they're not going to divulge.' He picked up another cookie.

'Take some back to the cottage.'

'Thanks, I will.'

'Lawrence, I'm getting very concerned about Dot. I think we should have mentioned it to the inspector. Perhaps we should still do that, or drive over to her cottage.'

'I think it's a bit premature. There could be any number of reasons. In any case Chadwick would probably advise waiting for another twenty-four hours before going looking for her.'

'All right, we'll wait. But if we haven't heard from her by first thing tomorrow, I'm going to check up on her.'

Before leaving, Kingston picked up his mail from the hall table. Walking along the path to his cottage, he flipped through the half-dozen or so letters, most of them bills. The second to last had the Art Loss Register logo on the envelope. As he started to open it, there was a loud clap of thunder and it started bucketing down. Stuffing the letters inside his jacket, he started to run up the path. By the time he reached the cottage door, he was drenched. He went inside, shed his jacket and dropped the letters on the coffee table. After taking a moment to wipe his face and towel his hair, he sat down on the sofa, anxious to know what Jennifer Ingels had to say.

He opened the envelope and took out a cover letter and two follow-up sheets, listing names of individuals and companies. He read the letter.

Dear Dr Kingston,
Enclosed is information I have been able to access from our database concerning your recent request.

On the matter of the art dealer named Girard, our records indicate that a Laurent Girard operated an art gallery on Rue St Dominique, Paris, from 1933 to 1946. Later that year, with a partner, named Jeremy R. Villesgrande, they moved into a larger gallery on Place du Palais-Royale. That gallery closed in 1981. We have no information as to Girard's whereabouts or whether he is still living, facts that I am sure you should be able to determine given further research.

Concerning your second request: other persons engaged in the purchase and selling of art in Paris during the years from

184

1945 to the present day, enclosed you will find a list of individuals and galleries obtained from our records.

Should you, in the course of your search, come to suspect that any of the art concerned might have been stolen from individuals, collections, galleries or museums, please contact me immediately.

I hope the information provided helps in your investigation.
Your truly,
Jennifer Ingels,
Public Affairs Director

Eyes following his forefinger, Kingston read slowly down the list of names typed on each of the two sheets. Ryder's name was not there. He read them again. Girard's name and that of his partner, Jeremy Villesgrande, were included but no Ryder. Kingston was confused and disappointed. The date when Villesgrande joined forces with Girard – late 1946 – would have been right about the time that Ryder had supposedly joined Girard. Were there, perhaps, three partners? Ryder could have been a sleeping partner, who didn't want his name associated with the gallery. What other explanations could there be? Kingston stared up at the ceiling, trying to come up with other ideas. Drawing a blank, he put the papers aside, making a mental note to drop Jennifer a note of thanks in the morning.

Some of Kingston's most productive hours were those spent on his back. Either on the sofa, at the end of the day – preferably with a glass of Macallan at his elbow – or later at night, in bed just before dozing off. Those were the times, usually with eyes closed, and with no extraneous pressures or distractions, when he did most of his productive thinking – when problems that might have eluded him for days were somehow solved. Now, in another of those moments, he lay on the sofa staring up at the ceiling, head resting on his clasped hands, propped up by one of Jamie's Laura Ashley brocade pillows. The time would eventually come when his assignment would be over. That

185

didn't mean that the gardens would be complete. Gardens are never complete. They are, like life itself, always evolving, ever changing, never the same from one day to the next, let alone one season to the next.

The thought took him back to his lecturing days and his repertoire of anecdotes, quotations, witticisms and jokes – all related to gardens or plants. Propagation: he had at least three anecdotes for that subject. Roses: more than a dozen. Fertilizer, pruning, mulching, soil . . . you name it, he had just the right saying or joke. One he used frequently had come from a lecture he once gave to a large garden club. Discussing soil amendments, he suggested that aged cow manure was an inexpensive and readily available commodity in most rural areas. Much laughter followed when an elderly, well-dressed lady thrust her hand up and asked how old the cow should be. He smiled at the recollection. All were permanently etched in his mind and he had learned to deliver them with the skill and timing of the best stand-up comic.

He also recalled, with fondness, a quote from Margery Fish. Reputedly, at an East Lambrook Manor garden party – the now famous Somerset garden that she and her husband created in the late thirties– a visitor asked Margery's husband when the garden would be finished. 'Never,' was his reply. Kingston smiled. In years past, before her death, he had spent time with Margery at Lambrook, marvelling at the collection of hardy geraniums and other perennials that tumbled freely over the twisty paths and stone steps of her magical garden.

When he and Jamie had drawn up their contract, it was mutually agreed that it would be up to him to determine when he felt his services were no longer required on a full-time basis at Wickersham, at what point the day-to-day operation of the gardens could be turned over to a head gardener and staff of his choosing. Up until now, he'd never thought too much about the idea of leaving Wickersham. But when that time did come, he knew it was going to be a bittersweet farewell. The hardest part would be having to say goodbye to Jamie. More than once, the idea of staying on in Somerset longer than planned – even moving down permanently – had entered his mind, but each time better judgement had prevailed. He knew, damned well, that the idea was ill advised and impractical.

There was another thing that bothered him about leaving. After today's meeting, it was beginning to look, more and more, as if the mysteries surrounding Wickersham were not likely to be solved in the near future. The meeting with Chadwick had revealed nothing he and Jamie didn't know already. It came as no surprise, because he more or less knew that that would be the case. What was more frustrating was that all the threads of investigation, slender in the first place, had been played out. With no further developments or leads, it would simply become a waiting game until such time that new evidence came to light or someone blinked.

What infuriated Kingston was that he was convinced he was close to finding answers to the riddles – at least some of them. The link between Ryder and Girard and the distinct possibility that the two of them were dealing in looted art dovetailed with Ryder's years in Paris: everything fell into place. It would have been easy to bring the paintings over from France one at a time. Canvases could be concealed or disguised. And what could be a more convenient and secure location for Ryder to store the paintings than Wickersham? Keeping them anywhere in the house would be considered too risky, no doubt. More likely, Ryder would have stored them in a place where *nobody* would find them, not even by accident. Ferguson, if he was right, had unwittingly located that place: underground, in the old catacombs of the priory. It was a perfect set-up. And the chapel held the last piece of the puzzle: the way into Wickersham's subterranean chambers.

Under different circumstances, Kingston would have

told Chadwick all of this but he wanted to buy a little more time to see if he was right. Besides, he knew that with Jamie present as well as his new DS – whom he was obviously trying to impress – Chadwick could rightfully come down hard on him for not having mentioned it all much earlier. The temptation to make Kingston look like a bumbling amateur might be too hard for Chadwick to resist. For a while he could delay the inevitable but not indefinitely. One thing was certain, though. He would never leave Wickersham knowing that Jamie's life was still threatened.

Up early the next morning, he found Jamie in the kitchen. He was surprised to see her wearing a flour-dusted apron, in the midst of preparing what appeared to be dessert of some kind – a cake maybe? It also suggested that Dot had not made an appearance.

'Any word from Dot?'

Jamie wiped her hands on the apron. 'No. I phoned several more times yesterday evening. Nothing. I'm scared something might have happened to her, Lawrence – an accident. She lives on her own, you know.'

'I didn't. No.'

'After I've cleaned up here, I'm driving over to her cottage.'

'I'll come with you if you like. As a matter of fact, I've got to pick up some emitters and parts for the irrigation system at Water Savers. We can stop there on the way back from Dot's. Where does she live?'

'Over by Crowcombe, I looked it up on the map. It's off the A road that goes up to Watchet.'

'Shouldn't take more than twenty minutes. I'll wait here till you're ready, if that's okay?'

'Sure you don't mind, Lawrence? I have to admit I would feel better having someone with me.'

'No problem whatsoever, my dear. See how we do for

time and I may treat you to lunch.' He looked at the countertop, reached over and picked a strawberry from the bowl and popped it in his mouth.

'Hands off,' she said, making a mock hand-slapping gesture with the spatula in her hand.

'What is it?'

'Strawberry shortcake. One of my favourites.'

'My daughter Julie's, too. I've had it a couple of times when I've been over visiting.'

'It was going to be for the dinner. I was going to tell you about it but I decided to cancel it – for the time being anyway. With all this weird stuff going on, it didn't seem to be such a good idea.'

'I can well understand.'

She wiped her hands on the striped apron. 'I'd invited Francis and Alexandra, the couple who own the antiques shop in Bridgwater. You remember? I told you about them. It was going to be the two of them and David – David Latimer. Bella's staying with her sister for a few days. And you and me, of course.' She turned to stir whatever was in the pot on the Aga. 'We'll just have to do it some other time.'

'I'll look forward to it,' Kingston replied.

'David's still coming tonight, but just for drinks. When we talked on the phone I told him about the accident and some of the things that have been happening and he insisted on coming over to see me. I told him you'd join us, if that's okay.'

Fifteen minutes later, with Kingston driving, they left for Dot's.

Finding the cottage was easy. The village was tiny, only a scattering of houses, and the rustic Ash Tree Cottage sign hanging over the gate was hard to miss. Kingston pulled alongside the picket fence in front. The cottage stood by itself, set back from the road. Tall trees concealed the house

189

on the northerly side. The cottage on the other side was a hundred or so feet away, partially shielded by a high yew hedge. On the left side of Dot's cottage was a wooden gate, obviously the way to the back garden. On the right side a gravel drive, just long enough to accommodate one car. Dot's white Honda Civic was parked there.

Kingston, with Jamie a few steps behind, walked up to the periwinkle blue front door. He lifted the lion's head knocker and gave two sharp raps. They waited an interval of thirty seconds then he rapped again, this time even harder.

'She'd have to be deaf not to hear that,' said Jamie.

'And we know she's not, right?'

Jamie nodded.

Kingston had stepped back and was looking at the windows on both sides. In all cases, the curtains were drawn. 'Wait here, Jamie,' he said, crossing a small patch of lawn, 'while I go and check the back.' He opened the side gate and went through. In less than a minute he was back. 'It's all locked. I took a peek in the kitchen. Nothing unusual there. The other windows are curtained, I'm afraid. Looks like a wasted trip.'

They started up the path, closing the gate behind them. For a moment they stood looking back at the cottage. 'What do you think we should do?' asked Jamie.

'I suppose we should call the police. Could be any number of explanations.'

'Well, I'm not usually one to look on the dark side but I think you're right.'

Jamie was about to get back in the car when Kingston held his hand up. 'Wait a moment. Let me just check her car.'

She watched him walk over to the Honda where he bent down and peered in the passenger side window. Next, she saw him try the door handle. It was clearly locked because she could see the car shaking with the force that Kingston was exerting. Quickly he tried the other doors. All were locked. As he came back to the car she could see by the grim look on his face that something was dreadfully wrong.

'She's in the car, Jamie. I'm afraid she's dead.'

'God! Are you sure?'

'Almost certain – committed suicide by the looks of it. There's a section of garden hose from one of the rear windows hooked up to the exhaust. Her face is unusually pink, too, one of the signs of carbon monoxide poisoning.'

Jamie already had her phone out. 'What's the emergency number here?'

Within fifteen minutes an ambulance arrived and shortly after, a police car. The police had the Honda door open in seconds and waited while the paramedics examined the body, quickly determining that she was dead.

When the police finally got round to questioning Kingston and Jamie, over half an hour had passed. For the next five minutes, they answered the sergeant's questions, then provided their names, addresses and contact numbers.

'Well, that's about it,' he said, folding his notepad. 'I appreciate your patience. No need for you to stay any longer – and I'm awfully sorry about the bad news.'

Jamie sighed and shook her head. 'A suicide. I would never have thought it.'

'We won't know that for sure, miss, until the medical examiner has made his report. But yes, it certainly looks that way.'

They took one last look at the policemen still going over Dot's car and the waiting paramedics, then headed back to Wickersham. Kingston could pick up his stuff tomorrow and they had long ago abandoned the idea of lunch. A mile outside the village they heard the faint wail of a siren as the ambulance took Dot away.

Chapter Twenty

At a quarter to six, David Latimer pulled up to the front door at Wickersham just as Kingston was about to go in. They shook hands, exchanged greetings and went into the house.

With drinks served – a glass of white wine for Jamie, Dewar's for both Latimer and Kingston – the three of them sat in the living room, Jamie doing most of the talking as they explained how they had found Dot.

'All things considered, it's not a bad way to go,' said Kingston with a sigh. 'Only have to run the engine for about fifteen minutes or so in a small car like that and you've got a lethal level of carbon monoxide.'

'What an awful thing to have happened, though,' said Latimer. 'Had she given you any indications that she might be undergoing stress of any kind? Any unusual behaviour?'

'No,' Jamie replied. 'To the contrary, she's just been her usual grouchy self.' Her sorrowful smile was fleeting. 'With her, that was one thing you could always rely on.'

'I didn't know Dot as well as Jamie did, of course,' said Kingston, 'but when I was with her the other day, she seemed to be – how can I put it – well, defensive. It struck me as a little odd at the time but I didn't think too much of it. A bad hair day, maybe.'

Latimer took a sip of his scotch. 'And Jack Harris. You say it's still not determined exactly how he died. If it was an accident, or murder?'

'No,' said Jamie. 'Inspector Chadwick thinks that it all had to do with gambling and drugs. He doesn't think it's connected to anything here.' She glanced at Kingston. 'Lawrence does, though.'

'You think Jack's death and Dot's suicide are connected?'

Shaking his head, Kingston let out a long sigh. 'God, I don't know, David. This thing with Dot has really thrown me for a loop. I'm still convinced that Jack had something to do with all of this, though.'

Latimer put his drink down on the table. 'Really? Do you have any hard evidence that makes you think that?'

'I have to admit, at this point it's all hypothetical. But it goes beyond just Jack's and Dot's deaths. I'm convinced that all the things that have been going on here are connected in some way: the break-ins, Jamie's accident, that business with the paintings. Not only that, I'm sure that they all have something to do with Ryder. Something about his past – something that happened a long while ago.'

Latimer frowned. 'The paintings?'

'I told you about it,' said Jamie. 'The man that showed up saying that Ryder had some paintings that belonged to a French art dealer and they wanted them back.'

Latimer nodded. 'Yes, that's right. Of course, I remember, now. Did he call again then or come back?'

'No,' said Jamie.

Latimer looked at Kingston. 'So, how do the paintings fit in with all this, then?'

Here we go again, Kingston thought. If he answered, he would probably get the same reaction from Latimer as he had from Jamie. She had already told him that David felt the same way as she did, that the paintings were long gone. He took a long sip of scotch before deciding to dodge the question for the moment, to spare Jamie the embarrassment of having to listen to a long-drawn-out hypothesis that she had heard one time too many already. But it was a good opportunity to ask Latimer the question that he'd been wanting to. He had to tread carefully though, knowing that Jamie wasn't aware of what had happened in Latimer's office when Mainwaring had threatened to contest the will.

'To answer your question, I'm not sure yet how the paintings fit in. But let me ask you something, David – this Mainwaring fellow. I know that after Ryder died he took his inheritance and disappeared but I'm curious – do you know anything more about him?'

'There's not much more to tell, I'm afraid.'

'You said that he was in Ryder's employ for about fifteen years.'

'Yes, that's about right.'

'In his role as butler, major-domo, whatever, how much would Ryder have confided in him? What I'm trying to get at is, how much would he have known about Ryder's past and his business affairs?'

Latimer smiled. 'Would he have known about the paintings? Is that what you're asking?'

Kingston swirled the melting ice cubes in his crystal glass. 'Not just the paintings but other things that might have taken place at Wickersham, too, not only during his tenure but before he was hired as well.'

'That's a vague question, Lawrence. One that I'm afraid I can't answer. All I know is that – well, certainly in the latter years of Ryder's life – Mainwaring pretty much ran the show here. Yes, I would imagine that he would have had access to Ryder's business and personal affairs, but to what degree, I have no idea. He didn't have power of attorney, that I do know.'

'And he vanished?'

'As far as we know.'

Jamie interrupted, asking if the two men would like another drink. Both saying yes, she went to the butler's table that served as a bar, poured two more scotches over ice and brought them back to the coffee table with a carafe of water.

Jamie looked at Latimer and smiled. 'You see, David, you not only found me a wonderful garden guru but a private investigator, too.'

Latimer chuckled. 'You're lucky, Jamie: two for the price of one. Talking of the gardens, I want to take a look at them before it gets too dark.'

'Absolutely. You're not going to believe what Lawrence has achieved since you were here last.'

An hour later, Jamie said goodnight to Latimer and Kingston at the front door.

The next morning Kingston woke up late. Since moving down to the country he not only slept more soundly but longer, too. Pulling aside the bedroom curtain he saw the panes were misted on the outside. A thick fog shrouded the garden, reducing it to ghostly grey shapes. He dressed warmly: a heavy wool sweater over his corduroy shirt and cavalry twill trousers. It was going to be a full day. As arranged, he was meeting Jamie at nine to go over a pile of invoices before they approved them for payment and to discuss the forthcoming visit by the director of a documentary crew who had written expressing an interest in producing a film of the gardens' renaissance. Immediately after that he was scheduled to supervise the long-awaited planting of the lime walk, a grass-verged avenue some twenty feet wide, with fifteen Tilia trees on each side. Jamie had jokingly said that was a good feng shui number, not that she believed in it. Then, at noon, Ferguson was at long last going to show up to see the chapel. But most important of all, after he was through with Ferguson, Kingston was going back to the chapel to take one last shot at solving its mystery – if indeed there was one.

When he had first mentioned the lime walk, Jamie, quite naturally, thought the trees would be citrus. He had explained that while Tilia was commonly referred to as a lime tree, it was not related to the citrus, but belonged to the Linden genus – all very confusing, he admitted. Eventually the upper branches of each semi-mature tree would be pruned and trained to cross over and entwine with those of its partner on the other side of the walk to form a living trellis – or, as Kingston liked to call it, 'a hedge in the air'. On their day out at Hidcote Jamie had fallen in love with the pleached hornbeams in the stilt garden and wanted to do something similar.

After a hasty cup of tea and a bowl of muesli, Kingston was ready to leave the cottage at a quarter to nine. He put on his Barbour jacket, wellington boots and battered waterproof hat, closed and locked the cottage door and set off for the house.

The meeting with Jamie was shorter than he'd anticipated. By eleven thirty, eight of the thirty lime trees were planted. Even with only four trees, equally spaced on each side of the walk, the visual effect was striking. Kingston left the crew to finish the planting when Ferguson arrived at noon sharp. After a brief exchange of pleasantries with Jamie, Kingston whisked him off to view the chapel.

Ferguson's reaction was more or less exactly what Kingston had anticipated: a mixture of awe and curiosity. For the first five minutes there was little talk as the archivist went to work silently studying every inch of the chapel and the well. It wasn't long before Ferguson asked the question that Kingston had been expecting.

'I take it you haven't made any progress regarding the old priory basement?' Ferguson asked, taking a tiny silver camera from his jacket pocket.

The word 'basement' struck Kingston as amusing. Surely an academic could come up with a more fitting noun? 'Unfortunately, no,' he replied. 'You'd have been the first to know if I had, Roger. Without some kind of documented or physical evidence to tell us the exact location of the priory, it's going to be impossible to find the underground rooms – if they still exist, that is.'

'You've gone over the chapel pretty thoroughly then?'

196

'At least half a dozen times.'

'It would have been the perfect location for a secret entrance but I can see the problem. There aren't many places to hide it in here, that's for sure,' Ferguson said, gazing up and around the chapel.

'That's what's so baffling. I was so damned sure that the entrance to the priory cellars, catacombs or whatever you want to call them was hidden in this chapel that I could *smell* it. But now I think it's most likely somewhere in the house.'

Ferguson nodded. 'I suppose it's still the most logical site. I don't think, somehow, it would be anywhere else.'

'I guess so,' Kingston sighed. 'But there's no saying *where* those damned monks built their priory. It could have been anywhere on the entire bloody estate.'

'What does Jamie think about all this?'

'At first, she was – well, ambivalent I suppose is the right word. I think, in the beginning, she thought I was some kind of English Don Quixote. But lately she's come round to the idea that there may be something to it after all. Although, I must say, she's not one for digging into the past.'

'She's an exception, then. Most of the Americans I've met lap up anything that's historical. English history must be on the curriculum of every college in the country. Sometimes I think they know more about us than we do ourselves.'

Kingston waited patiently while Ferguson spent the next ten minutes snapping digital photos of every inch of the chapel. It seemed a trifle excessive to Kingston but Ferguson was an archivist after all, and by the miniature size of the camera, it was reasonable to assume that it was a new toy. After a few minutes spent viewing the results on the LCD monitor, they left the chapel and went back to the house, to join Jamie for lunch. By the time Ferguson left, it was close to three.

Kingston decided to take a walk to the walled garden

where the peach house was nearing completion. When discovered, it was little more than a grey skeleton of rotted wood and broken panes of filthy glass supported only by the ivy and strangle of vines that had almost sealed its fate. Kingston was all for taking it down but was persuaded by one of the master joiners on the team that it could be refurbished. What followed in the ensuing weeks was a singular achievement of extraordinary skill, patience and love. Despite the severe rot in the wooden sections, two joiners were able to make accurate templates to rebuild the framework. Behind them two glaziers went to work installing glass that was saved from the original framework and matching panes cut from old ones found in a salvage yard. Finally, the paint crew had given it a primer coat and two top coats of white paint. The brick flooring was now being installed and soon the handsome structure, butted against the high garden wall, with its steep sloping, south-facing roof would be home to peaches, nectarines, guavas, passion fruit and pineapples as it was in its glory days.

At four thirty, Kingston left the gardens and made his way back to the cottage where his bag of tools was ready waiting. The canvas bag contained a hammer, set of screwdrivers, chisel, pliers, electronic stud finder, several types of brush, can of air spray, a heavy Mag-lite flashlight and other miscellaneous items. Recalling the maxim that flashlights are tubular metal containers often kept in a briefcase to store dead batteries, he wasn't going to trust his memory as to when the batteries were last changed, so he threw in four new spares.

It was drizzling steadily as he made his way to the chapel. Somehow the weather seemed appropriate for what he hoped would be the Gothic encounter to come. This could be his last trip to the chapel. If he didn't find the secret entrance to the catacombs this time, he would give up.

Closing the door to the chapel behind him, he switched on the flashlight and walked down the aisle to the first row of pews. There, he placed the toolkit on the bench, turned on the floodlights and sat down next to the aisle. He shivered. The place was like a tomb. Unlike his previous visits, where he'd spent many hours examining the limestone walls and timbers up close, and scrutinizing the floor on his hands and knees, he decided, this time, to simply sit and study the interior as an integral unit. He wasn't quite sure what this might accomplish but he'd tried just about everything else and his instincts told him that perhaps he was looking too hard: that the answer was staring him in the face. Maybe not 'staring' but it was here *somewhere*. He felt it in his bones.

Sitting on the hard pew, he looked around the interior. It was now so familiar that he could visualize it with eyes closed. After a minute or so he gave up. With one elbow resting on his knee, he lowered his head, closed his eyes and massaged his brow. 'Damn,' he muttered under his breath. He sighed deeply, opened his eyes and stared blankly at the wooden rail of the pew front barely inches from him. It was the colour of dark chocolate with a lighter grain. He was sure it was oak. The eighteenth-century Welsh dresser in his flat had similar graining and patina. He leaned back, stretching an arm along the back of the pew, looking across the aisle to the row on the other side.

Perhaps he should forget the whole thing. It was taking up far too much of his time and if he hadn't found anything by now, chances were he never would. Just how important was it anyway? Important to him but not necessarily to Jamie. Since their talk in the car on the way back from the hospital, she had not mentioned the attempt on her life. It was clear that she was making an heroic effort to put it behind her – trying to behave normally. And now, right on top of it, Dot's death. It was remarkable how well Jamie was holding up.

Right after the accident, Kingston had suggested that she get away for a while, even go back to the States and

perhaps stay there until such time that credible explanations were found for the deaths and bizarre happenings
that had taken place at Wickersham. He could keep things
going in her absence; hire a new full-time housekeeper,
keep working on the gardens and maintain the house.

But she would hear none of it. As much as she tried to
behave as if nothing had happened, the stress was clearly
getting the better of her. The laughter was gone between
them and the smiles were fewer.

He had purposely avoided bringing up the matter of
hiring a contractor to go through the chapel, as she had
recently suggested. He saw no point in it right now but
knew if this last search of his were abortive, that would be
the next step. He would insist on it.

With the thoughts of Jamie swirling in his mind, Kingston had forgotten all about what he was supposed to be
doing. He stood for a moment to stretch his legs. The pew
was hard and unforgiving. He felt sorry for the devout
worshippers, required to sit interminably through droning
sermons in those bygone years.

Why was he looking so hard at the pew on the other side
of the aisle? It was identical to the others but . . . somehow
different. It took him several seconds before he realized
why. He crossed the aisle and looked closely at the wood
surface, then cast his eyes down the row. He turned
around and looked at the row behind, then the one behind
that. He went back to where he'd been sitting and studied
the surface of the wood again.

With his knowledge of the cellular origins of graining,
he knew that the wood was tangential cut: a longitudinal
section cut parallel to the long axis of the trunk. In this
respect, all the pews were the same. But the wood of the
pew where he was sitting was slightly, very slightly lighter
in colour than the others in the chapel. Perhaps it was the
angle of the floodlights? Was that creating the illusion? He
went over to the heavy tripod that Jack had rigged up and
dragged it closer to the front row of pews. He rotated it

ninety degrees, then back a few degrees until the two lights shone equally on both sides of the aisle. There was no question, his pew was fractionally lighter in colour.

He took out the flashlight, bent down and shone it on the base of the pew where it met the flagstones. He saw what looked like a tiny crevice. How was the pew joined to the flagstones, he wondered? He leaned his hip up against the pew and shoved. Nothing moved. It was rock solid. Pulling out the can of air spray, he whiffed it along the crevice. The jet of air propelled a puff of dust and dirt in front of it as he moved along the pew. He stopped to examine the result. Between the base of the pew and the stone floor was a gap, little more than one eighth of an inch. It continued along both sides.

He stood, gripped the front rail of the pew with both hands and shook it hard. Again, nothing budged. He tried lifting it – same result. Whatever method had been used to affix the pew to the floor was both rigid and cleverly concealed. He scratched his head and stood looking down the length of the bench. How was the damned pew anchored to the ground?

He couldn't come up with the answer. Instead he came up with an intriguing hypothesis. The footprint of the pew was roughly three feet wide by about six or seven feet long, at the most. If the pew were removed, it would leave an opening in the floor sufficiently wide and long enough for a person to comfortably pass through. In his mind's eye he visualized the primitive mechanics: the pew being hinged by a transverse rod at one end, and when lifted from the opposite end, tilting it to vertical, revealing a flight of steps down into the underground chambers. The more he thought about the idea the more it made sense. Problem was – how to raise the pew? How would the monks of those medieval times have designed and constructed it?

Logically, he figured that there had to be a concealed release mechanism somewhere not too far from the pew.

He started with the presupposition that the device would be primitive. More likely a cord or cable of some kind attached to a spring that released and activated a locking device, the same principle as a conventional door latch. The obvious hiding place was the pulpit. Only a few feet from the front pew, it would have been relatively easy for the monks, or those who had conceived the system, to fabricate. Problem was that the pulpit was so simply constructed. It was no more than a panelled box with turned balusters on the corners, topped with a slanted panel to hold the scriptures or sermons. There was nowhere, inside or out, to hide a secret panel, lever or toggle. He'd already gone over it before, top to bottom.

The next possibility was the baptismal font. That was immediately behind the pulpit, off to the right. It was made entirely of stone and resembled a crude birdbath, certainly nowhere to hide anything there. Likewise, the well. Once again, it looked like a stalemate.

Kingston stood next to the pulpit thinking back to the meeting with Chadwick. Perhaps not telling Chadwick and Jamie about the chapel and the underground rooms might have been a mistake on his part. He knew damned well why he hadn't. First and foremost, he wanted to impress and surprise Jamie with the discovery – if it happened, that is. And second, he didn't want Chadwick to step in just yet and shove him aside, which he knew was exactly what would happen. Regardless of what took place from now on, he would tell Jamie everything that he'd been up to. Then she could decide what she wanted to do about it, which, ironically, would probably be to involve the police.

Forgetting all this, calmed by the solemn quiet, he let his eyes wander round the chapel. The all too familiar unadorned plaster walls, the stern pews, the ancient well that had surrendered its grisly contents. How many sermons had been voiced from the simple pulpit, he wondered? Was it just the family and staff at Wickersham who filled the pews? Or were the local parishioners included? How many generations had shuffled through these dark oaken doors to celebrate the joyous moments of their lives or salve their guilt?

He inhaled deeply, rubbed his brow and sighed. That was it, then. The monks of Wickersham Priory had won. Either that or he'd been wrong all along. He took one last look around the chapel, then hoisted up the tool bag from the floor by the pulpit. As he turned to leave, the back of the bag banged against the front of the pulpit. It was no more than a light knock – caused by one of the heavier tools, the hammer or the flashlight – but it was enough to give him pause and stop. There was something about it that hadn't sounded right. Lowering the bag to the ground, he stooped and knocked three times with his knuckle on the same spot. It was a hollow sound. Not unexpected because the pulpit itself was nothing more than a vertical box enclosed on three sides. But it didn't sound right. It was what? Too hollow a sound?

He let go of the bag and stood for a moment examining the front of the pulpit. Then he went round to the back and positioned himself where the vicar or priest would have stood to address his small flock. With his hands resting on either side of the pulpit, like a prisoner in a dock pleading his innocence, he stared out to the empty pews. Then he looked down to the place where the bible or scriptures would be. Then he got it.

Inside the pulpit, his knees were barely three inches from the wood panel. Yet looking down from his height, he could see that the front of the pulpit extended several inches beyond that. Why on earth hadn't he thought of it before? In the old days, bookcases were often constructed that way. Shelving on the front of the case and behind it a hidden space of several inches, neatly concealed, usually by a self-locking hinged back. The optical illusion was almost impossible to spot. Only the most perceptive eye would notice that the side dimension was somewhat

203

deeper than that suggested by the front view where the books backed up to the rear panel. In fact, with books filling the shelves, it was almost impossible to tell that there was a false back to the case.

Now on his hands and knees, inside the pulpit, Kingston traced the panel in front of him with the tips of his fingers. If he was right – and he was now certain that he was – there was a way of removing or swinging out the inner panel. The carpenter who had crafted the pulpit had been skilled in cabinet making because all edges of the panel were perfectly butted against those on the three sides and the underside of the lectern. Barely a hair's breadth separated them. How did it work? There were no hinges or spaces where a finger could be inserted under the panel. It had to work with pressure, he figured. He placed his hands squarely on the centre of the panel and pushed. Nothing happened. He tried doing the same thing to the base of the panel, the sides and the top centre of the panel, all with no success.

He stood and stepped back for a moment. If he had constructed the pulpit, where would he have positioned the opening device? Certainly not at the bottom because that could easily be kicked, as it doubtlessly was over many decades. Same with the centre of the panel, where a heavy person's knee could accidentally bump into it. It had to be located somewhere at the very top, underneath the lectern. But there was no space underneath. The sloping top was a solid piece of oak.

On his haunches, Kingston eyed the smooth panel facing him. It was almost as if it was taunting him. He took his time, placing his left-hand thumb on the top left corner. Then he did the same with his right-hand thumb on the opposite corner, careful to line it up at the same level. He leaned forward and applied equal pressure with both thumbs. 'Damn,' he muttered. Leaving his thumbs in place, he relaxed for a moment and this time pushed much harder. A small click and the panel fell forward resting on his hands. 'Gotcha!' he said.

Gently, he lowered the wooden panel to the floor of the pulpit. Now he was looking at the unfinished back of the pulpit's front panel. He saw it immediately; an oval iron handle, the size of drawer-pull, in the centre of the panel. He slipped three fingers inside it and pulled. He didn't have to pull very hard. A muted clanking sound echoed around the bare walls. He let go of the handle and took four steps to the front pew.

Gripping the end rail with both hands, offering a prayer of sorts, he closed his eyes and lifted. With an case that he least expected, the pew started to rise. He opened his eyes and watched with amazement. The motion was unbelievably smooth and silent. In a matter of seconds it finally came to rest at a ninety-degree angle to the floor.

It was exactly as he had pictured. In front of him was a rectangular opening in the flagstones. At his feet a flight of stone steps disappeared into the darkness below.

Chapter Twenty-One

Flashlight in hand, Kingston entered the catacombs. Being a touch claustrophobic, he prayed that the tunnels or corridors – whatever was down there – would not be too cramped. He was aware that in the Middle Ages men were a lot shorter, and his six-foot-plus height could become a handicap. At first, he'd questioned the wisdom of exploring the underground by himself but, after weighing the pros and cons, he convinced himself that the risk was minimal. In any case, after all he'd done to get to this momentous point the impulse to explore was overwhelming.

He'd already made sure that the pew was stable, unlikely to fall. An examination of the latch indicated that it could be released from below. The idea of being accidentally trapped down there was unnerving but as far as he could tell there was no likelihood of that happening. If the flashlight batteries started to go, he would have sufficient time to retrace his steps before they died altogether.

It was more than a dozen steps down before he reached the foot of the stone stairway. An uneasy feeling passed over him. It was as if he were about to leave the twenty-first century and the real world. Shining the light around, he saw a long tunnel ahead, more like a hall since the construction was rectilinear. To his relief the ceiling looked tall enough for him to navigate without crouching. Even so, his head grazed the ceiling where he was standing.

Both walls and ceiling were of greyish stone blemished in places with calcareous ochre and chalky deposits. The floor was a simple cobblestone. Every twenty feet or so, a single stone projected from the wall at a level with Kingston's head. Judging from the caked layers of wax, these were clearly candle sconces. The air was cool and stale-smelling, not dank as he had expected. The smell was not unpleasant, vaguely herbal, which was not surprising since he knew that herbs were often used in medieval times to repel insects and vermin.

About twenty steps farther down the hall, he came to a small room on his right. The simple wooden door was ajar. Pushing it open with his foot, he shone the flashlight around the space. It was empty. Another ten feet along was a second room, this time on the left. This space was considerably larger and the ceiling higher than that of the first room. A low partition divided the room in two and a mezzanine projected eight feet or so from the back wall. Kingston took it for a workshop or storage area. Soon he reached another room, much like the last one but the door was iron-bound and had a lock with a bronze escutcheon. Inside were the remains of what had once been heavy wooden racks of some kind. Aware that the production of wine and mead was a popular and profitable pastime for the monks, Kingston speculated that this room was a storage cellar for wine casks. He smiled to himself – hence the lock.

Passing two more empty rooms he came to a junction. The hall continued but also headed off to the left and right, offering three choices. At this point, he judged that he was well over a hundred feet into the labyrinth. Its sheer size and complexity was far more than anything he'd ever imagined and there was obviously more to come.

In the next fifteen minutes, he explored both the left and right hallways, which in turn led to others, and more rooms of differing size, most of them empty and all unlocked. It was a reasonable assumption, he decided, that the rooms he'd seen so far were used either for storage, work or sleeping.

Venturing farther into the maze – marvelling at its size and accomplishment – he suddenly realized that he hadn't been paying attention to directions. Getting lost hadn't crossed his mind till now and there were few, if any, markers. He was beginning to wish he'd left some of his own but it was too late for that now.

He glanced at his watch: almost six thirty. He'd been down there for close to half an hour. Had he covered the entire labyrinth, he wondered? Hard to tell. Regardless, he decided to go back to the chapel. He could return later with Jamie, maybe Ferguson, too – Roger would go bananas when he saw it. Doubtless, it would be considered among the most significant British archaeological discoveries of the century. The first job was to rig up some temporary lighting – a challenge, even with the length of the hallways he'd covered already.

From that first rush of excitement and trepidation, when he had stepped into the dark unknown of the catacombs, until now, Kingston had forgotten his principal goal: to find Ryder's secret hiding place – the room or vault where he stored the paintings that were shipped from France. Now he was experiencing a sinking feeling at the prospect of having to face up to the bitter disappointment of discovering that, after coming this far, there was no such place. That he'd been wrong about Ryder all along. How many rooms were still unexplored? There was no way of knowing. But at least there were *some*. So there was hope yet. If one of his earlier theories held water, then there could well be a good reason for his not having uncovered anything so far.

When all else failed, Kingston fell back on what he called his 'crossword puzzle logic' – teasing answers from confusing and complicated clues. His fundamental premise was that, once, there had been two ways of entering the catacombs: one through the chapel, the other from some-

208

where in the house. He had searched the house but that proved little. Knowing, now, how cleverly the chapel entrance was designed, he would have been surprised if he *had* found anything. His conclusion was that a secret entrance via the house still existed, or it had long since been sealed and – unless the house was dismantled piece by piece – would be all but impossible to find now. If the latter *were* true, then it would suggest that, at one point during his days at Wickersham, Ryder might have given up trading in art. He could have had a falling out with Girard; the market in high-priced paintings had crashed in the early nineties and values had decreased by as much as half at some auctions. Another likelihood: with all the recent publicity and attention focused on stolen art, it became too risky a venture. He could think of many reasons for Ryder having gone straight.

Given these presuppositions it was not surprising he had found nothing yet that resembled a secret storage area. If such a place existed, it would probably be closer to the house than the chapel. Sound or not, this conclusion bolstered his optimism as he found his way back to the chapel. He reminded himself to bring a compass on his next visit.

Kingston lowered the pew and watched it drop back into place with a dull clank. For a few seconds, he stood and stared, admiring its simplicity. Considering its age, it was a remarkable piece of engineering. He went to the pulpit and returned the panel to its original position, concealing the release latch. Picking up his tool bag, he started up the aisle. At the door, he stopped. It was . . . open. He stood for a moment looking around the interior, certain that he had closed the door when he first arrived at the chapel. He even remembered wondering whether he should lock it or not. And just before stepping down into the catacombs, he had checked it again, to make sure. Someone had been there. And that someone now knew the secret of the chapel.

*　　*　　*

Back at the cottage, Kingston picked up the phone and called Jamie. For the next several minutes he told her about his discovery, describing precisely how he had found the hidden latch, about the pew, and what the catacombs were like. After he was finished, she congratulated him, offering a thin apology for doubting him. She wanted him to take her there that very minute, but Kingston managed to dissuade her using the late hour and absence of lighting as an excuse. They agreed to meet at eight thirty in the morning, giving him time to rig up temporary lighting and be better equipped to explore. Kingston waited till the end of the conversation to ask the all-important question.

'Was anyone looking for me this afternoon, after I left you? Anyone come to the house?'

She paused before answering. 'Only Roger Ferguson.'

'Ferguson?'

'Yes. He came back to get his camera. He'd left it on the coffee table. The thing's so tiny, I'm not surprised, he should have kept it in his pocket.'

'Did he leave right away?'

'What are you getting at, Lawrence? Yes, I suppose he left right away. I didn't look out of the window to see if he drove off, if that's what you mean.' She paused. 'Why, is it important?'

'I don't know, it could be. It's just that I believe there was someone in the chapel while I was down below.'

Unlike the gloomy day before, it was a sparkling morning when Kingston left the cottage at eight o'clock on Tuesday. Despite the prospect of a warm day, he wore his old wax jacket over a wool turtleneck knowing how cool it was down in the catacombs. He had told Jamie to dress warmly, too.

Walking up the path to the house he stopped and bent down to study the leaves of the yellow *Alchemilla mollis* that spilled over the gravel. Each leaf resembled a delicate

210

bone china cup, filled with a teaspoon of rainwater. The sight never failed to stop him in his tracks, in awe and joy at this sculpture of nature.

Last night, after his fifteen-minute dinner, catered by the local fish and chip shop and washed down with two glasses of Pinot Grigio, he had dwelled on the fallout that would ensue when word of the discovery of the old priory's underground rooms hit the press. Wickersham would become a madhouse. Every newspaper, magazine and TV station would be clamouring to take pictures, demanding interviews, letting nothing get in their way in order to get a front-page story.

His mind flashed back to a conversation that had taken place two years ago, in Alex and Kate Sheppard's living room, when he had told them that the blue rose they had just discovered in their garden was about to turn their world upside down and that their lives would be forever changed. The chapel and the circumstances surrounding Wickersham were different, but nevertheless pandemonium could and certainly would break loose unless immediate steps were taken to head off such a catastrophe. Word would spread like wildfire and the resulting media frenzy on top of all the local nosy parkers could have a devastating effect on the gardens, not to mention Jamie's privacy and life in general on the estate. He would have to sit down with her right away and draw up a plan of action. First they would have to inform the local council members, the police and emergency services. Controlling the influx of traffic would be the first problem to address. He could think of a dozen others.

When would he tell Ferguson? In fairness, he should be among the first to know. But how much did he know already, Kingston wondered? It could have been him at the chapel yesterday. He admitted to being on the estate before, the time when Kingston and Jamie were gone. The more he thought about it, the more the idea of Roger's going behind his back seemed ludicrous – totally out of character. The man was an archivist, a scholar. Naturally he would have an all-consuming interest in such a discovery. For him, this was a once-in-a-lifetime historical and archaeological breakthrough in which he was directly involved. That said, Kingston couldn't dismiss entirely the suspicion that Ferguson knew more than he was admitting.

Chadwick, too, should be told about the chapel. He would hear about it soon enough but if – as Kingston was now almost certain – the catacombs revealed Ryder's secret cache of paintings, then police involvement would be essential.

At the house, he found Jamie ready and waiting in the kitchen. She was wearing blue jeans, a black wool pea coat over a cream turtleneck and a red wool scarf, loosely knotted in the front. A navy woollen hat concealed her hair.

'You look very fashionable, I must say,' observed Kingston, smiling.

'Well, you said to dress warmly.'

'No, I approve. You look great.'

'Okay, then,' she said, taking one last glance around the kitchen, 'let's go see this chapel of yours.'

'Of yours, I believe.'

'I'm not so sure. From what you've told me, the place is likely to become some kind of archaeological shrine. Somehow we're going to have to separate it from the gardens.'

'You're right. I've been thinking about that. It's obvious we won't be able to keep it a secret for long, so the sooner we start thinking about dealing with it the better.'

In five minutes they reached the chapel. Kingston unlocked the door and they stepped into the cool silent interior. It was the first time in his many visits that he had seen the stained glass windows in their full glory. The morning sunshine streaming through lit up the room with

212

kaleidoscopic colours. Whether by accident or design, the effect was spiritually uplifting.

At the pulpit, Kingston showed Jamie how he had spotted the subtle difference in the wood graining of the pews, then made a modest ceremony of releasing the catch and starting to raise the pew. As the pew began its upward arc, Jamie gasped. She watched as it locked into the vertical. 'Amazing!' she breathed. 'Awesome!'

'Well, Jamie, here it is,' Kingston said, as they both stood at the top of the stone steps, looking down into the darkness. 'Let me switch the lights on and we can go down.' The night before, after their phone conversation, Kingston had gone to the garden workshop, picked up some cables and low voltage lighting apparatus, and taken it to the chapel. Within an hour, he had managed to string temporary lighting almost a hundred feet into the catacombs. From there on, they were going to have to rely on a portable Coleman lamp, good for at least eight hours of light, and a flashlight that Jamie carried. With Kingston leading, they went down the steps.

The lights made navigating the hall much easier and far less daunting than on his first visit. After recovering from her initial awe and uttering a few more exclamations of amazement, Jamie followed silently. Every now and then, aided by illumination from the Coleman lamp, they stopped to look into one of the side rooms. Now, construction and workmanship details could be seen clearly; far more advanced than he'd thought. As they walked silently along the cobbles Kingston was gaining a much greater appreciation of the extent of excavation and engineering that had gone into the construction of the catacombs – and all of it by hand. It seemed unlikely that the monks could have done it unassisted.

Soon they reached the point where the halls branched off to the left and right; also where the temporary lighting ran out. As they continued down the central hall with Kingston holding the lamp aloft, the surroundings took on a more sinister turn. With their shadows dancing off the walls and pitch darkness only several feet ahead of them, they were walking into the unknown. The brittle silence amplified even the tiniest sound: a pebble dislodged somewhere behind them, a creak of what might be a door sagging on its hinge, or a single drip from condensation or leaching on the walls.

'You sure you want to keep going?' Jamie said, in a loud whisper, as they passed yet another room on their right.

'I think we should, Jamie. Are you okay?'

'Yes. I'm fine.'

'I don't think it can go on much farther. We're a hell of a long way in as it is. It has to end soon.'

No sooner had he said the words than the hall took a sharp right turn. Round the corner, the hall was considerably wider. The ceiling was higher, too – like a gallery. A half-open door appeared on their left. Kingston shoved it with his foot and walked in, holding the lamp as high as he could. He caught his breath. This room was different from all the others, markedly different. To start with, a metal conduit ran up one wall and across the ceiling. In the centre of the ceiling was a wide, cone-shaped lampshade, the electric light bulb clearly visible. But that wasn't all. The few pieces of furniture in the room were all modern. No question that they were from the twentieth century.

Jamie had joined him. 'What do you make of this then?' he asked.

'Weird. Looks like it was an office of some kind.' She looked up at the ceiling. 'I wonder where the electricity comes from?'

'I can only guess it comes from the house. We're probably standing right underneath it.'

Jamie pulled the door back. 'There's a switch here,' she said, flicking it up and down.

'Probably disconnected.'

'Right. What do you think this was, then?'

'I'm not sure. My guess is that, at one point, Ryder

discovered these underground rooms and decided that they would make the perfect place to run his art-dealing operation. Can you think of a better set-up?'

'If you're right, then chances are that they were accessible from the house.'

'Almost certainly, I would say.'

'So we should be able to get into the house from down here, then?'

'Unless he closed it all up.'

They left the room and continued along the gallery and entered another room on the right. Save for a six-drawer metal filing cabinet pushed up against a corner, it was empty. This room, too, was wired for electricity.

Kingston had a gut feeling that, in the next few minutes, they would discover Ryder's secret cache: where he stored his paintings while they were waiting to be sold on the illicit international market. When they finally opened that door, would they find any paintings? Would Fox and his client Girard be proved right? Would it reveal anything more about the mystery surrounding Ryder? Contemplating these thoughts, Kingston ushered Jamie out of the room and they continued along the gallery. How much farther could it go on, he wondered?

The answer came sooner than expected. Ahead, the light from the lamp was dancing off a wall some thirty feet in front of them, blocking their path. As they approached, a hollow feeling welled up in Kingston's gut, the kind when the winner's name is announced and it's not yours. Glancing sideways at Jamie, he could see that she was experiencing a similar emotion.

Now that they were closer, they could see that the gallery ended in a solid wall of stone. Kingston took a deep breath, exhaled loudly and put a hand up to his forehead. This was it then: a dead-end in the true sense of the word.

Chapter Twenty-Two

Kingston stood staring at the wall, the lamp hanging by his side. His reaction was confusion, bewilderment and exasperation. He had come all that way to find this?

The disappointment registered on his face was clearly obvious to Jamie, who had chosen not to say anything but instead had gone up to the wall to examine it more closely. As he watched her studying the grey stone, he tried hard to overcome the bitter taste of defeat that in a few seconds had deflated his optimism like a shrivelled balloon. All that was left now was to retrace their steps back to the chapel. Holding the lamp up higher he went over to join Jamie.

She turned to face him. 'Look at this,' she said, placing a hand on the wall just above her head. 'The stone is the same but the cement or plaster looks newer on this section.'

Kingston held the lamp close to the wall, moving it horizontally along the line of the cement. 'You're right,' he said. 'It's been sealed up. I bet this is where the entrance to the house was. Behind, there's probably a flight of steps like those in the chapel that lead up to a room in the house. It makes sense. It was relatively easy to run electricity down here to this end of the catacombs. And once that was in, he could run power tools, a simple heating and ventilation system – the works.'

'Maybe his hiding place was the other side of the wall. That way he could still get to it from the house.'

'It's possible. But I still think it makes more sense for it to be on this side. That way the room would be completely closed off from either end.'

'So where is it, then?'

Kingston shook his head. 'I wish I knew.'

'I suppose we'd best start back, then.' She reached a hand out. 'Why don't you let me carry that back,' she said, taking the lamp.

Kingston sighed. 'Not much else to do here by the looks of it. At least for now, anyway.'

'One thing's for sure. Your friend Ferguson is going to have the surprise of his life when he sees all this. Can you imagine?'

'I'll call him when we get back to the house. I'm sorely tempted to call Chadwick, too, but that can wait.'

They had reached the door of the second room, the one with the filing cabinet. 'Let's take another look,' said Kingston. He pushed the large iron-bound door all the way back and entered. Jamie followed. A quick glance told them that they hadn't missed anything the first time: the room was empty.

Jamie looked up at the glass lampshade hanging from the ceiling. Remembering the first room where she had found the light switch behind the door, she walked over and pulled the door back, fully expecting to see a switch. 'Jesus – Lawrence,' she gasped. 'This is it! I think I've found it. We just didn't look hard enough the first time.'

Behind the entrance door, hidden when it swung back against the wall, was another, smaller, much newer door.

Two steps and Kingston was at her side.

'My God! This *has* to be it.'

Together, they studied the door, Kingston caressing the smooth surface as if it were the patina of a fine antique. There was no question that it had been installed for security purposes. With no handle or doorknob, the only feature on the flat surface was a circular brass key escutcheon the size of a 10p coin. The key to open it would have to be small, like a padlock key. Kingston traced his hand over the surface then knocked on it with his knuckles. 'Sounds like metal,' he said. 'Hard to tell.'

'How are we going to open it?'

'Get a locksmith down here – or take a stab at trying to drill through it, I guess.'

'Isn't that difficult?'

'It is. Damned tricky. If you don't know precisely what you're doing, you can bugger up the lock and then you'll never get it open.'

Jamie watched while Kingston examined the escutcheon again. Staring at it, he was actually thinking back to a time over thirty years ago when he was a captain in the army. Whatever had possessed him at the time he couldn't imagine but he'd done a stint with Special Forces which, as part of its rigorous training regime in covert operations, survival training and commando techniques, had included, of all things, a course on picking and opening locks. Could he still remember how to do it? He knew that there was an optimum position to drill – and only one. It could also require two different types of drill bit. Jamie broke his train of thought.

'Do we have a cordless drill?'

'I'm sure there's one in the workshop.'

Jamie touched his arm. 'Let's get out of here. It's starting to give me the creeps. We can talk about it on the way back.'

They left the room and retraced their steps back to the chapel. Within ten minutes they were back at the house, and Kingston took off to find a drill. Luckily, Eric Newsome, the gardener in charge of the vegetable garden, was in the workshop when Kingston arrived. He found a drill immediately but the only drill bits they could find were for wood. Kingston called Jamie on his mobile and told her he was taking off for Taunton to buy the drill bits..

Driving into town, Kingston mulled over the other options. The simplest would be to get a locksmith to open the door. But the last thing he wanted was to have to take a stranger down into the catacombs. Nobody would be able to keep a secret like that very long. The other choice, of course, was to call Chadwick, get the police involved and have them open it. But whatever was behind that door, Jamie should see it first. It seemed the right thing to do. Once they knew just what it was – if indeed there was anything – then they could decide what best to do next. He walked hurriedly into the town centre from the car park, fingers crossed that he could open the mysterious door.

With several different size and type high-speed drill bits in a small brown bag on the passenger seat, Kingston headed back to Wickersham. When he alerted Jamie on his mobile that he was on his way back, she reminded him of his two o'clock staff meeting. These were frequent get-togethers at which he, Robin Gilchrist – the man Kingston had hired as the temporary head gardener – and Eric Newsome would give progress reports. The meeting also gave the team an opportunity to ask questions and air problems. Kingston asked her to postpone it.

Mid-afternoon, armed with a cordless Bosch drill driver, the bits, his tool bag and protective eyewear, Kingston went to the house to meet Jamie. While waiting for her to get ready, he called Ferguson to tell him about their find but couldn't reach him. He left a message saying he had some very important news about the chapel and would call back later. He signed off saying, 'You won't believe it, Roger. It's awesome.'

Shortly after four, they took off for the catacombs.

Kingston lined up the drill bit as he'd been instructed all those years ago. On his first attempt, the bit skidded off the hard surface, chattering against the steel door. Next time he applied more pressure and the bit started to eat its way into the steel plate, sprinkling fine shavings to the floor. Jamie stood by watching, saying very little.

Kingston took a brief rest to cool the drill and bit and started drilling again. In less than a minute he felt the drill bit clear the lock and spin freely. He took a hesitant glance at Jamie then pushed open the door. With Jamie holding the lamp, they entered. The room was much larger than Kingston had anticipated, twice the size of either of the other two rooms. Built-in furniture covered the surrounding walls. Facing them was a desk with drawers and lower cupboards on either side. Deep worktables ran the length of the walls on the left and right. Below the tables were horizontal rows of shallow map drawers. Above the work surface, the walls were covered with a grid of vertical wooden racks like those used in framing and art shops. All of them were empty. It was obvious what the shelves were designed to contain – almost certainly, paintings.

Jamie had started to open cupboards and pull out drawers. From where he was standing, Kingston could see that they, too, were empty. Ryder or somebody had obviously done a good job cleaning the place out. There was hardly a speck of dirt to be seen anywhere. As he stood there, looking around the empty room, the hollow feeling that had seized him earlier came back. This time it didn't go away. He knew this last room was where their search must end. It was as if Ryder was taunting him from the grave. He had to face it, either the paintings were here or there were none. It was as easy as that.

'I'm sorry,' said Jamie, softly.

Kingston snapped out of his thoughts. 'I know,' he said. 'I was *so* certain that this was it.'

'I know you don't want to give up, Lawrence, but it looks like we have no other choice. Do we?'

He summoned a disheartened smile. 'You're right. I don't think we do.'

Jamie had put the lamp on the floor while she took off her wool cap and tousled her hair. 'To be honest, Lawrence, I'll be glad to get out of here. I'm beginning to feel a little claustrophobic. God knows how those monks could stay down here for long.'

Around them, a wide circle of light illuminated the

flagstone floor. As Kingston bent down to pick up the lamp, he couldn't miss seeing the horizontal crevice between the stones at his feet. He moved the lamp to his left and followed the crevice where it took a right angle away from him, continued for another five feet or so then took another right angle turn. Holding the lamp slightly higher, he could now see that the crevice formed a uniform rectangle.

Jamie had seen it, too, and bent down next to him. 'What do you think?' she said.

Kingston was already prising between the stones with one of the tools of the Swiss army knife from his tool bag.

'There's something underneath here – a trapdoor most likely.' He grunted, working at loosening the stone. 'These stones are meant to be raised,' he said.

Once the first flagstone was removed, the others came out easily. When the last stone came out, they were looking at a rectangular wooden trapdoor. It was locked in place on two sides by swivel iron brackets. Recessed in its centre was a circular black iron handle. Kingston rotated the brackets, put three fingers in the handle and, straining audibly, lifted the heavy trapdoor. Jamie helped him to move it aside on to the floor.

Kingston held the lamp over the opening revealing a wooden ladder that disappeared into the hole. 'Hand me the flashlight, Jamie,' he said, leaning over the opening. He took it from her and shone it down in a circular motion. 'Looks like a storage area. Not very big.' He handed her back the flashlight. 'I'll go down and take a look. Hand me the lamp when I get on the ladder.'

Gripping the lamp carefully, he reached the bottom rung and looked around. The room was no more than twelve feet in either direction, the ceiling barely an inch above Kingston's head. The walls were stone and he saw at a glance that the only way out was through the trapdoor.

A filthy oriental rug covered most of the hard dirt floor.

He found that curious, since anything and everything of value had been removed from all the rooms they'd seen. It looked like an old Kazak from what little he could see of the pattern. As consolation, at least they'd found something of value, he thought. The only other items in the room were a large flat wooden crate and a small metal steamer trunk with leather handles. It was padlocked. He tried lifting the crate to see if there were any markings on it. It was not as heavy as he had imagined.

'Find anything?' asked Jamie, leaning over the edge of the trapdoor opening.

'Could be. I'm not sure. Come down and take a look? Oh, and bring down the toolkit, would you.' He put the lamp on the floor closer to the ladder so that she could see her way down.

Jamie sat on the trunk while Kingston went to work opening the crate, using a large screwdriver and a hammer. The crate was about five by four feet and eighteen inches deep. About the right size for paintings, Kingston knew, but this time he wasn't getting his hopes up. The rasping of nails being prised from wood filled the small room and soon he had the lid free. Jamie, at his side, held up both hands, fingers crossed. He lifted the lid and put it on the floor. Inside, all that could be seen was a snug-fitting blanket tied with string, a cushion to protect whatever was inside. He tried to lift it out it by squeezing his fingers down the sides but couldn't. Moving to one end of the crate, Kingston raised it to the vertical position then tilted it, hoping that the contents would slide out. They didn't.

As Kingston shook the heavy crate trying to dislodge its contents, Jamie was on the other side, her hands out, ready to prevent whatever was inside from falling to the ground. One mighty shake and the blanket-wrapped object was finally free, falling into Jamie's hands. He lowered the crate and she slid the bundle across to him. Quickly, he cut the string and removed the blanket, throwing it aside. On the

222

floor in front of them was a metal case similar to that used by professional photographers to transport cameras and lenses, only much larger. The case was bound with heavy wire to prevent it from opening. Now his pulse was racing. These *were* the paintings. They had to be.

Jamie broke the silence. 'This is getting like one of those Chinese box puzzles.'

'It is, but we're almost there, Jamie. This case *has* to hold the paintings,' he said, snipping the wires, unlatching the two chrome clasps on the lid. He lifted the lid, the underside lined with a foam material, exposing yet another package, this time, a tightly sealed plastic sheath. He lifted it out, carefully cutting the plastic with his knife. As the plastic casing was pulled away, it revealed three stretched canvases, each separated by a sheet of plywood. Kingston stole a quick look at Jamie. He removed the top piece of plywood, picked up the top painting and held it up facing them.

He couldn't believe what he saw.

Chapter Twenty-Three

Kingston took his eyes off the painting just long enough to catch Jamie frowning. 'What is it?' she asked.

'Rubbish, that's what it is. I hope this isn't Ryder's idea of a joke. This is bloody awful.'

They were looking at an oil or acrylic painting about sixteen inches by twenty-four. The scene was a Parisian street in the rain, with vivid multicolour vertical brush-strokes where street and window lights reflected off the rain-slick pavement and road. It was the kind of garish art that is churned out for the tourist trade, peddled at street fairs and in lesser quality galleries all over Europe.

Kingston removed the next plywood panel and picked up the second painting. It was no better. Slightly smaller in size, it was a landscape in the style of Seurat. He grimaced – amateurish would have been a kindly description. The composition was dreadful, the colours lifeless. He put it aside and picked up the third painting. A quick glance was enough. It was equally hackneyed and lacking in any painterly talent.

'These certainly aren't what Fox had in mind,' he sighed.

'If they're worthless – and even I can see that, now – why would Ryder or anyone go to all the trouble to conceal and protect them so well? It makes no sense.'

'I don't know,' Kingston muttered. He was holding up the tacky Parisian painting again. This time he examined the edges of the canvas where it was affixed to the wooden stretcher. He knew that a relatively simple method used to disguise paintings was to paint over them. It was a technique used effectively over the centuries, one all too familiar to art-theft and insurance investigators. Only recently, he'd read an account of the inspired and courageous actions of an art-loving Afghani doctor who, single-handedly, had saved over hundred paintings in the National Gallery in Kabul, disguising the works by painting new scenes over them. His artistic camouflage was sufficient to hoodwink the Taliban religious police who would otherwise have destroyed the artworks, as they had thousands of others during their five-year rule. Had he been caught the penalty might well have been execution.

Kingston knew, however, that this was not the case with the painting in his hand, nor the other two. They were too detailed and the paint too heavily applied. The wooden stretcher was also relatively new. Attempting to remove the paint would destroy, or damage beyond repair, any painting that might be underneath. He turned the canvas on its side. Not unexpectedly, the staples looked fairly new, in keeping with the canvas that showed little signs of age. He put the painting down and picked up the landscape, staring at it, perplexed. As Jamie had said, it didn't make sense.

'Why don't we see what's in the trunk?'

'Right, but let me try something first.' Kingston had pulled out his Swiss army knife and opened the large blade. He started prising out one of the staples. One by one he worked his way round the stretcher until they were all removed and the canvas was free. Jamie watched, saying nothing, while he scrutinized the canvas. He turned it over and was focusing on one corner. 'Bring the lamp over here would you, Jamie?'

He held the edge of the canvas up close to the light and poked at it gently with the knife. 'Well, I'll be damned,' he muttered. 'I think we've got two canvases here.' Kingston had switched to a smaller blade and was working it down the edge of the fabric. As he did so, the canvas started to separate. Gripping each edge, he carefully peeled the two pieces apart. Setting aside the phony Seurat, he held up the other canvas to the light where Jamie could also see it.

'Can you see the signature, Jamie?'

'Turn it a little bit . . . there. No, I can't quite make it out.'

'It's C. Pissarro – Camille Pissarro. And if it's the real thing – which I'm ninety-nine per cent sure it is – it's worth a mint.'

In turn, Kingston removed the top canvas from the other two paintings. Underneath one was a Matisse portrait of a peasant woman and under the other, a winter landscape that he guessed to be by either Signac or possibly Sisley: the signature was not immediately apparent.

'What do you think they're worth?' Jamie asked.

'I've really no idea but if I were to hazard a guess, the three of them together, in the many millions – twenty, thirty – could be much more.'

'My God. Why didn't Ryder sell them?'

'Maybe he couldn't. There was a time when the market in fine art sales took a dive. There's also the possibility that these three paintings were on circulated lists of stolen works. That would make them doubly difficult to unload.' Kingston had replaced the wooden lid on the crate and laid out the three canvases on top of it with the Pissarro uppermost. 'Perhaps, for whatever reason, Ryder decided to keep these three,' he said, finding it hard to take his eyes off the Impressionist masterpiece.

'If he did, why would he keep them sealed in a crate in a locked room? One would think that he would want to have them exhibited so that he could enjoy them.'

'Maybe they were at one time. Hanging in one of the upstairs rooms of the house where nobody would ever see them.' Kingston was carefully putting the three canvases back in the metal case. 'Who knows? There could be all kinds of explanations.'

Jamie was on her haunches studying the padlock on the

steamer trunk. 'I wonder what's in here?' she said. 'It has to be something valuable or Ryder wouldn't have it locked up here, would he?'

Kingston turned the padlock toward the light to get a better look at it. 'Valuable, yes – but perhaps something that Ryder didn't want anybody to know about.' He took out the Swiss army knife again and, with his ear close to the padlock, he began picking away at the lock with the knife's tiny probe tool. After a silent minute, broken only by an occasional mumble or grunt, he finally gave up. 'It's a pin-tumbler lock but it looks like it's got spool pins which makes it damned near impossible for someone like me to pick. We'll have to drill it open.'

Kingston was about to reach for the drill in the nearby tool bag when his hands froze and his pulse skipped a beat. Suddenly there was another light, brighter and moving, shining on the surface of the metal trunk. Then, before he could turn to see where it was coming from, he heard Jamie gasp just as the man spoke.

'You can pass those canvases up to me, if you would, please.'

Kingston stood, turned and looked up to the top of the ladder. With the flashlight shining directly into his eyes, he couldn't see who was holding it. The voice was not familiar.

'It's Fox,' Jamie whispered. 'I swear it.'

Kingston placed a hand on her arm. 'You may have to come down here and get them,' Kingston replied, shielding his eyes.

'That won't be necessary. Just hand them up, please.'

Fox moved the flashlight off Kingston to Jamie. 'Roll them up carefully, loosely if you would, hand them to the lady and have her bring them up the ladder.'

Kingston could now see more clearly. He flinched and stepped back. Fox was holding a small pistol and Kingston was looking right up the barrel.

Jamie glanced at Kingston, waiting for his lead. He said

nothing, his face like granite, eyes glowering. It was as if his mind were in overdrive.

Fox spoke again. His voice was calm, almost matter of fact. 'Don't force me to use this thing. I'll ask nicely one more time.'

Kingston let go of her arm and turned to the open metal case. He took out the canvases and took two steps to the packing crate where, with his back to Jamie, he laid the canvases down flat and slowly started to roll them up. Turning back to her he held the rolled canvases in his hand, clutched to his chest as if he was having serious thoughts about giving them up. He had no choice, though. Risking his own life was one thing but a bullet fired in these close quarters could easily endanger Jamie, too. He looked up to see Fox's face, to look him in the eyes, but the flashlight beam was back on him. All he saw was a halo of light surrounding a shadowy figure.

'Give them to the lady,' Fox said calmly.

Kingston handed the canvases to Jamie, letting his hands fall to his side.

'Hurry up, for Christ's sake,' Fox snapped.

Jamie stepped up to the fourth rung of the ladder and stopped, offering the canvases with her outstretched arm.

'Bring them all the way up.'

Jamie took a nervous backward glance at Kingston then continued up the ladder to where her head was level with the opening. She handed Fox the canvases. Stooping, he took them and stepped back. 'You can go back down, now,' he said.

Kingston watched Jamie descend and looked up at Fox again. It appeared that he had put down the gun but was still holding the flashlight. Kneeling, in full sight through the opening, he was shoving the hefty trapdoor cover with his free hand, sliding it over the opening.

'Sorry, doctor, but we're going to have to leave you down here to stew for a while.'

228

'You bastard, you . . .'

'Oh, and those tools, please. Have the lady hand the bag up, would you?'

Kingston handed the tool bag to Jamie, watching silently as she took them up the ladder and handed them through the half-open trapdoor. As they disappeared, the heavy wooden cover slid in jerks across the opening. It finally came to a stop, leaving a two-inch gap through which Kingston could see only the dancing light from Fox's flashlight.

'Sorry we never got the chance to meet, doctor,' Fox said through the narrow gap. His voice was calm, as though he really meant what he was saying. 'We would have had a lot to talk about – more than you would ever imagine.'

Before Kingston had a chance to say anything, he saw the gap vanish as the cover slammed shut and Fox's parting words echoed down. 'Get comfortable, won't you, because you could be down there for a long time. A very long time.'

Chapter Twenty-Four

The minute Fox locked the trapdoor Kingston was at the top of the ladder examining the underside, thumping it in different places with his fist. He remembered the two black rotating metal brackets that locked the door in place and knew that it would take extreme leverage and force to break them. Soon, he backed down the ladder and joined Jamie who had been unsuccessfully trying to call out on her mobile. Though her face was noticeably pale, he was relieved to see that she appeared reasonably calm.

'No signal, I'm afraid,' she said.

'I'm not surprised. These walls are probably two feet thick and then there are the walls up above, too.'

'How much longer do you think the lamp will last, Lawrence? Perhaps we should turn it off for a while.'

'I wouldn't worry. We should be good for at least another six hours or so but I don't think we're going to need anywhere near that long.'

'I know you're trying to make me feel better but I don't mind telling you, I'm scared. Really scared. To hell with the paintings now, Fox can have them. We're in serious . . .' Her voice trailed off and she lowered her head. 'I'm sorry,' she said, looking up at him again. 'Forget what I just said.'

Kingston took her arm and steered her to the trunk. 'Here, come and sit down,' he said softly.

She sat looking up at him, her eyes unflinching, no longer showing any visible signs of distress. Kingston wondered how many other young women would be able to exercise such self-control given the same terrifying circumstances.

'Fox doesn't have the paintings,' he said calmly.

'What do you mean? I handed them over to him.'

'No you didn't. I gave you the canvases that covered the real ones.' His face broke into an impish smile. 'Fox has the Paris street scene and the other two losers. The real ones I slipped behind the crate.'

'Brilliant. You sure had me fooled.' She looked at him for a long moment, obviously weighing the implications. 'So, sooner or later, once Fox finds out he's been tricked, he's going to come back, right?'

Kingston nodded. 'Hopefully sooner rather than later. Thing is, when he does, we must be ready for him. He'll be furious – my guess is that he won't hesitate to use that gun if he has to. But that could all be in our favour.'

Her brief moment of elation over, Jamie's expression was sombre again. 'In our favour! What will he do when he comes back, then? We're sitting ducks down here.'

'First we have to find a place to hide the canvases.' He reached behind the crate and took out the three loose canvases. 'Hold these for a moment, would you?' he said, handing them to her. He took off his jacket, laying it across the wooden crate, the inside lining facing up. 'This should work for the time being,' he said.

Jamie watched as he smoothed out the back section of the nylon lining. Neatly hidden by pleats was a long zipper that extended all the way across the back lining. 'It's called a "poacher's pocket",' he said, taking the canvases from Jamie and carefully folding them loosely in two so as not to risk cracking any of the paint. He winked. 'Big enough to hide a brace of partridges.' He slid the paintings into the pocket and closed the zipper, folding the pleats back in place. 'There,' he said, looking up, satisfied. 'That should out-fox Fox.'

231

'Clever,' said Jamie. 'So what are we going to do when he gets back?'

'I'll tell you in a minute,' he said, going to the ladder and climbing to the top.

She watched as he took the knife out of his pocket and started to lever the screwdriver blade under one of the metal straps that secured the ladder to the ledge of the trapdoor. In thirty seconds the strap was swinging free. 'Don't know what I'd do without this little baby,' he said, moving over to the second strap. 'Glad they used nails and not bolts,' he mumbled. Soon, the second strap was loose. Slowly he descended the ladder that was now movable. At the bottom, he gripped the rung level with his knees with both hands and suddenly jerked the ladder upwards. Sliding on the edge of the ledge surrounding the trapdoor, it struck the underside of the door with considerable force making a loud thump. He put the ladder back in position, looked at it for a second, then said, 'Next time Fox pokes his nasty face down here, he's going to regret it.'

'I'm starting to get the idea,' said Jamie.

'It's not the greatest,' said Kingston, 'but given the vast number of choices, it's the best I can come up with on the spur of the moment. It'll depend mostly on timing and a simple cue from you which we can work out.'

For the next couple of minutes, Kingston demonstrated how they would deal with Fox. He went over it twice to make sure each of them knew exactly what had to be done, then they settled in for the wait.

Kingston sat on the wooden crate, Jamie on the trunk, ready to get into their positions the minute they heard the slightest sounds overhead.

'I'm sorry that I got you into this damnable situation, Jamie,' Kingston said, shaking his head.

'Look, Lawrence, neither of us had the faintest idea that there could be any real danger in coming down here – nothing like this – so don't blame yourself. In a way,

232

I should carry the blame for not having seen through Fox, not believing that the paintings could be here.'

Kingston shrugged. 'Under different circumstances we might have been able to make a deal with Fox. Let him have the paintings if he would agree to walk away. Somehow I don't think that's an option any more. The man's a psychopath and he knows damned well that, given the chance, the first thing we'd do now is to call the police.'

'I know it's too late now, Lawrence, but perhaps it would have been a good idea to let someone know we were coming down here. Not a soul knows we're here.'

'There are quite a few things I wish I'd done differently, Jamie. I regret not having been more forthright with you and keeping stuff to myself. In all fairness, Ferguson should have been in on our discovery, too. He helped us find all of this.' He paused, looking up the ladder, thinking. 'I did try to call him by the way,' he said, turning back to her.

A minute or so passed as they were left to their own thoughts. Kingston was tempted to test the waters and tell her how much he had come to value and enjoy her companionship, how his feelings had changed towards her over the last weeks, just to see how she would respond, curious as to whether his feelings might be reciprocated. Springing it on her suddenly seemed inappropriate. Perhaps he could segue into it once he'd broached the question of their eventual parting, which he thought about constantly now.

Would she would ask him to stay on after the gardens were opened, to help with the vineyard and the winery? Now he'd had time to think it over, that prospect was both appealing and challenging. He prided himself on knowing a lot about the noble grape but to actually plant a vineyard and work alongside a professional winemaker would be an experience and an education that would never come his way again. While he pondered these questions his ears were alert for any sounds from above. Quickly he abandoned the idea of bringing any of it up. It was foolish of him to have thought of it in the first place. The only thing that mattered now was getting out of the damned tomb that they were in.

Kingston looked at his watch. Twenty-five minutes had passed since Fox had left. By this time he could be miles away. Maybe he hadn't bothered to look at the canvases after all. Unlikely, but it *was* possible. He'd undoubtedly seen them lying on the top of the crate, with the Pissarro on top, and would have no idea that a switch had taken place.

'Hell,' he muttered under his breath.

Jamie, whose chin was resting on her cupped hands, her eyes fixed on the floor, looked up at him. 'What?'

'Nothing. I just hope to God that he's not driving to London or somewhere bloody miles away before he looks at those paintings.'

'If he was telling the truth when I met with him, he could be taking them back to France. To the dealer.'

'Girard,' Kingston muttered instinctively.

Jamie sat up and lightly massaged her forehead. 'If he is, that would be catastrophic.'

'No, don't you worry, Jamie, he'll look at them. He has to – thirty million pounds' worth of art? He won't be able to resist it.'

'Sounds like you may be right, Lawrence.'

'What?' As he looked up at her the saffron light from the lamp glinted Vermeer-like on the whites of her eyes. She was looking up unblinking at the trapdoor. He heard it, too, now – a faint shuffle.

There it was again. No doubt about it. Someone was up there.

Kingston looked at Jamie, put his index finger to his lips and quickly moved up against the wall behind the ladder where he would be out of Fox's line of sight when he looked through the trapdoor opening. Jamie remained sitting on the trunk that they'd positioned about eight feet in

234

front of the ladder. When Fox removed the trapdoor he couldn't miss seeing her.

A few more seconds of silence – and then the unexpected.

A knocking on the trapdoor.

Jamie, biting her lip, looked across at Kingston. He frowned and motioned for her to be quiet and still.

More knocking, this time harder.

Then the barely audible grind of the brackets being slid aside.

Kingston watched as the trapdoor was lifted and a shadowy head leaned over the opening right above him.

'Jamie?'

It wasn't Fox's voice.

Kingston stepped around to the front of the ladder. It was only one word but the voice sounded familiar. Ferguson? He looked up. Hell's bells. It *was* Roger Ferguson.

Jamie was on her feet, clasping her hands to her head. 'Thank God you didn't wait for an invitation,' she said.

'You're both damned lucky I found you,' he replied. 'Who on earth locked you in this place?'

'Let's get the hell out of here first and then we'll tell you everything,' said Kingston.

Jamie was already at the top of the ladder, Roger helping her up into the room. Carrying his jacket and the lamp, Kingston was right behind her.

'How in the world did you find us?' Kingston asked.

'It was the tool bag.'

'Of course, no reason for him to take it,' said Kingston. 'You got my message?'

'I did. I called back but your answering machine's not working. After a message like yours, you didn't think I was going to sit on my hands and wait for an engraved invitation, did you? So I drove over. Neither you nor Jamie was around and China didn't know where you were, so I thought – well, it struck me that if your discovery was so "awesome" as you put it, you would be at the chapel, so that's where I went. When I saw that vertical pew and the stairway . . . well, I don't mind telling you, it was one hell of a surprise.'

Jamie tugged Roger's sleeve. 'We have to go, quickly,' she said.

'All right. Anyway, it was bloody dark looking down those steps, so I went and borrowed this flashlight from China. If it hadn't been for the tool bag sitting in the middle of the room, I might have missed the trapdoor altogether. One hardly expects to find a Bosch drill in the middle of a subterranean medieval chamber. If it weren't for that –'

'Look,' said Jamie, 'we don't have time to stand around and chat about it. Fox could come back any minute – he's got a gun – and then there'll be three of us down there,' she said, nodding at the trapdoor hole.

'Fox?' Roger asked.

'Never mind, we'll tell you later,' Jamie replied, testily.

'We'd better not leave that trunk,' said Kingston, putting on his coat, making sure the canvases were flat in the poacher's pocket. 'Give me a hand with it, will you, Roger?'

Kingston went back down into the room and dragged the small trunk across the floor to the foot of the ladder. What was inside, he wondered? What could possibly be so important to Ryder? With a grunt he hoisted it up on to his shoulder and started up the ladder. At the top Roger gripped the handle and the two of them manoeuvred the trunk over the trapdoor ledge and on to the floor.

With Kingston and Ferguson carrying the trunk between them and Jamie a few paces ahead holding the lamp and carrying the tool bag, they started back to the chapel.

Nothing was said as they hurried along the corridors, Jamie looking over her shoulder now and then, careful not to get too far ahead.

Kingston's mind was on the trunk. What on earth could it contain? More paintings, possibly, but from the painstaking manner in which the other three had been sealed and crated, it seemed unlikely. Whatever it was must be valuable. He started to imagine possibilities when he realized that Roger had suddenly stopped. So had Jamie. She was standing motionless a dozen paces ahead of them one hand held up, palm facing them. She looked over her shoulder. 'Someone's coming,' she whispered, just loudly enough for them to hear. 'It has to be Fox.'

Now they could all hear the sound of rapidly approaching footsteps.

'Come back, Jamie – here,' Kingston whispered. 'There's a room just behind us on the right.'

The three retraced their steps and stumbled into the empty room.

'Quick, put the lamp out,' Kingston said in a stage whisper.

The three stood like statues in the pitch-black stillness behind the half-open door, the trunk beside them. The footsteps, part running, were now very close. In seconds, a faint glimmer of bouncing light illuminated the rectangular gap of the door. It grew brighter to where they could read each other's expressions, all tense, fearful. Rooted to the spot, they heard the footsteps pass and the glow from Fox's flashlight gradually diminished.

'Let's get out of here fast,' said Kingston, gripping one of the trunk handles. 'It's only a matter of minutes before he discovers we've gone and comes charging back.'

Jamie bent down to pick up the lamp.

'Forget it, Jamie. Just use your flashlight.'

They darted from the room half running, half stumbling and made their way along the last stretch of corridor. Up ahead, at last, they could see daylight coming through the trapezium-shaped opening of the pew.

Jamie was first to the top of the steps. She shone the flashlight down so that Kingston and Roger could have as much light as possible as they heaved the trunk up. Roger helped lift the trunk up on to Kingston's shoulder where

Kingston steadied and adjusted it for a second, then started up the narrow steps. On the fifth step he faltered. The trunk was slipping off his shoulder. He leaned forward trying to correct it but knew he could not prevent it from falling. 'Quick, grab the trunk, Roger,' he said. 'I'm going to drop it.'

As the trunk slid unchecked off his arched back, Kingston turned to see Roger caught off balance on the step immediately behind him, grappling with it. For a brief moment he had a grasp of the trunk but couldn't hold on, more because of its bulk than its weight. Falling backwards, he let go of the trunk, pushing it away from him, and fell hard on the stone floor. Kingston cringed as the trunk crashed down inches from Roger's head and did a cartwheel before coming to rest, upright and undamaged.

Kingston rushed to his side, Jamie right behind.

'Are you okay?' Kingston asked, kneeling by Roger's side.

Roger had slowly raised himself and was half sitting supported by an outstretched arm with one leg tucked awkwardly under the other. For a horrible moment Kingston thought his leg might be broken.

'I think so,' he replied, rubbing the back of his head. He shifted his position slightly and winced. 'Bloody hell. I'm sorry.'

'Let's get you up and out of here,' said Kingston. 'Put your arm round my neck.'

With Jamie supporting him on one side and Kingston on the other, they got Roger to a standing position.

'I think I'm fine,' said Roger taking a couple of tentative steps.

'Thank God for that,' said Jamie. 'That trunk came awfully close.'

Kingston had a grip on one of the trunk's leather handles and was starting to drag it toward the steps. Jamie and Roger watched and waited silently as Kingston reached the bottom step.

'That'll be far enough. All of you, stay right where you are.' The hollow voice came from behind, echoing off the walls.

Fox stepped out of the darkness of the corridor. In one hand he held a flashlight, in the other his gun levelled at Kingston.

'Quite a trick, doctor. I have to give you credit.' He came closer, motioning to Jamie and Roger to move away from the trunk. 'Now, if you don't mind, I'd like the real paintings. I take it they're in there,' he said, his eyes glancing to the trunk.

'We don't know,' Kingston replied.

Fox laughed. 'You don't *know*? Don't patronize me. You'd hardly be dragging that thing with you if it didn't contain something valuable, now would you?'

'I told you, Fox. We have no idea *what's* in there. We haven't opened it.'

Fox's eyes darted back to the trunk and the padlock.

'Why don't you just do that now, then? You seem to be adept at drilling locks. Or do you have the key?'

'There is no key,' said Kingston.

'Liar!'

'There is no damned key,' Kingston shouted.

For a moment, Fox looked flummoxed. He looked at Jamie. 'Where's the drill?' he snapped.

'Up there,' Jamie replied, pointing to the top of the steps.

'Then get it.'

Jamie turned and started up the steps.

'Wait!' Fox said. 'Don't be stupid and try to make a run for it, woman. If you do, you may never see these two alive again.'

Jamie ran up the steps and returned with the tool bag.

'Okay, doctor,' said Fox, 'open the padlock.'

Kingston took the drill and triggered it on and off quickly. The small carbon bit was still in there. Gripping the lock with his left hand and twisting it into a fixed position to stop it from slipping, he started to drill. In less than a minute the shackle came free.

Fox moved closer, the gun in one hand trained on Kingston's back, the flashlight in the other aimed at the trunk. 'Open it up,' he said.

Kingston gripped the lid with both hands and lifted it. Looking down into the trunk, he smiled.

Chapter Twenty-Five

'Take it all out, damn it! Empty the bloody thing!' Fox shouted, inching closer.

Kingston glanced briefly over his shoulder and started to remove the contents of the trunk, two and three pieces at a time. Soon, on the floor beside him was a growing pile of framed pictures. A glittering assortment of sterling, ivory, wood, gilt, bronze and silver finish frames. Nearly all of them held photos of individuals or family groups. A number of the subjects were men in military officer uniforms. Next, Kingston started to remove all manner of documents. Some looked like letters, bundled together with string or elastic bands. There were folders, cigar boxes and document cases filled with old papers. When the trunk was empty, Kingston stood and turned to Fox. 'That's all of it,' he said.

Fox motioned with the gun for Kingston to move aside and stepped up to the trunk and looked down. 'It's impossible,' he muttered. He swung round and stepped to within a foot of Kingston, glowering at him, fuming. 'Where are the goddamned paintings? What have you done with them?'

With Fox's face now inches from his and the gun pointed at his stomach, Kingston fought to stay calm. 'There were three canvases in the crate back there,' he said staring into Fox's menacing dark eyes. 'That's all. And we gave them to you.'

'You're a liar, Kingston! I saw one of those paintings and

it's not any of the three you handed over – that worthless trash. Tell me now or you'll regret it. Where the hell are they?'

'He's telling the truth,' Jamie cut in.

'*Shut up!*' Fox snapped.

'You might as well give up,' Ferguson interrupted. 'Let us all go.'

Fox didn't answer right away. He had stepped away from Kingston and was sizing him up, looking at his jacket. It was evident that the two outside pockets were far too small to contain the canvases, even ones that were tightly folded.

'Unzip your jacket,' he said.

Out of the corner of his eye, Kingston saw Jamie flinch but Fox hadn't noticed it.

Slowly Kingston unzipped the jacket.

'Open it up, all the way, so I can see inside.'

Kingston did so, revealing the lining and the two inside pockets on either side, both small and obviously empty.

After a second or so Kingston let his hands fall to his side.

'So, you're not going to tell me where you hid them? Is that it?'

Nobody answered.

'They're back there somewhere, aren't they?'

Silence.

'Answer me, damn it!'

'Why don't you go back and take a look?' said Kingston.

'Don't be smart with me.'

'Okay, we'll come with you but let Jamie go.'

'Let her go?' he scoffed. 'You really think I'm that stupid?'

Kingston was now determined to get Fox riled up. Out of the corner of his eye he had seen Roger slip the weighty ten-inch long black flashlight from his jacket pocket and conceal it behind his back. His intent was clear and it worried Kingston. If Roger was going to make an attempt to take Fox out it could be extremely risky and he'd only get one chance at it. Kingston needed to distract Fox and the only ways he could think of doing that were either to get him as infuriated and paranoid as possible or gain his attention by hinting where the paintings might be.

'Yes, I do think you're stupid. And let me tell you why.' Kingston turned away from Fox and stepped back, looking at the trunk. He needed to get Fox into a position where he wasn't looking straight on at Roger, while bringing the two of them closer.

'First of all, even if you do find these fictitious paintings – which we don't have, by the way – do you really think you're going to walk out of here scot-free? How are you going to do that? You've already committed more than one capital crime down here, enough to put you behind bars for a long time. Are you going to commit more?'

'I've had just about enough of you, Kingston,' Fox hissed. 'We're staying here till I get those paintings.'

Kingston was ready to play the only card he could come up with.

'You may be overlooking something.'

'What might that be?'

'Well, if I were concealing something valuable in a trunk I wouldn't lay it on the inside where everybody could see it.'

Fox glanced at the trunk, brows furrowed. 'What are you getting at?'

'Come on, Fox, use your bloody imagination, man.'

Fox edged a little closer to the trunk. Off to the side, Roger inched a couple of feet closer to Fox.

For a few seconds, Fox's attention was focused entirely on the trunk but the gun was still levelled at Kingston and his hand wasn't wavering.

Fox took his eyes off the trunk and looked at Kingston. 'A false bottom. It's got a false bottom. Is that it?'

'I don't know. I'm just guessing.'

'Turn the trunk on its side, so I can see, then *you* examine it.'

Kingston leaned down and upended the trunk so that the inside was visible to Fox then stood back. In the split second that Fox's attention was on the trunk, he flashed a quick look at Roger who was now within striking distance.

'Well, don't just stand there, examine it, man,' Fox said impatiently.

Kingston approached the trunk and knelt down, peering inside and tapping the base and the sides as if he knew what he was doing. He could tell, looking at the dimensions, that a false bottom was unlikely. He was about to stand and explain that to Fox when he heard the loud thump of the heavy flashlight striking Fox, followed by an ear-splitting scream of pain. Unknown to him, Roger had missed his target. The flashlight had struck Fox's shoulder near the neck. When Kingston turned, he saw Roger and Fox on the ground struggling for the gun still in Fox's grip. The flashlight was close by, too risky for him or Jamie to retrieve. She had backed off knowing that any second Kingston would become involved.

'Run for it, Jamie!' Kingston shouted. 'Call Chadwick.'

She didn't hesitate, leaping up the steps and disappearing into the chapel.

As Kingston was about to join the fray, waiting for the right moment to dive into the mêlée, the gun went off.

The blast, reverberating down the corridor, was followed by the thwack and whine of the bullet as it ricocheted off the stone floor and walls. For an instant the three of them ducked and froze, Kingston praying that the errant bullet would stray harmlessly. The brief moment was enough to allow Fox to roll free, gun still in hand. He took a wild swing with it, the barrel glancing off Roger's forehead. Roger cried out and rolled over on his side, clutching his head. Before Kingston could grapple with Fox, Fox was on his feet running up the stairs after Jamie.

Kingston helped Roger to his feet. The gash on his forehead was oozing blood but he insisted that he was all right. 'Let's get out of here,' Kingston said. 'Fox isn't stupid enough to let us escape, too. He'll be back here any moment.'

Roger nodded, touching his bleeding forehead, taking a handkerchief from his pocket.

'Take your time, Roger, keep the flashlight, I have to stop that bastard from getting his hands on Jamie.' He turned to run up the steps when a shot rang out from above.

'Jesus!' Kingston breathed.

Roger was staring up the steps holding a handkerchief to his forehead, his face ghostly. He looked as if he wanted to say something but the words wouldn't come.

Kingston bolted up the stairs into the chapel.

'Not so fast, doctor.'

Kingston stopped in his tracks.

Fox was midway down the aisle, gun in hand.

'Did you really think I'd leave you two before I got what I came for?'

'What did you do to Jamie?' Kingston snapped.

'Never mind. Start worrying about your own health, because it's not looking so good right now. Tell me where those paintings are and just maybe we can strike a deal.'

'First, I want to know where Jamie is and if she's all right.'

'We seem to be going round in circles and frankly I'm getting tired of it. I've waited a long time for you to find these paintings and I want them – *now!*'

Gripping the pew next to him, Kingston stared him down and said nothing.

Fox waved the gun at him. His eyes were boring into Kingston's, his face a mask of pent-up rage. 'All right, if you want to play this kind of game you may end up paying a big price – all three of you. Makes no difference to me.' He held the gun steady. 'Well, say something *goddamit!*'

245

'I've said all I'm going to say,' Kingston answered in a level tone. 'Tell me about Jamie and then we can talk about the paintings.'

'Listen, Kingston. I've been waiting years for this moment and I'm going to get them whatever it costs. Do you understand?'

Kingston didn't reply. Fox had told Jamie that he had learned about the paintings right after Ryder died. What did Fox mean by waiting years?

Fox spoke again.

'You don't look surprised. Yes, I've known about the paintings for a long time but unfortunately I've never been in a position to do much about them. But I knew that when you started to nose around, getting more and more inquisitive about Ryder and this place and why that ungrateful bastard left it all to a bloody American woman, of all people – I had a gut feel that sooner or later you'd find them. All it took was patience and a little help along the way. Oh yes, I know all about the paintings and I know damned well that I saw one of them in your possession in that room.'

He started to walk towards Kingston, waving the gun in the direction of the steps. 'Why don't we do this?' he said calmly. 'Let's go down and have a little talk with that idiot friend of yours. I have a feeling after that you'll want to tell me.'

Kingston descended the steps followed by Fox.

At the foot of the steps, Kingston stopped. Ferguson was gone.

'Looks like that talk may have to wait,' said Kingston.

'A foolish move on his part and he'll regret it.'

'I have to know. Is Jamie hurt? We heard the shot.'

Fox didn't reply. Clearly he was flustered, trying to figure out his next move. He moved next to the trunk and knelt beside it, looking up at Kingston. 'Step back,' he said motioning with the gun. 'Make a move and I'm going to use this.'

Kingston watched as Fox examined the inside of the trunk, glancing up every few seconds to check on him.

'You don't believe me. There is no false compartment,' said Kingston.

Fox stood. 'You're coming with me,' he said, aiming the gun at Kingston. 'Get up there.'

Kingston started up the steps. Despite the fact that his life and quite possibly Roger's were in jeopardy, he couldn't stop agonizing about Jamie. The idea that Fox might even have taken a shot at her enraged him. He reached the top of the steps and entered the chapel. When he reached the aisle he stopped and, hearing Fox coming up the steps behind him, took a quick glance over his shoulder.

He almost gasped but managed to suppress it. Fox was on the second to last step, his head and shoulders just above the chapel's floor level. Behind him, concealed by the pew, Jamie was waiting, hands above her head, brandishing one of the bronze candleholders like a baseball bat. She'd apparently ripped it off the wall. No sooner than Kingston saw her, she brought down the candlestick with a surprising display of force on the back of Fox's head. Kingston turned to meet Fox's eyes just before they closed and his body slumped to the floor.

Jamie dropped the makeshift weapon clattering to the stone floor and ran to Kingston. For a moment they embraced, her head resting on his chest. Kingston felt a huge surge of relief, followed by an impassioned desire not to let her go. He'd forgotten completely how it felt to hold a woman like this.

At long last he let her go and held her at arm's length, looking down into her brown eyes. 'That's quite a swing you've got,' he said, smiling.

'I owe it all to softball,' she answered.

'More like hardball, if you ask me.'

They separated and turned their attention to Fox. Kingston knelt down and checked his pulse.

'He's not dead, I hope – is he?'

Kingston found the question strangely poignant. Unconscious in front of him was a psychopath who'd clearly demonstrated that he was not above burying people alive, maiming or killing to get what he wanted and Jamie was concerned about his health. If it had been up to Kingston, he would have given Fox a couple more whacks.

'No, don't worry, he'll make it.'

'Then I hope he spends the rest of his life locked up,' she said.

'We were *terrified* when we head that shot, Jamie. What happened?'

'I don't know. I was outside the chapel when I realized that, even though I had a good lead on Fox, he could still shoot me in the open. He'd know I would head for the house. So I changed my mind. I figured that if I hid in the chapel, I stood a much better chance. Seeing the chapel empty, he would conclude that I'd run outside. And that's exactly what he did. The problem was that sooner or later he would come back and it turned out to be sooner. I was wondering what I should do, when I heard the shot, too. A few seconds later, he stormed back into the chapel and went below.'

'So, he fired the shot – what, in anger?'

'That's what I think. He was so furious that I'd got away.'

'You took a big risk staying here –'

'– but it paid off, didn't it?'

Kingston nodded. 'Certainly did.'

Jamie's expression changed. She looked perturbed. 'Where's Roger?'

'He's still down in the catacombs somewhere. He probably heard everything that Fox and I said and, knowing we were on our way back down, he did the smart thing and made himself scarce.'

Kingston walked halfway down the steps and shouted, 'Roger! You can come out, it's all over.'

It was a minute or so before Roger made an appearance. His forehead looked a mess where the blood was starting to congeal. He'd been hiding in one of the rooms close to the steps, he said. Seeing Fox's body and the candlestick he knew quickly what had happened. 'How did you manage it?' he asked Kingston.

'Ask Jamie,' he replied. 'A home run, you might say.'

The police arrived quickly. First, a van and an incident-response car followed by an ambulance and then, five minutes later, a car with Detective Chief Inspector Chadwick and Sergeant Eldridge.

After seeing Fox lifted on a stretcher into the ambulance, the DCI and sergeant accompanied Jamie, Ferguson and Kingston back to the house. A police constable was instructed to retrieve the trunk and its contents and anything else left in the catacombs at the foot of the stairs and bring it all up to the house.

Chapter Twenty-Six

In the dining room, Jamie sat at one end of the long dining table, Kingston at the other. Between them, on the shiny mahogany surface, was a hotchpotch of yellowing papers, envelopes, folders, documents and a couple of cigar boxes. On the floor close to Jamie stood the leather-handled trunk; next to it, strewn on the oriental carpet, the framed photographs.

The last policeman had left fifteen minutes earlier. Since then, Jamie and Kingston had been studying the photos and were only now starting to examine Ryder's personal papers, correspondence and keepsakes. For the occasion, Jamie had opened a bottle of Veuve Clicquot champagne.

The photographs spanned many decades, the earliest – guessing from the style of the clothing and the military uniforms, which, it turned out, Kingston knew quite a lot about – dating back to the mid-nineteenth century. Nearly all the pictures were sepia or black and white. When they first started to look at the photos, Jamie had remarked that she felt like a voyeur looking through a one-sided mirror into a family's private life. Kingston had no such misgivings. He viewed them dispassionately, simply as historical documents, much as he imagined Roger Ferguson would when he got to see them. Roger had left soon after they'd got to the house, complaining of a nasty headache and nausea. Jamie had volunteered to take him to the hospital to have the wound properly dressed and to get an X-ray but he had insisted that he could manage on his own.

Here were photos of babies and children of all ages, in christening robes and sailor suits, tow-headed and pig-tailed; dashing young men with starched collars; elegant ladies with parasols and fancy hats, mostly taken in various parts of the garden; wedding couples and groups; holiday snaps; uniformed soldiers, sailors and airmen; moustached and stern-looking patriarchs and their busty spouses; granite-faced, white-bearded grandfathers and frumpy grandmothers – it was an intimate family portrait spanning more than a century. Kingston had set aside all the pictures that showed parts of the garden where specific plantings or garden features could be seen. He had also separated the photos that showed men in uniform, specifically the more recent ones. Eliminating those of the young man in Royal Air Force uniform – one of the three Ryder brothers – left a handful of photos of the two other brothers. They bore a remarkable family resemblance; there was no telling which of the two was James Ryder.

The papers and documents, and they were numerous, were like signposts through Major Ryder's life. Despite his endeavour to preserve his anonymity, these were clearly things that he simply couldn't bring himself to destroy. His birth certificate with a King George V stamp dated Sunday, 14 December 1919 in the Registration District of Taunton, father's name, Randolph William Ryder, mother's name, Elizabeth Mabel Ryder, formerly Carlisle. A suede pouch held his British passport. Kingston flipped through it checking for entry stamps of foreign countries. As expected, there were none. In his latter years Ryder hadn't travelled out of Wickersham, let alone the country. A number of military documents tracked his service career, notably a Staff College Certificate from Sandhurst. Birth-day and Christmas cards were stuffed in a manila envel-ope. Each contained a handwritten note of varying length, obviously of sentimental value to Ryder. There were mis-cellaneous letters, nearly all personal; membership cards; newspaper and magazine clippings, including several obituaries of what must have been friends and family members; a small collection of ticket stubs and programmes from various concerts and performances, equestrian events, car and horse races.

They were nearing the last of the papers and only a few odds and ends remained in the centre of the table. All the papers, documents and memorabilia that had already been examined had been pushed to one side.

Kingston leaned back in his chair and sipped the champagne. The chill was off but the bubbles were still coming. Sign of a good champagne, he knew. He looked at Jamie over the rim of the glass. He rarely had the chance to watch her thus, while her attention was fully taken by something else; when he could study her features at length with little risk of being caught in the act. Discreetly, he took in her body language, the graceful hand movements, the animated lips and the soft hollows below her cheekbones, all her natural beauty and little mannerisms.

She looked up and smiled. 'Have you gone on strike?'

He smiled back. 'No, not at all.' He was about to add the word, 'dear' but caught himself just in time. 'I thought I'd let you finish the rest. I was hoping that we'd find something that would shed more light on his art dealing days. But he seems to have erased that part of his life. Come to think of it, if Fox hadn't showed up, we might never have found out about that side of his life in the first place.'

Kingston finished the last of his champagne and watched as Jamie opened a foolscap-size envelope and turned it upside down. A small black book fell on to the table. It was about the size of a deck of cards but nowhere as thick. The leather cover was blank.

'What's that?' he asked.

'Looks like some kind of diary,' she muttered, opening it and starting to read.

Kingston watched idly as she started turning the pages. Soon, he became aware that her expression was growing more and more perplexed. She looked up suddenly.

'What is it? Kingston asked.

'It's written by a soldier.'

'Really?' Kingston got up and joined her, standing behind her chair, looking over her shoulder.

'Listen to this, Lawrence. *This will be the fourth night we've been stuck in this godforsaken hole. Hawkins, Nobby Green and Stevenson all bought it today. When Terry got hit, he was not that far away from me. At least he didn't suffer by the looks of it. That's a blessing. I've lost count of how many of us are left now. It can't be more than three dozen or so. The good news is the Jerries have stopped using mortars but their snipers are picking us off like flies. It's quiet for the longest time, then there's a shot and we all pray that the bugger missed. Stevenson, poor sod, told me yesterday that he'd heard we were running out of ammo. I'm beginning to hope that he was right. Then we would have to throw in the towel.*'

She flipped through it, scanned a few more pages and handed it to Kingston. 'It's tragic,' she said. 'Just to think what those men went through is enough but then, to take the time to write about it . . .' Her words trailed off.

Kingston wasn't listening. He was now seated in the chair next to Jamie and had his eyes glued to the diary's open pages. The descriptions were simply phrased, almost naïve, which gave them even more gravitas. The thoughts and feelings that accompanied them were like a mirror reflecting the young man's embittered soul.

Reading on about the soldier's account of the catastrophic plight that had befallen him and his comrades, Kingston was transported back to those dark days in Europe sixty years ago. Suddenly he looked up. 'This is starting to sound awfully familiar.'

'Familiar? What are you thinking?'

'That it could be Kershaw's or more likely Kit's diary.'

'There's no name in it, is there?'

'I haven't come across one so far. But think about it. How and why did it end up in Ryder's possession?'

'I've no idea,' said Jamie, shaking her head. 'Here, finish

this up.' She poured the last of the champagne into his glass. 'There's not much left to do with this lot, I suppose. I think I'll leave it to you and go and have a bath.'

'Wait. Listen to this. *It's night-time and for the first time in days it's quiet. But the silence is terrible, perhaps worse than the fighting because all I do is lie awake and relive the horrors of the day and dread the coming of tomorrow. I can't even begin to describe what kind of hell this place is. Every day there are more dead bodies, men with missing limbs and horrible wounds. We're hopelessly outnumbered by the Jerries and almost out of ammo and I can't see the point of fighting any more with just a handful of men. Another thing, I'm almost out of fags so things are getting serious!*

'I'd hoped against hope that we would make it out of here alive but it doesn't look that way now because we are being ordered to fight on to the bitter end. I've never believed much in fate but I'm starting to now.

'Cousin Jeremy has been a lifesaver but I'm beginning to see signs that even his optimism has now deserted him and though he won't come out and say so, he knows that it will take a miracle for us to survive.'

Kingston looked up. 'This is the young chap who got shot, Kit. It has to be. It makes sense that he and Kershaw were cousins – it fits with what Loftus told me.' He scratched his chin. 'But how on earth did it come to be in Ryder's possession?'

'What about the watch? It was neither Kit's nor Kershaw's by the looks of it.'

Kingston ignored her question. He was tapping his forehead, eyes momentarily closed. 'Yes, of course. That *has* to be it.'

Jamie had stopped what she was doing and was looking at Kingston eager to hear what he had to say next.

'Here's what I think happened, Jamie. Kit gives the diary to Kershaw or more likely, Kershaw finds it on Kit's body after he was killed in that Dutch village. The page that I just read more or less confirms that that was where it was written. We now know they were cousins, too. Funny, Loftus didn't mention that.'

'Maybe they didn't want it known.'

'Possibly.' Kingston was pulling on his earlobe. 'Let's see. When Kershaw gets out of jail he comes to Wickersham and probably confronts Ryder on two scores. First over his imprisonment, which we'll assume for a moment was unjust, and second, on account of the death of his cousin Kit, which he blames on Ryder. Kershaw must have had this diary with him. He'd carried it all those years.'

'You may be overlooking one thing, Lawrence.'

'What's that?'

'Well, we don't know if Kit was married or not. If he was, surely Kershaw would have given the diary to his wife?'

Kingston thought for a moment. She had a point. 'One explanation, Jamie, would be that Kit's wife was no longer living when Kershaw returned to England. If she had been in London through the war, it's quite possible she could have been killed in an air raid.'

Jamie smiled. 'I knew you'd come up with an answer.'

He paused. 'So, when he turns up at Wickersham he shows Ryder the diary.'

'But why?'

'To lay the blame at Ryder's feet for Kit's death, the unnecessary deaths of many of his men and his own incarceration. To make him feel guilty, ashamed of his actions.'

'More likely he would've wanted to kill Ryder, if you ask me. Sounds like he had enough reasons. After twenty years in prison he had had plenty of time to think about it.'

'Possibly. Given what he had endured, most men would want revenge.'

'But if it really was Kershaw who ended up in the well, something must have gone awfully wrong.'

'It looks that way. We'll never know for sure but we do

know that one way or another Kershaw ended up dead. Ryder might have done it intentionally or it could have been an accident. Either way, it appears that Ryder decided, for good reason, not to call the police but instead disposed of Kershaw's body down the well. Most likely he would have done that from inside the house before he blocked up that passageway. In fact, come to think of it, that would be the reason *why* he sealed it.'

'If it was an accident, why wouldn't Ryder have called the police?'

'My guess is that it happened while Ryder was actively dealing in stolen art. And the last thing he'd want would be the police investigating a suspicious death at Wickersham; having the story splashed all over the newspapers. No, it was the perfect solution as far as he was concerned. Nobody would ever find out, certainly not in his lifetime.'

Jamie sighed. 'Well, we're no closer to knowing why Ryder decided to leave me his estate. We'll probably never know the answer to that question, either. All we seem to end up with are endless hypotheses.'

'I think we will, Jamie. Now we've got this diary.'

'What about the watch, though? The initials?'

'I know,' Kingston muttered. 'That does complicate things. If it *was* Kit's or Kershaw's, maybe one of them bought it second hand, after all.'

'You seem to be able to find an explanation for everything. You would have made a good politician, Lawrence.'

Kingston smiled. 'I know but at least we have more than we had before. I think we're getting close to working this whole thing out. You *must* want to know now what motivated Ryder?'

She shrugged. 'To be truthful, I'm not so sure. All along I've been trying to avoid the question: forget about the past and do what I feel is best for Wickersham – something that would make the Ryder family proud. You know how I feel, Lawrence, we've talked enough about it. I must tell you, though, I felt a bit uncomfortable looking at all those pictures of Ryder's family; before there were no faces and now, too many. I kept wondering where I fitted in, if I'm related in any distant way or if he chose me for some other reason. I think the photos have brought me closer to the family, I feel more a part of it. But there's his dealing in stolen art and the possibility that he may have been responsible for doing away with Kershaw. I'm confused.'

'I think we're nearly there, Jamie. I'm convinced there's just one small thing we've been overlooking. One last piece of the puzzle that, when it locks into place, will explain everything that's happened since you arrived and long before, too.'

Chapter Twenty-Seven

Kingston looked out of the window of the living room, thinking of nothing in particular. Over the last forty-eight hours, he and Jamie had exhausted their post-mortem of the events in the catacombs. There was nothing more to discuss. They had heard from Roger Ferguson who was none the worse for wear, straining at the bit to return to what he warned would be a lengthy and painstaking examination, photographic documentation and cataloguing of the priory catacombs involving specialists in several sciences.

Jamie had left the room minutes earlier to check on her baking. He thought she said Toll House cookies but couldn't be sure. Maybe it was Tow House? She was still looking for a local woman to take Dot's place and meanwhile making do herself.

They were both waiting for Inspector Chadwick, who had called the day before requesting to 'have a word' about the incident with Fox.

It was a particularly sparkling day. Outside Kingston could see across the new lawns and was admiring the herbaceous borders which, although now in their infancy, would fill out nicely in a season or two. The big shrubs they'd planted – including *Magnolia sinensis*, berberis, phlomis, cotinus and various forms of viburnum – would form a dark variegated backdrop for the smaller shrubs and flowering plants in the centre and at the front of the border: varieties of old roses, potentilla, philadelphus,

abutilon, *Geranium psilostemon*, penstemon, knautia, helle-
bores, lychnis, salvia, delphinium, anchusa, iris and a
dozen more.

The day before, he'd called Jennifer Ingels at the Art
Loss Register to tell her about the paintings. Naturally, she
couldn't wait to see them and offered a half-hearted apology, confessing that she had been dubious about a good
part of what Kingston had told her when they met. Until
ownership was established or it was determined what
should be done with them, the paintings were to be stored
at a fine arts storage depot in London.

Chadwick and Sergeant Eldridge showed up punctually
at three o'clock and Jamie joined them in the living room,
apologizing for keeping them waiting.

'Whatever that is you're baking in there smells frightfully good,' said Chadwick.

'Just cookies,' Jamie replied. 'They'll be ready in about
ten minutes. We can have some with tea, later.'

Chadwick settled into the couch and crossed his legs.
'Well, at last I've got some good news for you.'

'Really?' said Jamie, glancing at Kingston.

'Seems that our man, Fox, is a bit of a chameleon. From
what we've found out so far, he's gone by at least a couple
of other names – one that you'll both recognize.'

Kingston was frowning, at a loss to come up with a
name.

'Mainwaring,' said Chadwick

Kingston's eyebrows shot up. 'Mainwaring?'

'That's right. Faced with two possible murder charges
and the incarceration and attempted murder of you and
Jamie, he's been most co-operative over the last couple of
days.'

'Two murder charges?' Kingston inquired.

'Are you talking about Jack?' Jamie asked.

Chadwick nodded. 'Dorothy Parmenter, too.'

'So it wasn't suicide?' Kingston interjected.

'No, it wasn't. We don't have a full confession yet but it

seems that Dot had had enough of Mainwaring – particularly after Jack's questionable death which she probably
linked to Mainwaring – and was going to tell Jamie her
suspicions about what was going on. Mainwaring decided
to put a stop to that by doing her in and making it look like
a suicide.'

'Poor Dot,' Jamie murmured.

'What about Jack?' Kingston asked.

'He's claiming that he had nothing to do with Jack's
death. He admits to having gone to Jack's house a couple
of times but swears innocence.'

'That could've been him I saw the day I went to Jack's.
Silver BMW.'

'I'm pretty sure that's the car he drove here,' said Jamie.

'Right,' Chadwick cut in. 'He knew, too, that Jack had
money and drug problems and had become involved with
some unsavoury characters. He befriended Jack at a pub in
Spaxton and Jack agreed to help him spy on you two. He
wouldn't say how much he was paying Jack but neither
did he deny paying him. Mainwaring obviously couldn't
keep you under surveillance himself; he needed people
who were around the estate on a day-to-day basis. Someone on the inside.'

'Enter Dot,' said Jamie.

'Exactly,' Chadwick sniffed. ' It's still speculation but
I think it's a reasonable assumption that, at one point, Jack
came to realize that he wasn't getting anywhere, on top of
which he was starting to arouse suspicion – particularly
with you, Lawrence. It became obvious that if he were
going to find out anything about the paintings, he would
need somebody close to you. Who better to eavesdrop than
Dot? Jack was probably able to rope her in without much
trouble because they knew each other from the old days,
when they were both in Ryder's employ. They may have
been more than simply friends, if you know what
I mean.'

'She was being paid, too?' asked Jamie.

'It looks that way. When we checked out her cottage there were a lot of new things lying around – brand new wide-screen TV, DVD player, lots of jewellery and new clothing. Some items still had the price tags on them. It all suggested that she'd recently come into money.'

Chadwick uncrossed his legs and leaned forward. 'We've been keeping tabs on Mainwaring for a long time. I couldn't tell you at the time, of course, but what we uncovered as we went along dovetailed into everything that was going on here. The big break came when we tracked down Mainwaring's employer before Ryder.'

Chadwick sniffed. 'By the way, Mainwaring's not his real name. He's actually Reginald Elliot. Before he went to work for Ryder, he was employed by a private nursing home in Surrey. He's a registered nurse by profession. While he was at the home – about twenty years ago – there was a big scandal. Some of the elderly patients were being bilked out of their savings, on top of which there were two suspicious deaths. You know, shortage of breath and suffo-cation are pretty much one and the same thing. Our friend Elliot was under suspicion of causing both deaths but there wasn't enough evidence to make a case. Mainwaring had been very clever in his modus operandi and in covering his tracks. He got the job with Ryder some time later through an employment agency that specializes in placing nursing personnel.'

'How long was he with Ryder?' asked Jamie.

'Going on fifteen years.'

'So, he probably knew a lot about Ryder's personal life and his business dealings,' said Kingston.

'Well, he did, yes. Towards the end, Ryder was pretty much incapacitated and he relied on Mainwaring for just about everything. One of the first things we asked Main-waring was how he got to know about the paintings.'

Kingston had been about to ask the same question. 'How did he?'

'He maintains that Girard had been at the house on

261

several occasions and it was no secret that he and Ryder had been dealing in art for a long time. Mainwaring insists that he never actually saw any paintings but had been in the room a number of times when paintings and deals were discussed. He got to know about the three paintings, the ones that you discovered, directly through Girard. Right after Ryder died Mainwaring says he got a call from Girard offering his condolences on Ryder's death and telling him about the three valuable paintings. He insisted they had been in Ryder's possession all along and that, with Ryder's passing, they rightfully belonged to him and that he wanted to pass them on to his son before he died. Apparently Girard had cancer and didn't have long to live – which, unfortunately, turned out to be the case.'

'That part of the story is true,' said Jamie. 'At least, that's what Fox – I should say, Mainwaring – told me.' She paused for a moment, her look puzzled. 'But wouldn't Girard be entitled to only one half of what the paintings were worth?'

'We asked the same question. Apparently Girard told Mainwaring that he had bought out Ryder's share and Ryder had agreed to return them.'

'That, we'll never know, I suppose,' said Kingston.

Chadwick continued. 'Mainwaring stated that Girard had hired him to find the paintings. And listen to this. He maintains that Girard promised him a fee of two hundred and fifty thousand pounds if he were able to deliver them to Girard in France.'

Jamie whistled.

'The paintings were described in detail and Girard provided the dimensions of each but did not divulge the artists' names. Mainwaring knew damned well that anyone prepared to offer a quarter-million-pound finder's fee would know that the paintings were worth far more. He insists he had no idea that they might have been stolen, though.'

Jamie gave Kingston a quizzical look. 'Lawrence, didn't

you tell me that Girard had another partner? How does he fit into all of this?'

'First time I've heard of it,' said Chadwick.

Kingston smiled. 'Yes, that's what we were led to believe. That information came from the Art Loss Register people. I only worked it out quite recently.'

'Worked what out?' Chadwick inquired.

'I was told that Girard's partner's name was Jeremy R. Villesgrande. I think it was the very English first name and the French last name that was the giveaway.'

'Giveaway? I don't follow,' said Chadwick.

'It's an anagram, you see. Jeremy R. Villesgrande is an anagram of James Grenville Ryder. It was Ryder's clever way of keeping anonymity.'

Sergeant Eldridge spoke for the first time. 'Mainwaring also said that he was sworn to secrecy by Girard. One mention of valuable paintings to anybody and the whole deal was off.'

'That should have rung some bells with him, wouldn't you think?' asked Kingston. 'He couldn't be that naïve. He must have known they were stolen.'

'It's irrelevant, actually,' Chadwick chimed in.

Kingston frowned. 'I'm confused. Is Girard still alive?'

'No, unfortunately not. Sorry, I should have made that clear at the beginning. He died only last month.'

Brow furrowed, Kingston glanced at Eldridge then back to Chadwick. 'By the way, did those books and papers ever turn up? The ones stolen from the cottage?'

'No. But it's a sure bet that once Mainwaring found they were of little use, he disposed of them. It's reasonable to believe that Jack stole them after Dot told him Ferguson had brought them over, seeing how interested you were in them, Lawrence.'

'All along I was convinced it was Jack I saw that night of the storm,' said Kingston. 'There was the hooded sweater in his house and then the incident at the chapel. It was obvious that he was up to no good. The chap was not only a bad apple, he was a bad actor, too.'

Chadwick stood, straightening his trousers and stretching. 'That about sums it up so far. In the next few days, we'll have enough information to file formal charges against Elliot but don't you worry, he'll go up for a long time. From now on, I think life will be a little more peaceful at Wickersham and you two can go about business as usual.'

'Wait,' said Jamie. 'What about my car? Mainwaring sabotaged it, right?'

'Another thing he hasn't admitted. That'll probably be an attempted murder charge. But, yes, Jamie, there's no question that he did it – in all probability, as Lawrence said, to get you both off the estate. I would imagine that by then he was sure something was going on with the chapel. Don't you worry, though, we'll find out.'

Jamie shook her head and let out a sigh. 'What a nasty piece of work.'

Chadwick simply nodded.

'Sure I can't talk you into some tea and cookies?' Jamie asked.

Chadwick flashed a look at Eldridge then back to Jamie. 'No thanks, Jamie, we'd better be getting along. I'm sure you and Lawrence have plenty to do without having to put up with us for another hour.'

Chadwick shook hands with Jamie, then Kingston, and started for the door, followed by Sergeant Eldridge. At the threshold, he stopped, turned and reached into his inside jacket pocket. 'I almost forgot,' he said, with an enigmatic smile. 'I think this will be of interest to you.' He handed Jamie a plain envelope. 'I checked with your lawyer, by the way. He said you should have it.'

Chapter Twenty-Eight

Jamie and Kingston stood in the arch of the doorway and watched as the police car rounded the curve in the driveway.

Back in the living room, Kingston watched with more than a casual eye as Jamie slit open the envelope. She read a few lines then looked at him. 'It's not long, why don't I read it to you?'

'Fine.' Kingston leaned back in his chair.

'*My dear Mainwaring,*' began Jamie.

'*First, let me state that I am deeply appreciative of the unflagging service and attentive care you have provided over these many years, particularly knowing that for the best part it has meant considerable sacrifice and forbearance on your part, depriving you of leading what might be termed a normal and social life. For this I am truly grateful.*

'*This letter concerns the decision that I have made with regard to the distribution of my estate and assets. My solicitor, Ernest Woodhouse, will of course (and may have done so by now) present you with specific terms of my will, informing you of your inheritance. But I feel that I owe you an explanation as to why I have made this doubtlessly unexpected, and what might be construed as perverse, decision.*

'*In the course of my lifetime I have committed acts which I deeply regret. For these transgressions I make no excuses and ask no forgiveness. Certain of these acts, despite my well-intentioned convictions at the time, have resulted in the unnecessary deaths of a number of men and a lifetime of grief and deprivation for their families. Most of these actions occurred during the war but by no means does that excuse my decisions and what I now see clearly as reprehensible behaviour.*

'The two men who have suffered the most through my dereliction and criminality are no longer alive as a result, and because of their actions, I am. They are Kit Archer and Jeremy Kershaw, a private and a sergeant, both under my command during enemy action in France and Holland.'

Jamie stopped reading and looked again at Kingston. Her face registered confusion and shock. She closed her eyes and pressed a hand up against her lips.

'Lawrence – that's my mother's maiden name! Archer.'

'Really? Is there more?'

She continued to read.

'For more than half my lifetime I have carried the burden of their deaths like an omnipresent albatross, their ghosts appearing before me in my nightmares and my every waking hour. Their faces do not betray hatred or revenge, however. And that has made the torment even more unbearable. Their expressions are always serene and benevolent; as if they have forgiven me for the tragedy I have brought to their lives.

'Private investigations conducted on my behalf revealed that Sergeant Kershaw left no heirs. The sole surviving Archer family member is a young woman named Jamie Allison Gibson, granddaughter of Private Kit Archer. The contents of my last will and testament will reveal that I am leaving her my entire estate and the bulk of my other assets.

'I trust that the sum I am bequeathing you will be more than sufficient to see you through your remaining years in comfort and with self-sufficiency. It is also my hope that you will understand and accept the reasons for my decision.

'I cannot go to my grave knowing that I haven't done

everything in my power, albeit far too puny and too late, to make moral and tangible restitution for my miserable failures.

'James Grenville Ryder.

'PS I would prefer that you not divulge the contents, or any part of this letter, to any other persons.'

Visibly at a loss for words, Jamie handed Kingston the letter. As he read it, he slowly shook his head. 'Extraordinary,' he muttered.

'To say the least,' said Jamie. 'I'm surprised that Mainwaring gave it to Chadwick.'

'Maybe he didn't. It could have been discovered among his belongings. You know the police will have searched his home after he was arrested.'

Kingston got up and went to the butler's table where he pulled out the stopper from the crystal whisky decanter. 'How about a grown-up's drink, Jamie,' he asked, looking over his shoulder.

She glanced at her watch. 'A little early but why not?'

'The usual?'

'Yes, thanks.'

Kingston poured the drinks, brought them back to the coffee table and sat down facing her.

Jamie took a sip of the vodka tonic and looked at Kingston. 'This is all very confusing. I may need you to explain to me again what happened in that Dutch village where my grandfather was killed.' She paused and looked aside. 'My *grandfather*, that's going to take some getting used to. Kit Archer,' she muttered.

'You knew nothing at all about him?'

'No.' She had a faraway look in her eyes.

'Hmm, I suppose it's not *that* unusual.'

She raised an eyebrow. 'Kit? Is that a real name?' she asked.

'It's an abbreviation, like Bill or Harry. In England, it's short for Christopher – Chris or Kit.'

'Well, that's it! The watch.'

'Of course! CMA. Why on earth didn't I think of that? Christopher M. Archer.'

'I wonder what the M. stands for?'

'I'm sure a little genealogical research on the Internet will tell you. But you obviously knew next to nothing about your grandparents?'

'No, my mom hardly ever talked about her parents. Growing up, I would ask about them every once in a while but whenever I did, she managed to change the subject or shrug it off. As far as I know she never had any photos of either of them – at least I never saw any, which I found a bit odd. Finally I came round to realizing that it was simply something she didn't want to talk about, that there was some dark secret there, so I gave up asking.'

Kingston smiled. 'Well, if nothing else, at least you know now that there's some British blood in you, after all.'

She didn't acknowledge Kingston's remark. She was looking off to her side, the light from the window edging her shadowed face. The letter had clearly flustered her and doubtlessly had resurrected long-forgotten moments of her childhood. Kingston waited for what he thought was a decent interval before interrupting her thoughts. He was about to say something when she turned and looked him.

'So, was my grandfather a deserter? Is that why my mother never spoke of him?' Her voice was subdued. She spoke as if she were asking herself the questions, not him. Betraying a hint of sadness, her dark brown eyes never left his. 'I was afraid it might turn out this way, learning something that was best left buried in the past – we talked about it, remember, Lawrence? It looks like it's turned out the way I predicted after all.'

Kingston wanted to go over to her, put an arm around her and comfort her. As it was, he simply sat there looking up at the ceiling. He took his time before he spoke.

'No, Jamie. Your grandfather was not a deserter. You *must* put that idea out of your mind.' He paused, his mind racing, trying to recall just how much he had told Jamie about Kit Archer after his meeting with Loftus. 'It took courage to do what he did.' He lowered his glass to the table. 'What exactly happened in that Dutch village, Jamie? We'll never know the whole story. The only person alive to tell the tale is Loftus and even he didn't actually witness what took place between Ryder, Kershaw and your grandfather. His story is based on hearsay. Let me tell you what I think, based on all the information we have.

'In those last desperate days and hours, the situation had become hopeless for the soldiers in that village. They all knew it. What's more, they knew that unless their commanding officer was prepared to raise the white flag, surrender, they would all most certainly die. I'm certain that in the history of war, this is by no means an unusual set of circumstances and that in the end it nearly always comes down to a question of two choices. The men must either obey their superior officer – which, from the very first day of square-bashing, is what a soldier is drilled into doing, without thinking – or they can mutiny. Given the little time they had left and the brutal punishment that they had suffered, I doubt that mutiny was ever an option. They were too few, too exhausted and far beyond any organized uprising.'

So far Jamie hadn't said a word and it looked as if she wasn't going to, at least for the moment, so Kingston continued.

'I've thought about this a lot, Jamie. And I've come to realize that what Kit Archer did was selfless and courageous. Whether his cousin, Jeremy Kershaw, was in on it, is impossible to say. But by Kit's taking it upon himself to surrender, we know he ended up saving the lives of all his comrades, including Ryder. We can debate whether Kit planned this or whether it was an impulsive act. I prefer to think that he thought it through. He knew damned well the risk but saw it as the only possible chance to save their lives. This is the greatest sacrifice a man can make in my eyes, and should be in yours too, Jamie – he should be considered a hero. Ryder certainly came to realize this. He intimated so in his letter.'

A brief pause followed while she thought about his reassuring words.

'Lawrence, I don't know how you do it,' she said, smiling. 'In less than two minutes you've elevated my grandfather from deserter to war hero.' She paused and grinned. 'And do you know what? You've convinced me that he *really* was. And for that, I will always be very, very grateful.'

She got up and went over to his chair, kneeled by his side and kissed him on the cheek. 'I'm so happy you came into my life,' she said. 'You're a good man.'

For one of the rare times in his life, Kingston was at a loss for words.

Jamie stood and faced him, gripping his hand, pulling him out of the chair. 'Why don't we forget about all this for now and go out and celebrate. We can talk about roses or those great wines that you and I are going to make one day.'

Acknowledgements

My special thanks are due to Tim Smit and his landmark book, *The Lost Gardens of Heligan* (published by Victor Gollancz, 1997), and the miracle that he wrought personally, in bringing back to life a mysterious estate and a Victorian way of life that had been overlooked for more than seven decades. Many of the passages in this novel that bear on the garden restoration are loosely excerpted or adapted from the pages of Tim's remarkable story. Unquestionably, he saved me countless hours of research and for that alone I am truly grateful. His book should be required reading for all those with a love for gardens and history.

Much of the historical detail on country houses is taken from *The Country House Kitchen Garden* (Sutton Publishing in association with the National Trust, 1988).

Some passages concerning the growing of grapes and winemaking are excerpted from *Grape: The Making of California Wine*, a 2004 series published in the *San Francisco Chronicle*, written by staff writer Mike Weiss. Expert winemaking flourishes were added by Sonoma County Chateau St Jean winemaker, Margo van Staaveren.